A Man Called White

A MAN CALLED WHITE

The Autobiography of

WALTER WHITE

Indiana University Press

Bloomington & London

Acknowledgment is made to the *Saturday Review of Literature* in which parts of Chapters I and XLIII appeared in an article called, "Why I Remain a Negro" and to *The Reader's Digest*, which reprinted it. This edition published by arrangement with The Viking Press, Inc.
Published in Canada by Fitzhenry & Whiteside Limited,
Don Mills, Ontario
First Midland Book edition 1970
Library of Congress catalog card number: 48–8621
SBN: 253–20135–7
Manufactured in the United States of America

For My Sister Madeline

Contents

A Man Called White

I

I Learn What I Am

I am a Negro. My skin is white, my eyes are blue, my hair is blond. The traits of my race are nowhere visible upon me. Not long ago I stood one morning on a subway platform in Harlem. As the train came in I stepped back for safety. My heel came down upon the toe of the man behind me. I turned to apologize to him. He was a Negro, and his face as he stared at me was hard and full of the piled-up bitterness of a thousand lynchings and a million nights in shacks and tenements and "nigger towns." "Why don't you look where you're going?" he said sullenly. "You white folks are always trampling on colored people." Just then one of my friends came up and asked how the fight had gone in Washington—there was a filibuster against legislation for a permanent Fair Employment Practices Committee. The Negro on whose toes I had stepped listened, then spoke to me penitently:

"Are you Walter White of the NAACP? I'm sorry I spoke to you that way. I thought you were white."

I am not white. There is nothing within my mind and heart which tempts me to think I am. Yet I realize acutely that the only characteristic which matters to either the white or the colored race—the appearance of whiteness—is mine. There is magic in a white skin; there is tragedy, loneliness, exile, in a black skin. Why then do I insist that I am a Negro, when nothing compels me to do so but myself?

Many Negroes are judged as whites. Every year approximately twelve thousand white-skinned Negroes disappear—people whose absence cannot be explained by death or emigration. Nearly every

3

one of the fourteen million discernible Negroes in the United States knows at least one member of his race who is "passing"—the magic word which means that some Negroes can get by as whites, men and women who have decided that they will be happier and more successful if they flee from the proscription and humiliation which the American color line imposes on them. Often these emigrants achieve success in business, the professions, the arts and sciences. Many of them have married white people, lived happily with them, and produced families. Sometimes they tell their husbands or wives of their Negro blood, sometimes not. Who are they? Mostly people of no great importance, but some of them prominent figures, including a few members of Congress, certain writers, and several organizers of movements to "keep the Negroes and other minorities in their places." Some of the most vehement public haters of Negroes are themselves secretly Negroes.

They do not present openly the paradox of the color line. It is I, with my insistence, day after day, year in and year out, that I am a Negro, who provoke the reactions to which now I am accustomed: the sudden intake of breath, the bewildered expression of the face, the confusion of the eyes, the muddled fragmentary remarks—"But you do not look . . . I mean I would never have known . . . of course if you didn't want to admit . . ." Sometimes the eyes blink rapidly and the tongue, out of control, says, "Are you sure?"

I have tried to imagine what it is like to have me presented to a white person as a Negro, by supposing a Negro were suddenly to say to me, "I am white." But the reversal does not work, for whites can see no reason for a white man ever wanting to be black; there is only reason for a black man wanting to be white. That is the way whites think; that is the way their values are set up. It is the startling removal of the blackness that upsets people. Looking at me without knowing who I am, they disassociate me from all the characteristics of the Negro. Informed that I am a Negro, they find it impossible suddenly to endow me with the skin, the odor, the dialect, the shuffle, the imbecile good nature, traditionally attributed to Negroes. Instantly they are aware that these things are *not* part of me. They think there must be some mistake.

There is no mistake. I am a Negro. There can be no doubt. I

know the night when, in terror and bitterness of soul, I discovered that I was set apart by the pigmentation of my skin (invisible though it was in my case) and the moment at which I decided that I would infinitely rather be what I was than, through taking advantage of the way of escape that was open to me, be one of the race which had forced the decision upon me.

There were nine light-skinned Negroes in my family: mother, father, five sisters, an older brother, George, and myself. The house in which I discovered what it meant to be a Negro was located on Houston Street, three blocks from the Candler Building, Atlanta's first skyscraper, which bore the name of the ex–drug clerk who had become a millionaire from the sale of Coca-Cola. Below us lived none but Negroes; toward town all but a very few were white. Ours was an eight room, two-story frame house which stood out in its surroundings not because of its opulence but by contrast with the drabness and unpaintedness of the other dwellings in a deteriorating neighborhood.

Only Father kept his house painted, the picket fence repaired, the board fence separating our place from those on either side white-washed, the grass neatly trimmed, and flower beds abloom. Mother's passion for neatness was even more pronounced and it seemed to me that I was always the victim of her determination to see no single blade of grass longer than the others or any one of the pickets in the front fence less shiny with paint than its mates. This spic-and-spanness became increasingly apparent as the rest of the neighborhood became more down-at-heel, and resulted, as we were to learn, in sullen envy among some of our white neighbors. It was the violent expression of that resentment against a Negro family neater than themselves which set the pattern of our lives.

On a day in September 1906, when I was thirteen, we were taught that there is no isolation from life. The unseasonably oppressive heat of an Indian summer day hung like a steaming blanket over Atlanta. My sisters and I had casually commented upon the unusual quietness. It seemed to stay Mother's volubility and reduced Father, who was more taciturn, to monosyllables. But, as I remember it, no other sense of impending trouble impinged upon our consciousness.

I had read the inflammatory headlines in the *Atlanta News* and the more restrained ones in the *Atlanta Constitution* which reported alleged rapes and other crimes committed by Negroes. But these were so standard and familiar that they made—as I look back on it now—little impression. The stories were more frequent, however, and consisted of eight-column streamers instead of the usual two- or four-column ones.

Father was a mail collector. His tour of duty was from three to eleven P.M. He made his rounds in a little cart into which one climbed from a step in the rear. I used to drive the cart for him from two until seven, leaving him at the point nearest our home on Houston Street, to return home either for study or sleep. That day Father decided that I should not go with him. I appealed to Mother, who thought it might be all right, provided Father sent me home before dark because, she said, "I don't think they would dare start anything before nightfall." Father told me as we made the rounds that ominous rumors of a race riot that night were sweeping the town. But I was too young that morning to understand the background of the riot. I became much older during the next thirty-six hours, under circumstances which I now recognize as the inevitable outcome of what had preceded.

One of the most bitter political campaigns of that bloody era was reaching its climax. Hoke Smith—that amazing contradiction of courageous and intelligent opposition to the South's economic ills and at the same time advocacy of ruthless suppression of the Negro —was a candidate that year for the governorship. His opponent was Clark Howell, editor of the *Atlanta Constitution,* which boasted with justification that it "covers Dixie like the dew." Howell and his supporters held firm authority over the state Democratic machine despite the long and bitter fight Hoke Smith had made on Howell in the columns of the rival *Atlanta Journal.*

Hoke Smith had fought for legislation to ban child labor and railroad rate discriminations. He had denounced the corrupt practices of the railroads and the state railway commission, which, he charged, was as much owned and run by northern absentee landlords as were the railroads themselves. He had fought for direct primaries to nominate senators and other candidates by popular vote, for a corrupt practices act, for an elective railway commission, and for state ownership of railroads—issues which were destined to be still fought for nearly four decades later by Ellis Arnall. For these reforms he was hailed throughout the nation as a genuine progressive along with La Follette of Wisconsin and Folk of Missouri.

To overcome the power of the regular Democratic organization, Hoke Smith sought to heal the feud of long standing between himself and the powerful ex-radical Populist, Thomas E. Watson. Tom Watson was the strangest mixture of contradictions which rottenborough politics of the South had ever produced. He was the brilliant leader of an agrarian movement in the South which, in alliance with the agrarian West, threatened for a time the industrial and financial power of the East. He had made fantastic strides in uniting Negro and white farmers with Negro and white industrial workers. He had advocated enfranchisement of Negroes and poor whites, the abolition of lynching, control of big business, and rights for the little man, which even today would label him in the minds of conservatives as a dangerous radical. He had fought with fists, guns, and spine-stirring oratory in a futile battle to stop the spread of an industrialized, corporate society.

His break with the Democratic Party during the '90's and the organization of the Populist Party made the Democrats his implacable enemies. The North, busy building vast corporations and individual fortunes, was equally fearful of Tom Watson. Thus was formed between reactionary Southern Democracy and conservative Northern Republicanism the basis of cooperation whose fullest flower is to be seen in the present-day coalition of conservatives in Congress. This combination crushed Tom Watson's bid for national leadership in the presidential elections of 1896 and smashed the Populist movement. Watson ran for president in 1904 and 1908, both times with abysmal failure. His defeats soured him to the point of vicious acrimony. He turned from his ideal of interracial decency to one of virulent hatred and denunciation of the "nigger." He thus became a naturally ally for Hoke Smith in the gubernatorial election in Georgia in 1906.

The two rabble-rousers stumped the state screaming, "Nigger, nigger, nigger!" Some white farmers still believed Watson's abandoned doctrine that the interests of Negro and white farmers and industrial workers were identical. They feared that Watson's and Smith's new scheme to disfranchise Negro voters would lead to disfranchisement of poor whites. Tom Watson was sent to trade on his past reputation to reassure them that such was not the case and that their own interests were best served by now hating "niggers."

Watson's oratory had been especially effective among the cotton mill workers and other poor whites in and near Atlanta. The *Atlanta Journal* on August 1, 1906, in heavy type, all capital letters, printed an incendiary appeal to race prejudice backing up Watson and Smith which declared:

> Political equality being thus preached to the negro in the ring papers and on the stump, what wonder that he makes no distinction between political and social equality? He grows more bumptious on the street, more impudent in his dealings with white men, and then, when he cannot achieve social equality as he wishes, with the instinct of the barbarian to destroy what he cannot attain to, he lies in wait, as that dastardly brute did yesterday near this city, and assaults the fair young girlhood of the south . . .

At the same time, a daily newspaper was attempting to wrest from the *Atlanta Journal* leadership in the afternoon field. The new paper, the *Atlanta News*, in its scramble for circulation and advertising took a lesson from the political race and began to play up in eight-column streamers stories of the raping of white women by Negroes. That every one of the stories was afterward found to be wholly without foundation was of no importance. The *News* circulation, particularly in street sales, leaped swiftly upward as the headlines were bawled by lusty-voiced newsboys. Atlanta became a tinder box.

Fuel was added to the fire by a dramatization of Thomas Dixon's novel *The Clansman* in Atlanta. (This was later made by David Wark Griffith into *The Birth of a Nation*, and did more than anything else to make successful the revival of the Ku Klux Klan.) The late Ray Stannard Baker, telling the story of the Atlanta riot in *Along the Color Line*, characterized Dixon's fiction and its effect on Atlanta and the South as "incendiary and cruel." No more apt or accurate description could have been chosen.

During the afternoon preceding the riot little bands of sullen, evil-

looking men talked excitedly on street corners all over downtown
Atlanta. Around seven o'clock my father and I were driving toward
a mail box at the corner of Peachtree and Houston Streets when
there came from near-by Pryor Street a roar the like of which I had
never heard before, but which sent a sensation of mingled fear and
excitement coursing through my body. I asked permission of Father
to go and see what the trouble was. He bluntly ordered me to stay
in the cart. A little later we drove down Atlanta's main business
thoroughfare, Peachtree Street. Again we heard the terrifying cries,
this time near at hand and coming toward us. We saw a lame Negro
bootblack from Herndon's barber shop pathetically trying to out-
run a mob of whites. Less than a hundred yards from us the chase
ended. We saw clubs and fists descending to the accompaniment
of savage shouting and cursing. Suddenly a voice cried, "There goes
another nigger!" Its work done, the mob went after new prey. The
body with the withered foot lay dead in a pool of blood on the
street.

Father's apprehension and mine steadily increased during the evening, although the fact that our skins were white kept us from attack. Another circumstance favored us—the mob had not yet grown
violent enough to attack United States government property. But I
could see Father's relief when he punched the time clock at eleven
P.M. and got into the cart to go home. He wanted to go the back
way down Forsyth Street, but I begged him, in my childish excitement and ignorance, to drive down Marietta to Five Points, the heart
of Atlanta's business district, where the crowds were densest and the
yells loudest. No sooner had we turned into Marietta Street, however, than we saw careening toward us an undertaker's barouche.
Crouched in the rear of the vehicle were three Negroes clinging to
the sides of the carriage as it lunged and swerved. On the driver's
seat crouched a white man, the reins held taut in his left hand. A
huge whip was gripped in his right. Alternately he lashed the horses
and, without looking backward, swung the whip in savage swoops
in the faces of members of the mob as they lunged at the carriage
determined to seize the three Negroes.

There was no time for us to get out of its path, so sudden and
swift was the appearance of the vehicle. The hub cap of the right

rear wheel of the barouche hit the right side of our much lighter wagon. Father and I instinctively threw our weight and kept the cart from turning completely over. Our mare was a Texas mustang which, frightened by the sudden blow, lunged in the air as Father clung to the reins. Good fortune was with us. The cart settled back on its four wheels as Father said in a voice which brooked no dissent, "We are going home the back way and not down Marietta."

But again on Pryor Street we heard the cry of the mob. Close to us and in our direction ran a stout and elderly woman who cooked at a downtown white hotel. Fifty yards behind, a mob which filled the street from curb to curb was closing in. Father handed the reins to me and, though he was of slight stature, reached down and lifted the woman into the cart. I did not need to be told to lash the mare to the fastest speed she could muster.

The church bells tolled the next morning for Sunday service. But no one in Atlanta believed for a moment that the hatred and lust for blood had been appeased. Like skulls on a cannibal's hut the hats and caps of victims of the mob of the night before had been hung on the iron hooks of telegraph poles. None could tell whether each hat represented a dead Negro. But we knew that some of those who had worn the hats would never again wear any.

Late in the afternoon friends of my father's came to warn of more trouble that night. They told us that plans had been perfected for a mob to form on Peachtree Street just after nightfall to march down Houston Street to what the white people called "Darktown," three blocks or so below our house, to "clean out the niggers." There had never been a firearm in our house before that day. Father was reluctant even in those circumstances to violate the law, but he at last gave in at Mother's insistence.

We turned out the lights early, as did all our neighbors. No one removed his clothes or thought of sleep. Apprehension was tangible. We could almost touch its cold and clammy surface. Toward midnight the unnatural quiet was broken by a roar that grew steadily in volume. Even today I grow tense in remembering it.

Father told Mother to take my sisters, the youngest of them only six, to the rear of the house, which offered more protection from stones and bullets. My brother George was away, so Father and I, the only males in the house, took our places at the front windows of the parlor. The windows opened on a porch along the front side of the house, which in turn gave onto a narrow lawn that sloped down to the street and a picket fence. There was a crash as Negroes smashed the street lamp at the corner of Houston and Piedmont Avenue down the street. In a very few minutes the vanguard of the mob, some of them bearing torches, appeared. A voice which we recognized as that of the son of the grocer with whom we had traded for many years yelled, "That's where that nigger mail carrier lives! Let's burn it down! It's too nice for a nigger to live in!" In the eerie light Father turned his drawn face toward me. In a voice as quiet as though he were asking me to pass him the sugar at the breakfast table, he said, "Son, don't shoot until the first man puts his foot on the lawn and then—don't you miss!"

In the flickering light the mob swayed, paused, and began to flow toward us. In that instant there opened up within me a great awareness; I knew then who I was. I was a Negro, a human being with an invisible pigmentation which marked me a person to be hunted, hanged, abused, discriminated against, kept in poverty and ignorance, in order that those whose skin was white would have readily at hand a proof of their superiority, a proof patent and inclusive, accessible to the moron and the idiot as well as to the wise man and the genius. No matter how low a white man fell, he could always hold fast to the smug conviction that he was superior to two-thirds of the world's population, for those two-thirds were not white.

It made no difference how intelligent or talented my millions of brothers and I were, or how virtuously we lived. A curse like that of Judas was upon us, a mark of degradation fashioned with heavenly authority. There were white men who said Negroes had no souls, and who proved it by the Bible. Some of these now were approaching us, intent upon burning our house.

Theirs was a world of contrasts in values: superior and inferior, profit and loss, cooperative and noncooperative, civilized and aboriginal, white and black. If you were on the wrong end of the comparison, if you were inferior, if you were noncooperative, if you were aboriginal, if you were black, then you were marked for excision, expulsion, or extinction. I was a Negro; I was therefore that part of history which opposed the good, the just, and the enlightened. I was a Persian, falling before the hordes of Alexander. I was a Carthaginian, extinguished by the Legions of Rome. I was a Frenchman at Waterloo, an Anglo-Saxon at Hastings, a Confederate at Vicksburg. I was the defeated, wherever and whenever there was a defeat.

Yet as a boy there in the darkness amid the tightening fright, I knew the inexplicable thing—that my skin was as white as the skin of those who were coming at me.

The mob moved toward the lawn. I tried to aim my gun, wondering what it would feel like to kill a man. Suddenly there was a volley of shots. The mob hesitated, stopped. Some friends of my father's had barricaded themselves in a two-story brick building just below our house. It was they who had fired. Some of the mobsmen, still bloodthirsty, shouted, "Let's go get the nigger." Others, afraid now for their safety, held back. Our friends, noting the hesitation, fired another volley. The mob broke and retreated up Houston Street.

In the quiet that followed I put my gun aside and tried to relax. But a tension different from anything I had ever known possessed me. I was gripped by the knowledge of my identity, and in the depths of my soul I was vaguely aware that I was glad of it. I was sick with loathing for the hatred which had flared before me that night and come so close to making me a killer; but I was glad I was not one of those who hated; I was glad I was not one of those made sick and murderous by pride. I was glad I was not one of those whose story is in the history of the world, a record of bloodshed, rapine, and pillage. I was glad my mind and spirit were part of the races that had not fully awakened, and who therefore had still before them the opportunity to write a record of virtue as a memorandum to Armageddon.

It was all just a feeling then, inarticulate and melancholy, yet reassuring in the way that death and sleep are reassuring, and I have clung to it now for nearly half a century.

II

A Family in Atlanta

The Atlanta riot naturally stands out in my memory as a shocking awakening to the cruelty of which men driven by prejudice, ignorance, and hatred can be guilty. What I saw then has made me hate violence of every sort with implacable and ineradicable loathing. But it also served as a contrast to the everyday life of a normal thrifty and happy middleclass family.

Father and Mother were both so light-skinned that either could have passed for white. Father was born in Augusta, Georgia; Mother in the cotton mill town of Lagrange, seventy miles southwest of Atlanta. Father's family were exceedingly poor and devout. They wished desperately to give their only child the education he wanted so much. They could do little to aid, but he persuaded them to let him go to Atlanta when he had completed grammar school. Neither Augusta nor any other Georgia city or town provided high school education for Negroes at the time, although they did for white youth. Even today the same condition applies in most of the towns and villages of the state. Fortunately for Father and others like him, tuition and living expenses at Atlanta University on both the high-school and college level were modest. Father worked at odd jobs to eke out a meager and, I fear, a not too cheerful life. He had completed high school and his freshman year in college when a double tragedy overcame him. His father and mother both died within a short time. When the debts were paid nothing was left, and Father was forced to leave the University.

He had no profession, of course, nor had he learned any trade. Virtually the only means by which Negroes in the South could earn a fairly decent wage combined with security in those days was employment in the post office. So Father took and passed the civil service examination for letter carrier and went to work. Dollar by dollar he laid aside whatever money he could until the total reached $500.00, with which he purchased a lot on Houston Street, at that time on the far outskirts of Atlanta. Once more he began a long period of saving, living at a level of frugality little better than mere subsistence, until he had accumulated enough to build a modest five-room house.

Mother had meantime completed her education and returned to Lagrange to teach. They were married there in October 1882, and returned to Atlanta to the sparsely furnished cottage where Mother characteristically plunged in on her lifelong war against every vestige of dust or dirt within range. The next year my brother, George, was born, to be followed during the next seventeen years by five sisters and myself. I stand in respectful awe and admiration of the job they did, financing such a home and family on the microscopic salary which Father earned. During most of his life it was one hundred dollars a month, that sum being increased many years later by twenty-five dollars for maintenance of a horse and mail collector's cart (for which Father had to pay). A decade later the family income was modestly increased by thirty or forty dollars a month. This came from the rental of the cottage which had been moved back to permit building a larger house, made necessary by the regular additions to the family.

Although there were times when Mother told us we could not afford some of the innumerable things children always ask of their parents, so skilled was Mother's management and so sharp her pride that we never knew how really poor we were. It was true that the price of foodstuffs was far lower than now, yet, even so, the way she managed to feed us on her small food budget was little less than a miracle. Although Mother's skill with the needle was perhaps somewhat less than genius, she more than made up for it in quantity production of dresses and other garments for my sisters and shirts for Father, George, and me.

On Mondays by five o'clock in the morning Mother's arms were immersed in the first of many tubs of washing, aided by each of the children as soon as she or he was large enough to help. Wednesdays were for ironing and Saturdays for putting up quantities of jellies and preserves and canned vegetables in season, shopping, and all the other tasks of maintaining a well-run household. Similarly every other day had its allotted program.

To no other man I have ever known has a very personal God been so real as was Father's to him. To Father He was no vengeful, humorless being off in some far place. He was instead a very friendly sort of Deity with whom one enjoyed a quiet, warm relationship too precious to be endangered by overfrequent or demanding supplication. Unlike many of the churchy people I knew who constantly babbled of what good Christians they were and thereby built up a vigorous suspicion of their sanctity, Father seldom talked of religion or attempted to press his beliefs upon others, even his own family. He would discuss God and religion more often with me than with my brother or sisters, chiefly because we habitually spent four hours together each weekday, and three on Sunday, in the mail cart, which naturally provided the setting for talk on many subjects.

In that sanctuary of heaped-up mail, faintly redolent of mucilage and canvas, Father and I invariably but amicably would take the opposite sides of the questions we discussed. It was only by accident years later I learned that Father did this deliberately to spur me to study and read whatever was available to find substantiation for my arguments. He never forgot to remind me of my own statement during one of our discussions of God. Father had mentioned the omnipotence and omniscience of God. Brashly I ventured to deny this. "If God is omnipotent as you say He is, why doesn't He just decree that each of us be free of sin and weakness, and then devote the enormous amount of time thus saved to more productive uses? If God is really all-powerful, He wouldn't have to work through fallible human minds and hearts, without which He apparently can do nothing."

I shall never forget the benign yet triumphant smile on Father's face as he paused so long to reply that I turned to where he stood on the step of the cart to see how he reacted to such blasphemy.

"That is just my point," he answered. "God *is* omnipotent, but He *chooses* to work through human instruments like you and me and every other human being on earth. Never forget that He needs your brain and heart to work His will."

To the day of his death, and particularly after I had begun to work with the National Association for the Advancement of Colored People, Father used to write to me of his happiness and pride that, in the work I was attempting to do to wipe out race prejudice, "God is using your brain and heart." For days after such a letter arrived I would be subdued in spirit because of this exaggerated opinion of Father's, which I was often tempted to deny. I did not do so, because that simple belief seemed to compensate him for the workridden and selfless life he had lived to give his children the best opportunity for education he and Mother could afford.

The heavy hand of a strict Puritan Sunday which Father absorbed from the New England teachers at Atlanta University patterned the Sabbath in our home. Industrious preparations for that day began on Saturday, when every rug in the house was hung over a clothesline in the yard and beaten until the last microscopic speck of dirt was driven out. Coal scuttles in kitchen, dining room, and bedrooms had to be filled to the brim, and kindling chopped with which I laid early Sunday morning fires. Saturday afternoon was the time when shoes for all the family had to be "blacked" with a sticky paste which smelled of some acid and which could be softened only by generous and frequent applications of spit. Trips to the market, whitewashing fences, feeding and watering the horse, and whatever other chores Mother's extraordinarily fertile brain could devise, filled the other hours. Saturday's final chore was to stoke the kitchen stove until it was red-hot to heat enough water for baths for all our large family.

On Sunday morning we dressed and solemnly descended to the parlor for prayer. This was a room used only for weddings, funerals, Sunday prayers, and equally important occasions. Antimacassars decorated each of the chairs and the sofa. A bell-shaped glass dome shielded a spray of artificial flowers. A stout family Bible with its diamond-shaped mirror on the cover dimly reflected the morning sunlight, and a glass-doored bookcase filled with bound sets of the classics and Dr. Eliot's Five-Foot collection created an atmosphere which banished whatever ebullience any of us might be feeling, as effectively as though we were entering a cathedral.

There was no time on weekdays for more than the briefest blessing of food by Father. But Sundays were different. None of us dared be late for eight o'clock devotions. That gave an hour and a half for prayer and breakfast before the children were sent to Sunday school at the First Congregational Church, which was half a block away at the corner of Houston and Courtland Streets. Relieved of the pressure of time, Father quietly gloried in the luxury of leisure in which to advise with God.

Those Sunday mornings are always associated in my mind with sore knees and slippery horsehair. Each of the children would arrange himself quietly and as comfortably as possible on sofa or chair, the upholstering of which sloped sharply downward both in the rear and in the front. The younger children were bedeviled by fear of Father's displeasure at squirming on the one hand or, on the other, of slipping on the treacherous horsehair if the ridge became so uncomfortable as to make shifting one's position necessary. Mother always sat near the door so that she could go out quietly if the smell of scorching rolls required.

When we were seated and silent, Father would hand the Bible to one of us to select and read a chapter. The reading finished, we knelt while Father reported with considerable detail to the Lord on a variety of matters in the White household and neighborhood, his reports interlarded with respectful but firm intimations that one or two of them had not been handled by Heaven with as complete wisdom as might have been desirable. With equal firmness, but fitting deference, Father made suggestions on how events of the coming week should go.

Father's concentration on his conversation with the Deity was never too great, however, to keep him from half-opening his eyes in a minatory survey of his audience to see if each of us was respectfully on his knees. I was always a skinny child whose kneecaps had no protection of flesh. After the first few minutes of kneeling the agony became so unbearable that I would shift unobtrusively sidewise to a position from which I could speedily bounce back to my knees if Father's head turned in my direction. But not always was I alert enough.

When we had recited the Lord's Prayer, Father would open ceremoniously the sliding double doors between parlor and dining room, occasionally with gently acid comment by Mother if the prayers had been too long and the rolls were scorched.

We loved Sunday breakfasts. Mother's rolls emitted a lovely fragrance of yeast and golden butter, and there was fried chicken or fish, the omnipresent hominy grits, and steaming coffee, followed by thin slices of sweet Rocky Ford cantaloupes. By dividing them with mathematical precision Mother could make one large melon do for eight or nine of us. Unhappily, the melon season in those pre-hothouse days was all too short. Consequently most of the year the breakfast fruit was either stewed prunes, or dried apples cooked after soaking overnight and served liberally sugared and cinnamoned.

I did not mind Sunday school, but found it almost insufferable to sit still on the handsome but hard pews during the long church services at eleven.

Spring or summer, autumn or winter, the schedule for Sunday afternoons was identical. As soon as the dinner dishes were washed Father solemnly marched up the stairs to his room for an afternoon nap, followed by the rest of us. However much we might have been tempted to dawdle or to seek refuge in some part of the house where it was cooler in summer or warmer in winter, it never occurred to us to do so.

For no other reason than to escape boredom, I experienced on these Sunday afternoons the only desire to study my school lessons. But that was sternly forbidden by Father as sinful on the Sabbath. The same prohibition applied to the reading of any novel less than twenty-five years old. I never learned the formula by which Mother and Father arrived at the conclusion that a work of fiction became pure by attainment of the age of a quarter of a century, while the most moral novels, if new, were sinful.

I had read over and over again by the time I was twelve or thirteen years old each of the meager stock of books in the glass-doored mahogany bookcase in the parlor. These included Shakespeare, Dickens, Thackeray, Trollope, and some of the Harvard Classics.

These were supplemented by books from the church library, and by the time I was twelve I had read a rather large number of good books.

Before it was rebuilt, the First Congregational Church was a charming red brick structure with a wide lawn surrounded by an iron picket fence. The lawn was a kind of private playground for the children of church members. But we often had to do battle to protect our bailiwick from the gangs of white boys on Courtland Street. Although the warfare was intermittent and usually productive of nothing more serious than a bloody nose or bruised knuckles, we derived a certain joy from it. We were more often victorious than defeated, chiefly, as I remember it now, because a defending force had certain tactical advantages over an attacking body. If the white boys called up reserves, we could always find refuge in the church.

But it was too bad for anyone who was caught alone. At the corner of Cortland Street was a watering trough for horses. Occasionally thirsty humans patronized it also; you pressed down on a handle and contorted your body so as to get your face under the spigot. Mother, who was a fanatical foe of germs and dirt in any form, forbade our drinking from the fountain lest we contract some fearful disease. But for some mysterious reason the water of this fountain always seemed much more delicious than that from one of Mother's spotlessly shining cut-glass tumblers.

One day as I was drinking from the forbidden fountain one of the white boys of the neighborhood crept up behind me and pushed sharply the back of my head, causing my nose to bang against the spigot and my face and clothing to be showered with water. Shaking the water from my eyes, I ran after the boy, who yelled derisive remarks about "niggers drinking from white fountains." Forgetting in my rage that I was following him into enemy territory, I became increasingly infuriated as he lengthened his lead. Knowing I could not overtake him, I picked up a stone and threw it with unaccustomed accuracy, hitting him on the back of the head. I saw him stagger and clutch his head, the blood oozing between the fingers. My anger changed to cold terror. I had hit and injured a *white* boy and, knowing that a white policeman, judge, and jury would take his word, I saw myself being sent away to prison for a long term.

Forgetting the groceries I had been on my way to purchase, I ran home sobbing to Mother, begging her to whip me. Somehow or other I felt that if she did so I would thereby escape other punishment. Instead of sympathizing with me, Mother roared with laughter, remarking that she would be grateful if I would specify for which one of my many misdeeds I was asking to be punished. Expecting a burly policeman to put in his appearance any minute, I had no time to supply a bill of particulars.

"Never mind what for," I pleaded, "just whip me—whip me quick!"

But now Mother was laughing so hard that she sat down to wipe the tears from her eyes with her apron. Sure enough the door bell rang long and insistently. Mother went to the front door to face the irate mother of the boy I had hit, while I, then about eight years old, peered in terror from behind Mother's skirts.

"I am going to have the law on that boy of yours," she screamed, "for hitting my poor little boy." Sternly Mother turned to me and demanded that I tell her what had happened. My story finished, Mother turned upon the woman and so vigorously defended me that the unwelcome visitor's anger soon cooled under Mother's threat to have the other boy arrested for attacking me first. So convincing was Mother that soon my fear vanished and I began to preen myself as something of a hero. That mood did not last long. As soon as her visitor had left, Mother turned and ordered me to go into the back yard and get some switches from the peach tree. These she peeled to make their sting more memorable. Thereafter I managed to quench my thirst at home instead of from the forbidden fountain.

Mother believed no less in God, but her rules of conduct were less Spartan than Father's. After his death she even permitted bridge-playing in her home. Once when she was visiting in New York I offered her a drink, assuring her that she need have no qualms, because it had been made by monks. Not wholly believing me, she turned to my wife to ask if I were telling the truth. Gladys assured her that it had been made by Benedictine monks. With this assurance that she was not sinning, Mother tossed off the powerful liqueur in one gulp. A few minutes later Aunt Alice, Mother's only sister and equally talkative, called to visit and, accepting Mother's lead, also drank a glass of the benedictine.

"It's nothing but sweet water, Alice, and made by the monks," Mother assured her.

My dismay rose higher and higher as the two in their innocence waxed gayer and gayer as the contents of the bottle rapidly disappeared.

Father had believed with absolute devotion that "wine is a mocker." Once, a few weeks after I was born, he had been dangerously ill with typhoid fever. They tried to get him to take a tablespoon of brandy as a stimulant. Though only half-conscious, Father demanded to know what they were giving him and on being told, clenched his teeth tightly, refusing to "face my Maker with liquor on my breath."

Father and Mother were of medium height though, as women do, she appeared somewhat taller. Father's skin, though naturally very light, was deeply tanned from many years of exposure to sun and wind in his work as a mail carrier. His hair was brown, as were his eyes. Mother had almost severely aquiline features, with light blue eyes and the most golden hair that I have ever seen. Theirs must have been a difficult life as they guided themselves and us along the course between the Scylla of white hostility and the Charybdis of some Negroes' resentment against us because we occupied a slightly more comfortable and better-kept home and were less dark than they.

The streetcars of Atlanta were places where interracial conflict most often occurred. Whites were supposed to sit from the front of the car toward the rear and Negroes were required to sit from the rear toward the front. If Mother and my sisters boarded a car and sat in the "Negro" section they were often objects at best of embarrassing stares and remarks and not infrequently of insults and other indignities from white male passengers. If they had sat in the "white" section they would have been accused by some Negroes of "passing." It was because of this that Father indulged in the only extravagance I ever knew about when he bought the surrey.

The shining vehicle was more a burden to me than a joy, because it was my job to keep it cleaned and greased and to drive it when Mother wished to go calling on her friends.

I did not understand at the time the probable significance of an episode involving Father and the surrey. One day I entered the carriage house, in the front of which stood the mail cart and at the rear the surrey. I was barefoot, so I made no sound on the soft earth. Father stood by the surrey stroking the patent-leather mudguard. It was the one moment of his life when I saw him extract joy from anything except complete selfless service to his family and his God.

When he became aware of my presence he snatched his hand away from the carriage with almost the same appearance of guilt as I had when Mother caught me with my hand in the great stone crock of pickled peaches. Almost gruffly he sought to explain his action. "The surrey is awfully dusty," he said. "Get a cloth and wipe it off."

III

A Jew Is Lynched

For my first job, which I took at the age of ten, I was paid the munificent salary of fifty cents a week. My employer was I. Kalish, who operated a small tailor shop on Peachtree Street opposite the Grand Opera House. I reported for work at seven in the morning, swept out the store and dusted, washed two small front windows, and started out about nine to collect suits to be drycleaned and pressed, returning them to their owners in the afternoon. After I had worked a month my salary was raised to seventy-five cents a week. This, with occasional tips, brought my earnings sometimes as high as a dollar and a half a week.

During later summer vacations I worked one year as office boy for a doctor and another in the same capacity for a bibulous and unsuccessful artesian well driller. However, I soon became impatient with wages no higher than three or four dollars a week. A number of my friends told me of earning as much as a dollar a day plus tips as bellboys or waiters in Atlanta's hotels. Over Mother's objections, because she feared the kind of "carryings on" I would see, I applied one summer for a job as bellboy at the Piedmont Hotel, then Atlanta's most luxurious.

I got a job as page-boy and wore the most gaudy and glamorous uniform of all time. It was a rich purple woolen, which, with a few alterations, fitted me like wallpaper. Three rows of globular buttons, one from the collar button straight down and the other two from the shoulders down to the waist, were matched by other buttons on the sleeves and as much gold braid as that of an admiral of the fleet. A brimless cap, also adorned with gold braid and brass buttons, was perched saucily on the side of my head. Tips were good, sometimes running as high as a dollar or more a day, which, added to the wage of a dollar, seemed like more money than any other person in Atlanta possessed.

I had been working a week or so when I discovered I was "passing"—the job of page having been hitherto a "white" job. Again panic assailed me. I went to Fred Toomer, now a successful insurance executive of the Atlanta Life Insurance Company, who was captain of the Piedmont Hotel bellboys. He was an athletic hero of mine as the hard-hitting third baseman of the Atlanta University baseball team. I found consolation in Fred.

"Mr. Dutton did not ask you if you were white or colored. It's a good job and you're doing it well. All he can do to you is to fire you. You are making good money, so go ahead and earn it until you are fired," was his advice.

I decided to stick on the job, but it was not easy. When Mr. Dutton offered me the position of key clerk the following year, however, at a salary of a hundred dollars a month plus board and room, I found that I couldn't sail under false colors any longer. To cleanse my conscience I blurted that I could not accept the job of key clerk, as I did not want to get him into difficulty. He heard me through to the end of my confession.

"You are better educated and better bred than most of my clerks," he told me. "I'm from New Hampshire, and the fact that you are a Negro makes no difference to me. But I am operating a hotel in the South and my guests would leave if they found out that you were colored. But I wish you luck."

I decided to get a job as colored in another hotel, because I needed the wages and tips which could be earned as a bellboy—higher than in any other temporary employment open to Negroes in Atlanta. I had to earn money to help Father pay my tuition and other expenses at Atlanta University. In the new job I began with startling speed my education in the facts of life and particularly, to borrow Langston Hughes's phrase, "in the ways of white folks." What I saw and heard there made it impossible for me ever again to be taken in by the white man's boast of the superiority of his morals over those of the Negro.

The summer before my senior year at Atlanta University was spent working harder and earning less money than almost any other period of my life. Although I could have returned to bell-hopping or waiting on table, I had become disgusted with that kind of life and particularly at the treatment a Negro had to endure from patrons in a Southern hotel. I applied for and was given employment during the summer selling policies for the Standard Life Insurance Company.

I soon learned that the market of prospects in Atlanta had been so thoroughly covered by more experienced salesmen that it would be a waste of time for me to remain there. I set out, therefore, for smaller towns and rural areas. I was given no salary or expense account, my compensation consisting of a percentage of the premiums on the insurance which I sold. I could not afford to rent an automobile or even a horse and buggy. That summer I walked more miles, usually under a broiling sun, than at any period of my life. But I learned a lot from talking with whites of these rural areas, especially when they believed me to be of their own race.

Invariably, since I was from Atlanta, they asked me about the Leo M. Frank case. A young white factory girl had been raped and murdered in an Atlanta pencil factory of which Frank was president. Suspicion had fastened on him and, to a lesser extent as a possible accessory, on a Negro janitor. Frank was not only a Jew but a "damyankee" from New York. Under "normal" circumstances no one would have thought of accusing a white man had he been gentile and Southern. The guilt of the Negro would have been the inevitable assumption and he would have been lynched or tried, convicted, and executed. Because of Frank's religion and place of birth the case developed into a clash of prejudice in which anti-Northern and anti-Semitic hatreds had been whipped to such a frenzy that the usual anti-Negro prejudice was almost forgotten.

Frank was tried in a courtroom packed to capacity, with many of the spectators openly armed. A howling mob filled the grounds around the courthouse. Open threats against the jurors, if they did not return a prompt verdict of guilty, were shouted incessantly. It was inevitable that under the circumstances a verdict of guilty of murder in the first degree would be brought in by the jury. The verdict was promptly appealed by powerful Jewish organizations, because Frank at the time of his arrest was president of the B'nai B'rith. Despite brilliant presentation of the appeal the United States Supreme Court confirmed the verdict of the Georgia court, ruling that as long as a state court observed the form of a trial the federal government had no right to go beyond the form and inquire into the spirit which dominated the trial.

I never dreamed at the time that five years later I would investigate a trial similarly dominated by a mob; but when that time came, I remembered many of the conversations I had held about Frank and his trial as I went about the country selling insurance, and what I learned through them.

Frank's conviction so shocked Governor John M. Slaton of Georgia that, although it meant political suicide for him, he commuted the death sentence to life imprisonment. A mob attempted to lynch the Governor. Only his courage in facing them, and the intervention of the police, saved his life.

Actually Frank was one more racial victim of Southern political ambition. Hugh M. Dorsey, who had prosecuted him, was riding triumphantly on the crest of popular approval in his campaign for the governorship. Thomas E. Watson, running for office as United States senator, seized upon the Frank case and used his weekly newspaper, *The Jeffersonian*, to win popular approval through preaching race hatred.

A few days after the commutation of his sentence a mob entered the state prison, took Frank to Marietta where Mary Fagan, the murdered girl, had been born and was buried, and lynched him.

Soon after that Thomas Watson was elected to the United States Senate, and Hugh Dorsey to the governorship of Georgia.

I returned to Atlanta to enter college with only a few dollars to show for my summer's work. In addition to playing not too good football, serving as president of my class, being a member of the university debating team, and a few other extracurricular activities of that sort, I worked throughout the school year preparing for the Standard Life Insurance Company simple mathematical tables dealing with net and deferred premiums and preparing actuarial tables which required simply care and the following of formulae.

At a forum in Kansas City several years ago a member of the audience asked me to tell of some of my experiences in investigating race riots and lynchings, and I complied with that request. After the meeting had adjourned a sensitive-faced man came to the platform to ask, "How have you managed to escape hate? I would imagine that you would despise every white face you see after the horrible experiences you have had."

For a brief moment a wholly unjustified glow of smug satisfaction came over me as I mentally congratulated myself at escaping the corrosive effect of hating groups of people because of the sins of some of their members. My smugness was short-lived. It dawned upon me for the first time how indebted I was to the unselfish and brilliant men and women who had forsaken their homes in New England to go south to teach in school like Atlanta University. There they had been subjected to ostracism and sometimes insult from Southern whites for teaching and associating on a basis of complete equality with Negroes. Many of them were so well-trained and able that they could have earned much larger salaries and lived in far greater comfort in the North. They had been moved by a selfless devotion to a cause in which they passionately believed— education for the Negro on the same basis as for others.

The Kansas City question caused me at the time, and many times since, to realize the debt I owe to men like Professor Edgar N. Webster, handsome and brilliant professor of physics. He and his family, and those of President Edward Twichell Ware, Dean Myron W. Adams, Miss Mabel D. Hancock, Miss Idella M. Swift, and others demonstrated to us, even in prejudice-ridden Georgia, that not all white people were infected with delusions of racial superiority and opposed to progress for the Negro. It was they who saved me from the defeatist belief that all whites are evil and bigoted in their attitude toward dark-skinned peoples.

IV

Atlanta Negroes Unite

My four years of college, though they seemed interminable at the time, passed all too quickly. Before I had time to realize what was happening I stood, diploma in hand, uncertainly facing the task of determining upon a career. I was offered the principalship of an American missionary school at Albany, Georgia, which flattered me immensely but which a brief teaching experience as a substitute during my senior college year caused me to decline speedily and firmly.

Fortunately my work as a salesman of insurance during the preceding summer, and my part-time work for the Standard Life Insurance Company during my senior year, brought me an offer of a job as clerk in that organization and I started to work the morning after my graduation. The pay was most modest, but my expenses were small since I was living at home. Evenings and Saturday afternoons I devoted to selling insurance. Not long afterward I was promoted to the position of cashier, which was less imposing and responsible than it sounds. My duties consisted of receiving premiums when paid in person and listing remittances by mail, turning over the checks and money orders and cash to the bookkeeper, who meticulously checked my reports and solemnly gave me receipts. My salary remained the same as it had been as a clerk, but I had the warming satisfaction of signing receipts in handwriting which I sought to make businesslike. The promotion had another advantage —it disproved, I hoped, the prediction which had been freely made that I was too young and too much interested in having a good time to do a responsible job satisfactorily.

In an effort to conceal my youth I began to grow a mustache, but even this, unfortunately, helped little: at its most luxuriant period it was hardly visible, since it turned out to be a delicate champagne color. As a matter of fact, it never has amounted to much. It was years later that it evoked a scoffing comment from Arthur B. Spingarn. A particularly inhuman lynching had just occurred in a Southern state which I was eager to investigate. The Board of Directors of the NAACP was reluctant to let me go because previous investigations had been so publicized that they feared it would be dangerous for me to go South. "I'll let my mustache grow," I pleaded, "and then no one will recognize me."

Arthur looked at me pityingly and then laughed. Said he: "Nobody but your sweetheart would ever know you had a mustache!"

One Sunday after church in the autumn of 1916 a group of us sat talking in the offices of the Standard Life. We had learned the day before that the Atlanta board of education was planning to save enough money to build a new high school for white students by eliminating the seventh grade from the colored grammar schools. Two years before this, the eighth grade had been abolished from the colored schools, the saving thus effected being given to the white schools. Because no protest had been made by Negroes then, it was obviously believed by the board of education that there would be none now.

Despair and consternation had descended on Negro Atlanta. There were no high schools of any description for colored students, although Negroes were taxed for maintenance of the school system at the same rate as whites on two million dollars of Negro-owned property. As for grammar schools, only fourteen were provided for a Negro population of more than seventy-five thousand. Thirteen of that number were very old and dilapidated wooden structures which, in addition to being fire hazards, were so overcrowded that double and triple sessions were necessary to accommodate the overflow. The one brick building for Negro children had been erected for and used by whites until a new modern one was built for them. Parents of Negro children who wished their children to receive an education beyond the seventh grade had to pay tuition for that instruction at schools like Atlanta University, which were forced to maintain high school departments because of the failure of Georgia communities to furnish high school training.

And now the Negro seventh grade was to go. " 'Unto every one that hath shall be given, and he shall have abundance; but from him that hath not shall be taken away even that which he hath,' " patriarchal Jackson McHenry sadly observed at church that morning. Many of the older generation like Mr. McHenry advised caution and submission to prevent angering the dominant whites. But those of us who sat in the office felt that the line of surrender and compliance had to be drawn somewhere. What could we do? Negroes were voteless, outnumbered, helpless.

Harry Pace presented the only hopeful and concrete suggestion —that we write to the then fledgling National Association for the Advancement of Colored People at its New York headquarters to obtain their advice and aid. Someone else—I believe it was Carter Brown who had worked in New York for the NAACP—said we ought to form a branch in Atlanta. I was delegated to write the letter, and sat down to do so immediately. We felt less helpless when the letter had been mailed.

Before a reply could be received we learned to our dismay that some informer—a local Uncle Tom—had rushed to the board of education to tell them that Negroes, for the first time in the history of Atlanta, were planning to protest. Despite the apparent futility of such objection or the ease with which the board could dismiss it, the officials became alarmed at such unprecedented and bold action. They decided to move forward the date of the meeting and give no publicity to the change, to vote abolition of the Negro seventh grades and make that action a *fait accompli* before the "impudent, radical Negro delegation" made its appearance. However, just as the board of education had its informers, so did we have ours, and thereby we learned of the change of date for the meeting.

They would not permit me to be a member of the delegation which was appointed to appear before the board because I was "too young and hot-headed," but I was made a member of the committee to draft the petition which would be presented to the board. A few thought we should limit our demands to retention of the seventh grades; others of us were equally insistent that as taxpayers and citizens we should demand high schools, both regular and technical, new and more modern grammar schools, and every other facility being given to white students. Our point of view won. In a document of nearly twenty-five hundred words, we boldly demanded for the Negro children of Atlanta educational facilities in every way the equal of those enjoyed by their white contemporaries.

Tall, dignified, and handsome Dr. William F. Penn, graduate of Yale University and stepfather of Dr. Louis T. Wright, who was destined later to serve as chairman of the board of directors of the NAACP, acted as chairman of the committee to present the petition to the board of education. Harry H. Pace, Dr. John Hope, Benjamin J. Davis, Sr., head of the Negro Odd Fellows of Georgia and chairman of the Georgia State Republican Committee, and other members of the committee, respectfully but vigorously backed up Dr. Penn's plea.

Little effort was made by the board to conceal its amazement and resentment at Negroes' daring to question or oppose the will of the white majority of Atlanta or the plans of the board to do as it willed about education for Negroes. To listen to hitherto docile Negroes bluntly saying that they would no longer submit to educational discrimination and injustice was as though a mouse had turned on a terrier many times its size.

To our astonishment, and the discomfiture of other members of the board, the presentation received unexpected support from James L. Key, who was later to be mayor of Atlanta. He had listened with deep concentration to the statements of Dr. Penn, Mr. Pace, and Mr. Davis. When they had finished, Mr. Key rose and with troubled voiced declared to his fellow board members:

"Gentlemen, I want to plead guilty to every word these men have spoken. We have the government in our hands, we control the finances, and we should be derelict to our duty if we did not grant their demands."

Mayor Asa G. Candler, head of the Coca-Cola Company, jumped to his feet and shouted angrily, "I do not agree with the gentleman who has just spoken. I do not wish to plead guilty. Let us not give way to hysteria but look at this matter in a sane manner."

Mr. Key refused to be sidetracked. He turned to the Mayor and heatedly answered, "The seat of all hysteria in this city is in the Mayor's office and the chief professor of that science is the Mayor himself. I do plead guilty, and as long as I am a member of this board I pledge my word here today that I shall fight for the rights of these men. Every move that is for the giving of justice to them has my hearty support and I shall cast my vote against every move that tries to take away from them what is theirs."

We never found out what was said in executive session after the delegation left. But a few days later, to our delight, the board announced that it had abandoned its plan to cut short the education of Negroes and had decided instead to float a bond issue to improve Atlanta schools.

Although there were some who advised that, having won the skirmish of the eighth grade, decision should be left to the school authorities as to what part of the money from the bond issue would be applied to the deplorably inadequate and run-down colored schools, others believed we should leave nothing to chance and should secure as definite commitments as possible from the school board. Meanwhile, organization of the Atlanta branch of the NAACP was speeded in anticipation of the struggle ahead. Harry Pace was chosen as president and I was elected secretary. Our first public meeting had as speaker the great James Weldon Johnson, who, after a distinguished career as writer of Broadway successes with his brother Rosamond, and as United States consul to Nicaragua and Venezuela, had joined the small staff of the NAACP as field secretary.

In the interim, our committee of Dr. Penn, Mr. Pace, and Mr. Davis appeared again before the board of education. They were told with brutal frankness and considerable profanity that none of the bond money was to be spent on Negro schools and that there was nothing colored citizens could do about it. Members of the board had been attacked in editorials in some of the Atlanta papers and ridiculed by many of their friends for being "whipped into line by niggers." They were in no mood to incur further attacks and, although at least one member was not unsympathetic to at least patching up the Negro schools, the board voted unanimously against the request of our delegation.

The job of keeping alive a determination to continue the fight was discouraging and eventually hopeless. We studied the law and found no legal basis there. We could find nothing in the Georgia State Constitution which could be used to force the Atlanta authorities to abide by the United States Supreme Court's decisions that "separate" educational facilities for Negroes must be "equal" to those provided for whites. As all hope seemed gone, someone—I forget now who it was—proposed that we examine the city charter of Atlanta in order to learn what was required for the floating of bond issues. There we found the answer: the charter required affirmative approval of two-thirds of the registered voters, and not, fortunately for our purpose, two-thirds of those who actually took the trouble to vote. We counted on white voters' neglecting—in the great American tradition—to vote on an issue in which no personalities were involved.

Our major hurdle was the poll tax. We started a house-to-house campaign through the third and fourth wards and on the west side where the Negro population was segregated. Patiently we explained the details of the issue. The response was immediate and heartening —in fact, so much so that we had to space out the appearance of Negroes at the City Hall lest there be time for a counter-campaign among the whites on the "Negro issue." I shall never forget the excitement when one none-too-prosperous man paid back poll taxes with accrued interest for thirty-two years—a sum he could ill afford—in order to vote, even though all his children were long past grammar or high school age. When our opponents woke up and started belligerent and viciously anti-Negro tirades against "Negro domination," the time was too short to register a large enough number of white voters to override the Negro vote.

The James Weldon Johnson mass meeting in the moving picture theater in the Odd Fellows Building was so packed with eager-faced Negroes and even a few whites that we had difficulty wedging the platform party through the crowd to enter the auditorium. Mr. Johnson, calm, slender, and immaculate, stood hazardously on the narrow strip of stage between the footlights and a painted backdrop, characteristic of theaters of that day. The backdrop advertised the Gate City Drugstore, the Standard Life Insurance Company, the Atlanta Life, and other Negro business enterprises. There was none of the sonorous, flamboyant oratory of that era in the meeting— only the quiet, irrefutable presentation of the facts and the need to wipe out race prejudice before the hate thereby engendered destroyed both the victims and the perpetrators.

One of the white members of the audience, a puzzled expression on his face, stopped me after the meeting to say, "This is a new doctrine. I wonder how many white preachers in Atlanta have vision enough to see or say what Johnson said today. Imagine a Negro being as concerned about white people who kick him around as he is about his own race!" He shook his head as though to clear it of something which had not happened, and wandered off toward the white section of town.

Two years later I heard Mr. Johnson tell a vast audience in New York's Carnegie Hall that "the race problem in the United States has resolved itself into a question of saving black men's bodies and white men's souls." This revolutionary doctrine caused that evening the same bewilderment and surprise on the faces of Charles Evans Hughes, the late Anna Howard Shaw, and a former governor of Alabama who spoke on the same program.

It happened that at the Atlanta meeting I sat nearest to the platform, next to the gentle Dr. Hope. Suddenly I was called upon, to my dismay, to say a few words. Caught off guard, I nervously asked Dr. Hope what I should say.

"Tell them about the NAACP," he advised with a perfectly straight face.

I launched into an impassioned and, I fear, a rabble-rousing speech.

"We have got to show these white people that we aren't going to stand being pushed around any longer. As Patrick Henry said, so must we say, 'Give me liberty, or give me death!' "

The audience loved it. But when I looked at the school principal his face was ashen with terror, as he saw his job go glimmering when news of the meeting got back to the superintendent and school board.

Before Mr. Johnson left Atlanta, Mother and Father invited him to dinner. Throughout the meal he watched me, and I was inordinately pleased at the attention he paid to what I said and the number of questions he asked me.

After he had returned to New York I received a letter from him saying that he had recommended to the NAACP board of directors that I be invited to join the staff of the Association as assistant secretary and that he had been authorized to ascertain whether I would be interested in such a job. To say I was startled is a most moderate description of my reaction. To accept would mean abandonment of all the plans of financial security I had made. The job in New York would pay only twelve hundred dollars a year, which was less than I was then earning in salary and commissions from the sale of insurance and stock in the Standard Life. I paid only a modest sum each week to Mother for board, lodging, and laundry —far less than I would have to pay on my own in expensive New York. Mother was very vocal against my leaving home to live in "that Sodom and Gomorrah" of New York, where, she was certain, I would immediately succumb to all the fancy evils which she believed lurked around every corner of Manhattan. Others whose advice I sought told me in varying degrees of frankness that I would be a fool to give up a bright financial future to devote myself to an almost hopeless cause.

The NAACP did, indeed, seem to offer at the time a precarious future at best. It consisted of only 8,490 individuals distributed in 76 branches, the membership of which ranged in number from one in St. Joseph, Missouri, to 692 in Boston. Its small staff of two officials—Roy Nash as secretary and Mr. Johnson as field secretary—one volunteer worker, Mary White Ovington, and two clerical workers, Richetta G. Randolph as stenographer and Frank M. Turner as bookkeeper, never knew from payday to payday whether salaries, rent, postage, and printing bills could be paid. It seems hardly conceivable, as this is being written, in 1947, when the Association has more than 1500 branches and a membership close to 600,000, that such penury and peril could have constantly threatened the movement so short a time ago.

The imminence of war and the possibility of being drafted was another circumstance which made me hesitate. While I debated the offer, a "flying squadron" of intensely patriotic young Negroes came to Atlanta during the courses of a Southern tour to induce Negroes to volunteer for the Negro officers' training camp which the War Department under pressure was planning to open at Fort Des Moines, Iowa. For the first time in history, the city of Atlanta permitted Negroes to use the city auditorium for a meeting to whip up patriotism. Some of us were invited to sit on the platform. When an eloquent appeal for volunteers was made, I found myself springing to my feet as one of the first to volunteer.

We were ordered to near-by Fort McPherson a day or two later for physical examinations. In the group were two other men whose skins, like my own, were light enough in color to make it possible for them to "pass." For some then unexplained reason we were asked to step aside, where we were scrutinized with none-too-friendly glances by several Army officers. We had no fear of failing to pass the physical—all three of us had participated in one or more sports, baseball, football, track—and were in top condition. We were totally wrong. All of us were rejected, while another fellow student, who had been the butt of campus jokes because of his frail and non-athletic physique, was accepted. We were all the more puzzled when we heard he had fallen in a dead faint the very first day on the parade grounds at Des Moines.

Later we learned the reason why the three of us, so patently healthy, had been rejected. Wild rumors, born of guilty consciences no doubt, were sweeping the South that the "Huns" were industriously at work among Southern Negroes to spread unrest. These German agents and spies, so the tales ran, were capitalizing on Negro bitterness against lynching and race prejudice. Fantastic stories were believed that as soon as white soldiers went off to war, Negroes would rise up and massacre white people in their beds under the direction of the Kaiser's agents. Obviously, light-skinned Negroes who could easily pass as white would be the kind the Kaiser would use!

Two persons urged me to accept the NAACP offer. One was Father. We hitched the horse to the surrey and went for a long drive one afternoon, far out into the country past the Piedmont Driving Club.

"Your mother and I have given you," he told me quietly, "the best education we could afford, and a good Christian home training. Fortunately, it is better than most colored children have had. Now it is your duty to pass on what you have been given by helping others less fortunate to get a chance in life. I don't want to see you go away. I'll miss you. But remember always, God will be using your heart and brains to do His will. You'll be misunderstood and criticized when you fight so difficult a battle as that created by the race problem. But decide, with the help of God, what's right and don't falter or turn back."

The other individual who urged me to go to New York was the brilliant surgeon, Dr. Louis T. Wright, who had only recently returned to Atlanta to practice medicine after a spectacularly successful career at the Harvard Medical School. Bluntly he told me, "You'd be a damned fool to stay here in Atlanta. Go to New York by all means. Life will mean much, much more to you when you are fighting for a cause than it possibly can if you stay here just to make money. You'll stagnate and eventually die mentally."

I wrote Mr. Johnson my acceptance and told him I would report for work on January 31, 1918. It was hard to leave Atlanta in the midst of the bond issue fight; but—to jump ahead of my story—I was delighted when later Negroes voted in sufficient numbers to defeat the bond issue despite a most bitter campaign of vilification by the Atlanta papers, particularly the *Atlanta Georgian.*

A new weapon for Negroes, the boycott, was used most effectively against that paper. Virtually every Negro subscriber canceled his subscription, and very few Negroes bought the paper from newsboys or news stands. Circulation dropped alarmingly. For the first time, the *Georgian* recognized the extent of Negro buying power. The newspaper's pride and prejudices would not permit it to abandon or backtrack on its attacks on Negroes for opposing the bond issue. It sought to placate aroused Negro subscribers by delivering the paper free, but such bribery proved equally ineffective. Many Negroes returned the papers, still rolled and folded as they had been, tossed into front yards and onto porches, to the *Georgian's* offices, or telephoned that they did not wish the publication on their premises.

Defeat of the bond issue placed the city of Atlanta in a most embarrassing position. The city's credit was not too good in the bond market anyway because of an already excessive bonded indebtedness and the inefficiency of management of the city's fiscal affairs. War with Germany moved closer and closer with grim inevitability. Little time remained. Swallowing pride, the city's officials asked representative Negroes what minimum concessions they would accept in return for support of, or at least nonopposition to, another bond issue.

As a result of the fight the Negroes of Atlanta made, the David T. Howard High School, named after a philanthropic and greatly loved Negro to whose farm we loved to go each summer for a magnificent barbecue, was erected, and the grade schools were patched up.

V

In Which I "Pass"

Mr. Johnson, who soon afterward urged me to call him "Jim," met me on arrival in New York on a bitterly cold day and took me to the place where he had arranged for me to board. My landlady was a retired caterer and one of the three or four best cooks whose food I have been privileged to taste. She could, for example, prepare ninety-two different soups, and I never did decide during all the years I lived at her house which of the ninety-two was most delicious.

Early the morning after I arrived Jim took me to the office, where I was introduced to Roy Nash, who was leaving the office of secretary to join the Army, and the handsome John Shillady, who was taking Roy's place. Richetta Randolph, who served as stenographer, confidante, and mentor to all of us, took me immediately under her protective wing, sensing with a woman's sure intuition how scared and unsure of myself I was. Until the day of her retirement she teased me about my addiction to blushing whenever spoken to, a trait which I fear I have long since lost.

Jim and I used to eat luncheon at the Automat, both because the food was good and inexpensive and because we could use the time saved by self-service to browse in Brentano's bookstore. All the sales clerks knew and admired Jim, so that we could spend as much time without interruption as we wished. Thus began for me a liberal education in contemporary literature as Jim either purchased for me or recommended my buying books of fiction, poetry, and history and discussion of social problems which he thought would be of permanent value.

On Lincoln's birthday, twelve days after I began work with the NAACP, an incredibly horrible lynching was staged at Estill Springs, Tennessee. Jim and I read on the bus on the way to work the next morning how Jim McIlherron, a Negro sharecropper, had been slowly burned to death by a mob for defending himself from a beating by his employer. As soon as we reached the office we talked with John Shillady as to what we could possibly do other than telegraph a protest to the governor, which, we knew, would do nothing more than possibly secure a few lines of publicity. I asked permission to go to the scene to make a first-hand investigation. Jim vigorously opposed this because he feared injury or death for me if my purpose and racial identity were discovered. Eventually, however, he gave reluctant consent, and thus I started a phase of work for the Association which neither it nor I had contemplated when I was employed.

My self-confidence steadily declined and my fear rose on the long train ride. I had learned, while an insurance agent in Georgia, enough of the cruelty of which Southern mobs were capable, and their fear and hatred of "outside interference in the affairs of the South," to know I would be given short shrift if McIlherron's murderers found out why I was there. As I remember the experience, however, I believed that I would be subjected to even greater fury for the sin of "passing" as a white man, which I had to do to induce the lynchers to talk freely. It was my first planned attempt to pass and, being so recently out of Georgia, I worried most because of that.

Everything moved smoothly at the outset. The third-rate boardinghouse, fraudulently bearing a weatherbeaten sign reading "Hotel," was run by a lanky and lazy individual whose ochre-colored skin was discolored by malaria and tobacco. Indolently waving in the general direction of my room to which I had to carry my own bag, he asked me in the same sentence my purpose in coming to Estill Springs and if I would be interested in buying a farm he owned which he described as "the best damned cotton land in Tennessee." Taking the unexpected cue, I allowed as how I might at least be interested enough to look at the farm, and thereby gained a guide and sponsor.

Although I was forced to spend more time than I wished looking at eroded farms, I learned a great deal about sleuthing during those days. Located about halfway between Nashville and Chattanooga, the rural hamlet of Estill Springs nevertheless was as remote from the outside world as though it had been in Tibet. Radios were then virtually unknown in that section and only one newspaper a week penetrated the abysmal darkness—a copy of the *Nashville Banner* which the mill owner of the town received. From early morning until nightfall and closing time, the country store was a forum and its stove a target for tobacco juice. There were no shades or grays of opinions—only the unequivocal black and white surveyed and discussed with the assurance of omniscience which comes from isolation and the absence of a desire for truth when truth is disturbing. I soon learned that a combination of such omniscience of the uninformed and the scarcity of excitement in such an atmosphere made it both unnecessary and unwise to ask questions about the recent lynching. It was apparent that the inhabitants could not refrain from talking in my presence if only I were patient.

The first few times the conversation veered toward the lynching I purposely exhibited eagerness to talk about politics or the weather or cotton-raising. My studied indifference and apparent ignorance of the fact that there had been any trouble began to become highly irritating to them. Even when they boasted and began to reveal far more than they realized as to the actual participants I deliberately intimated that I had known of much more exciting lynchings than that of McIlherron. When local pride had thus been sufficiently disparaged, the facts came tumbling forth. It was difficult to suppress evidence of my anger and nausea at the gruesome recital. The white man who had beaten McIlherron had no just cause for doing so, they admitted, and he was universally distrusted and disliked in the community. When I asked why then they had taken such terrible vengeance on McIlherron for refusing to submit to undeserved mistreatment from such a man, I was told "any time a nigger hits a white man, he's gotta be handled or else all the niggers will get out of hand."

New York City looked even more attractive and safe than when I first reached it after I had returned from Estill Springs. Publication of the facts I had uncovered created a modest sensation, particularly when my Estill Springs informants discovered that not only was I not a prospective buyer of land but a Negro who had been housed and fed in their local "hotel." On his next trip to Washington Jim suggested that I accompany him to tell senators and congressmen the first-hand story of the McIlherron burning at the stake to induce them to step up their efforts to enact federal legislation against mob violence. At that time the average number of lynchings annually was around two hundred, with additional mob murders unreported in the press. The overwhelming majority of Americans, including Negroes, accepted without question the belief that most lynchings were in punishment of rape of white women by Negroes. To ascertain and publish the truth the NAACP began a study, "Thirty Years of Lynching in the United States, 1889–1918," which amazed those who read it when it revealed that less than one-sixth of the victims of more than five thousand lynchings had been accused even by the mobs themselves of sex crimes.

It was Jim's skillful hand which guided the efforts for passage of federal legislation against lynching during the twenties. I frequently joined him in appearing before Senate and House committees and in the laborious work of buttonholing congressmen and senators to get them to work more vigorously. Year after year and session after session of Congress went by, and still no anti-lynching bill was enacted. We were able to secure the passage of the Dyer Bill by the House of Representatives; but invariably the bill would meet its death in the Senate through filibusters which still are possible because of the archaic rules of the upper house, which permit each senator to speak twice for as long as his strength permits on any bill and any amendment thereto.

However, the campaign for federal legislation publicized the facts about lynching. Each year we noted an increase in the number of Americans who dared speak out against the crime. Each year we noted a decrease even in the South of the number of public officials and ministers of the Gospel who dared to defend lynching. Publication of the first authentic study of mob murder helped to change editorial comment on lynching, particularly in its revelation of the falsity of the relation between lynchings and rape. Americans were astounded (some of them still are) to learn that fellow Americans have been put to death by mobs for such "crimes" as "being too prosperous for a Negro," talking back to a white man, and for refusing to turn out of the road to let a white boy pass.

These years, however, were not all devoted to work and tragedies. Jim and Grace, his beautiful and charming wife, were responsible more than any others for the so-called Negro Renaissance of the early twenties. Frequently their apartment was the gathering place of writers, poets, singers, and men and women of the theater. Many an evening we talked until long after midnight. The color line was never drawn at Jim's. It was there that many who were later to do much in wiping out the color line learned to know each other as fellow human beings and fellow artists without consciousness of race.

Sometimes there would be parties at my house or at the homes of one or another of those I met at Jim's. Heywood Broun, Claude McKay, Fania Marinoff, and Carl Van Vechten (who later established the invaluable James Weldon Johnson Memorial Collection at Yale University), Langston Hughes, Eva and Newman Levy, Ruth Hale, Countee Cullen, Carl and Irita Van Doren, Marie Doro, Edna St. Vincent Millay, Sinclair Lewis, George Gershwin, Mary Ellis, Willa Cather, Blanche and Alfred Knopf, Walter Wanger, Joan Bennett, and many others who then enjoyed fame or were destined to achieve distinction in the arts, letters, or human relations were among those I was privileged to know.

VI

I Decline to Be Lynched

The blood lust which World War One was too short to satiate made the year 1919 one of almost unmitigated horror and tension. Violent and bloody race riots broke out in Washington, Chicago, Omaha, Philadelphia; Phillips County, Arkansas, and other areas. John Shillady's considerable experience in social work organizations and his skill at organization itself had resulted in the first large-scale membership drive of the Association's history, which had raised our membership to 35,888. In 1919, the first large annual conference at Cleveland made the Association far more widely known than it had ever been before.

We needed all the strength we had gained and much more when the bloody summer of that year arrived. Jim investigated the Washington riot. I was sent to Chicago, where without much difficulty I was able to secure evidence against some of the ringleaders of the riot, which I turned over to the mayor and prosecutor. What I learned there caused me more than ever before to understand the economic factors in race prejudice.

Charles H. Dennis, the brilliant and famous editor of the *Chicago Daily News*, suggested to Carl Sandburg and to me that we ascertain the relationship between property values on the South Side, where the Negro section had materially expanded as a result of wartime migration, and the riot itself. What we found was startling. Property owners in the sections into which Negroes had moved or, more frequently, shrewd real estate agents, sold houses to Negroes at prices much higher than those which could have been obtained from white buyers. Barred by prejudice from purchasing homes in an open market, Negroes had to pay these prices or else stay in the crowded slums around State Street. Frightened owners, fearing devaluation of their properties as Negroes became their neighbors, sold their homes at considerable sacrifice to unscrupulous agents who promptly resold them at far above their real worth. It was inevitable that whites thus exploited would resent Negroes who they believed were responsible for the loss of much of their life's savings.

In many cases, large houses were subdivided into one- and two-room apartments to be rented to home-hungry Negroes. Income from the houses was thereby multiplied. Meanwhile, the owners rushed to City Hall to claim and obtain lowered valuations and smaller taxes, on the spurious grounds that occupancy by Negroes made the property less valuable. With Negroes in the buildings, they were able also to spend less on repairs and general maintenance than was spent on apartment buildings occupied by whites. Thus, they benefited from a three-way advantage: higher rentals, lower taxes, and reduced upkeep. Houses which had brought an annual income of five or six per cent under white occupancy now brought returns of ten per cent or better. I have never been able to find a law of economics which explains why, when a return on an investment is increased, the investment itself is considered less valuable merely because Negroes are involved.

The Chicago riot taught me that there could be as much peril in a Northern city when the mob is loose as in a Southern town such as Estill Springs. I was constantly made aware in white areas, especially the Halsted Street area near the stockyards, that eternal alertness was the price of an uncracked skull. I naïvely believed that I was well enough known in Negro Chicago, despite my white skin, to wander about at will without danger. This fallacy nearly cost me my life. One afternoon about dusk, I walked south on State Street to keep an appointment at the Binga State Bank located at the corner of Thirty-seventh Street. I never knew what made me look down Thirty-sixth Place toward the Provident Hospital. At any rate, I did look just in time to see a Negro draw a bead on me with a revolver from behind a tree. I ducked as a bullet whanged into the side of the building exactly where my head had been a fraction of a second before. With most undignified speed, I gained the magnificent shelter of the bank and thereafter made sure to have as companion a Negro who was discernibly a Negro whenever I had business on the South Side.

While I was in Chicago, notice was served on the national office of the NAACP that the organization could no longer operate in Texas until it had been chartered in that state. Although the ruling was manifestly designed to stop all operations of our branches in Texas, as it was quite certain that the state would never grant us a charter, and since other states would follow suit, the situation was such as to require prompt and vigorous action. The demand was also violative of usual procedure, since the NAACP was incorporated by the State of New York. John Shillady went to Austin, Texas, the state capital, to talk the matter over with Governor Hobby (whose wife later commanded the WAC in World War Two) and the Texas attorney general, having first wired ahead requesting appointments with those two officials.

Two days later an Associated Press friend telephoned me that a wire dispatch had just come in stating that John was missing after having been beaten unmercifully on the streets of Austin and that it was believed that he might have been killed. Another dispatch reported that John had been found and had boarded a train for New York. After he got back I heard the story. As he left his hotel on the way to keep the appointment with Governor Hobby, he had been set upon in open daylight on one of the main business streets of the Texas capital by a mob led by a judge and the sheriff. Not a hand had been raised in his defense. When the NAACP appealed to Governor Hobby to set in motion state machinery to apprehend and punish the known assailants, Hobby telegraphed that Shillady had got exactly what he deserved and that the same treatment would be accorded any other white man who dared interfere with Texas' handling of its Negroes.

John's physical condition from the beating and the deterioration which followed from the crushing blows on his head was pitiful to watch. His great gaiety and warm smile disappeared. The superb efficiency which had been his was replaced by an indecisiveness as though he were paralyzed. As time went on he grew steadily worse instead of better and the Association's work naturally suffered. A few months later he resigned and entered a hospital, from which he emerged several times only to return, until, not long afterward, he died—a victim of lynching as surely as any Negro who had been strung up to a tree or burned at the stake.

When John resigned, Jim Johnson was elected secretary. The task he faced was a heartbreaking one. We had lost considerable ground and prestige by the months of inactivity due to John Shillady's broken spirit. Delays in action had caused our already inadequate income to drop alarmingly, since the Association then, as now, was financed by its membership dues and not by endowments or philanthropy. When Jim took over the secretaryship not only were we broke, we owed sizable debts for printing, rent, and other operating costs. Jim saw to it that the stenographers were paid, but he and I went without salary for as long as four months while we all worked desperately to place the Association on a sound financial basis.

The bloody summer of 1919 was climaxed by an explosion of violence in Phillips County, Arkansas, growing out of the sharecropping system of the South. The incident was fated to affect materially the legal rights of both Negro and white Americans. Throughout the nation newspapers published alarming stories of Negroes plotting to massacre whites and take over the government of the state. The vicious conspiracy, so the stories ran, had been nipped in the bud, but it had been necessary to kill a number of the "black revolutionists" to restore law and order.

I was eager to go to the scene, and left for Arkansas on the first train after we had scraped up enough money for my fare. Scipio A. Jones, a wise and courageous Negro lawyer, introduced me to three white lawyers who had been retained by the Negroes, two of whose names happened with mordant humor and appropriateness to be Winchester and Winchester. From them and Mr. Jones I learned the facts which, briefly, were as follows.

A number of colored tenant farmers and sharecroppers in Phillips County had grown tired of working year after year, only to wind up each season in debt to their landlords, no matter what the quantity or price of cotton they had raised. There had been beatings and even lynchings when individual Negroes had dared to demand itemized bills for supplies bought at the landlords' stores and an accounting of the weight and price of the crops they had raised.

The harassed Negroes organized a meeting to confer with Messrs. Winchester and Winchester, from which developed the ambitiously titled Progressive Farmers and Household Union of America. Articles of incorporation for a fraternal organization were prepared (the cost of that type of association being considerably lower than others) which would pool the meager resources of the impoverished and exploited Negro farmers to pay for test cases in court when landlords refused accountings. The ray of hope which the plan promised caused the hitherto despairing farmers to flock enthusiastically into the movement. At first, the plantation owners and merchants paid scant attention to the movement. The legal work of incorporation finished, Messrs. Winchester and Winchester collected their fee and retired in favor of another white lawyer in Little Rock by the name of U. S. Bratton. Bratton's courage was as great as his skill in defense of his clients, many of whom were Negroes. He was respected and feared. His employment caused the landlords to take the new organization seriously because they knew Bratton would pull the cover from the unsavory system and, possibly, send some of them to federal prison for violation of the Thirteenth Amendment against slavery and the laws against peonage.

At Bratton's request a meeting was arranged at a small Negro church at Hoop Spur. The place was packed. Suddenly the audience was thrown into panic as fusillade after fusillade of bullets poured into the crowded church, killing a number of women and men and wounding others. Fortunately some of the Negroes had brought weapons with them, having learned of the mounting hostility of the white community against the attempt to organize. The fire of the attackers was returned and one of the assailants was killed. The match had been applied to the powder keg. Word was sped by telephone to every nook and cranny of Phillips County, the story being fantastically amplified with each telling of it. Within a few minutes efficiently directed, heavily armed mobs swept over the countryside hunting down and killing every Negro they could find.

I was never able to fix definitely the number of Negroes who were killed, but did gather evidence establishing a total in excess of two hundred.

Every colored man, woman, and child who could do so fled the county, many of them by foot through the swamps and woods under cover of darkness during several days and nights of slaughter. Those who could not escape were herded in stockades where a self-appointed "Committee of Seven," made up of white landlords and merchants, proceeded to conduct a kangaroo court to pass on which of the imprisoned Negroes were "guilty" and "bad niggers" and which were "good niggers." The chief test of the latter classification was proof that they had not joined and had disapproved of the farmers' organization, and their agreeing to work without pay a specified length of time for designated employers. These were released.

But seventy-nine men stubbornly refused to yield to intimidation, even though they knew their courage might cost their lives, either inside or outside the law. With a speed as great as that of assembling of the mob, the hapless and defenseless seventy-nine were indicted for murder, insurrection, and a variety of other "crimes." The dingy courtroom at Elaine, the county seat, was jammed with openly armed men who loudly interrupted the trial at will to let the judge and jury know what they would do if speedy convictions did not materialize. Twelve of the defendants were found guilty and sentenced to die, and sixty-seven others were condemned to prison terms ranging from twenty years to life imprisonment, in trials which consumed slightly less than five days.

I asked for and was granted an audience with Charles H. Brough, the governor. Introducing myself as a reporter for the *Chicago Daily News* and presenting as credentials a telegram from Charles H. Dennis, the managing editor of that paper, I purposely led him to believe that I had little knowledge of the Negro question and was open-minded to whatever facts he, as chief executive of the state, cared to give me.

"I am delighted that a Northern newspaper has sent so able and experienced a reporter to answer the foul lies the *Chicago Defender* and that infamous National Association for the Advancement of Colored People have been telling about the good white people of Arkansas," he boomed.

He then proceeded, at considerable length, to give me the "truth." Absolute lawlessness created by Northern "agitators" among the Negroes of Phillips County had existed, he alleged. The white people of the county had shown remarkable restraint and human kindness in putting down the insurrection, he assured me with great warmth. In a burst of warmth and Southern hospitality, he gave me a letter of identification, in which he called me "one of the most brilliant newspapermen he had ever met," for me to use in Phillips County in case I ran into any difficulty there.

Everything went well in Phillips County for me, thanks to the Governor's letter. On the advice of Scipio Jones, I made no effort to talk with any of the Negroes. I had already talked with many refugees from the county in Little Rock, and those who were still there were too frightened to talk to an outsider. My chief concern was that when my investigation was publicized, reprisals might be visited on any Negro who had been seen talking with me.

I did, however, want to talk with the prisoners who were still closely guarded in the county jail in Helena. I knew that it would probably be of little value, since the jailer or sheriff would probably insist on being present during the interview. I had sought to induce Sheriff Kitchen to let me talk with the prisoners alone, quite deliberately trading on the story he had told me of a Negro soldier saving his son's life during a battle in France. The Sheriff had been noncommittal, saying he would meet me at the jail.

As I walked down West Cherry Street, which ran parallel to the railroad track, a Negro overtook me. As he passed he said under his breath just loud enough for me and no one else to hear, "Mister, I've got something important to tell you—follow me." He turned right at the next intersection, crossed the railroad tracks, and led me into a clump of woods far enough away to be out of sight.

"I don't know what you are down here for, but I just heard them talking about you—I mean the white folks—and they say they are going to get you. The way I figured it out is that if the white folks are so against you, you must be a friend of ours."

I asked him if he knew why they wanted to get me, but he had no further knowledge. There were just two trains a day out of Helena—one which left in a few minutes and the other that night. I sped down the railroad tracks, keeping out of sight as much as was possible. Just as the train pulled in, I climbed aboard from the side opposite the station platform. The conductor looked at me quizzically when I offered payment of my fare in cash. I explained to him that I had important business in Memphis that evening and had not had time to buy a ticket.

"But you're leaving, mister, just when the fun is going to start," he told me. In answer to my question as to the nature of the "fun," he replied, "There's a damned yellow nigger down here passing for white and the boys are going to get him."

"What'll they do with him?" I asked.

Shifting his cud of tobacco, he shook his head grimly and assured me, "When they get through with him he won't pass for white no more!"

No matter what the distance, I shall never take as long a train ride as that one seemed to be. The train ambled along in an exasperatingly leisurely fashion on a single track which ran most of the way to the Mississippi River through heavy woods which grew down to the track on either side. The lichen-covered trees grew so close together than even in open daylight the darkness was ominous. Arriving at the river's edge, the train was run onto a barge which carried us across the Mississippi into the state of that name and northward to Memphis.

Late that evening in Memphis I learned that news had been circulated there that I had been lynched in Arkansas that afternoon.

VII

I Almost Join the Klan

Publication of my findings by the *Chicago Daily News* and through the Association's press releases created a gratifying sensation. Our empty treasury began to be replenished by the contributions of both white and Negro Americans who were shocked by the story and wanted to aid in appealing the conviction of the seventy-nine defendants. Moorfield Storey, the president of the NAACP and one of America's most distinguished authorities on Constitutional law, assumed personal direction of the appeals. We were faced with a seemingly insuperable obstacle in getting the federal courts to intervene. We knew that there was no hope for the defendants in the Arkansas courts, and that our only hope of saving the lives of the twelve who had been sentenced to death and of freeing the other sixty-seven lay in convincing the federal court that they had the constitutional authority to pass upon the trials and verdicts.

The insuperable obstacle was the decision the United States Supreme Court had rendered in the Leo M. Frank case, which had so stirred Georgia during the summer when I was selling life insurance there. Since in this case the court had held that, so long as a state court had complied with the legalistic forms required under the "due process" clause of the federal Constitution, federal courts had no authority to go beyond the form of the trial and inquire into the spirit which had dominated it, and since this was precisely the issue and the only issue on which we could ask federal intervention in the Arkansas murders, we were pretty discouraged. But we started what then seemed almost a hopeless fight.

The details of the five-year struggle in the Arkansas and the lower federal courts would consume too much space here if they were told. Three times gallows were built for execution of the twelve Negroes. Three times we were able to secure writs to stay the execution. Eventually a writ of certiorari was granted by the Supreme Court and a date set for argument before that tribunal. Moorfield Storey argued the case. He bluntly told the Court that it had erred grievously in the Frank case. He pointed out eloquently that a citizen is a citizen both of the state in which he resides and of the United States. For this reason, he insisted, there is a shared responsibility of state and federal courts to guard zealously the Constitutional rights of every citizen of the United States.

We were moved by Mr. Storey's magnificent humanitarian appeal, but neither he nor anyone else dared entertain any real hope that the Court would follow his reasoning. Legal precedents enjoying the sacrosanct status which they did at that time would be overruled, we were certain, only by a miracle.

I shall never forget February 19, 1923, the day the decision was handed down in the small Supreme Court in the Capitol in Washington in the case of *Moore* v. *Dempsey*, the Arkansas riot case. In more than five years of struggle against unbelievable odds, we had won!

Louis Marshall wrote me a warm letter of congratulation, in which he said of the position which he had taken unsuccessfully in the Frank case that "the stone the builders rejected has become the cornerstone of the temple." He enclosed a check as "a thank offering" and volunteered his legal services without cost to the NAACP, which he gave to the end of his life. We received many letters and telegrams of congratulation on the victory, but none was as welcome as a letter written on inexpensive paper in pencil and signed by those of the defendants who were literate enough to write, expressing their gratitude.

About that time, I almost succeeded in becoming a member of the Ku Klux Klan. A college classmate of mine sent me a Klan letter which a friend of his had retrieved from a white man's wastebasket. The letter read as follows:

As a leading citizen of your community, and having confidence in your patriotism, I take the liberty of bringing to your attention a matter which cannot fail to appeal to every real American.

The story of the Ku Klux Klan, of the reconstruction days, and its valiant services in behalf of white supremacy, insures it a place in the heart of every true American, thereby adding to the glory which clusters around the names of Gen. Nathan Bedford Forrest, its Grand Wizard, and Gen. John B. Gordon, who was at the head of the work in Georgia.

A branch of the reorganized Klan of today, which has been broadened into a standard fraternal order, thereby enlarging the scope of its work, yet retaining all of the protective features of the old Klan, should be in every community of the Nation.

Its need today, when the fourteen million people of the colored race are organizing, and when the Anarchist and Bolshevik forces are encroaching daily upon the basic principles of Americanism, cannot fail to be apparent to the thinking man.

If you are interested in this matter I would be glad to hear from you, at once.

Very truly yours,
sgd./ Edward Young Clarke

In the name of our fathers—for our country, our homes and each other.

I wrote the Klan on plain stationery saying that as a native Georgian, although now living in New York, I was greatly interested in the reorganization of the Klan and would like information regarding membership. Clarke answered my inquiry, expressing pleasure at my interest and enclosed a questionnaire asking for information about myself, which I completed and returned.

Clarke's letters increased in cordiality as our correspondence continued. Apparently he became convinced that I could be useful to the Klan. He inquired if I would be willing to devote full time as chief organizer of New York state. I replied cagily that I was very comfortably situated and could not consider a major change in my career unless I was certain it would be worth while. In the meantime both from Clarke and other sources we were able to gather documentary and other evidence which clearly showed the sinister and illegal conspiracy against human and civil rights which the Klan was concocting. I was invited to Atlanta at the expense of the Klan, but decided against going.

Clarke apparently decided in the meantime that it would be best to make some independent inquiries about me before hiring me as state organizer. Suddenly I ceased receiving signed letters directly from the Imperial Palace of the Klan. In their stead, I began to be deluged with anonymous letters threatening my life if I ever revealed any of the information about the Klan which I had gained in my correspondence with Clarke. But these facts had already been placed in the hands of the Department of Justice and of the New York Police Department.

The effect of the Klan's propagation of hate and violence was not long in being seen. Negroes had registered in large numbers in various Florida cities, particularly in Jacksonville. Just prior to the presidential election of 1920, one thousand hooded Klansmen paraded through the streets of Jacksonville. Negroes telephoned the chief of police and mayor asking that the Klan parade pass through Davis Street, on which the inhabitants were Negroes. This invitation the Klan thought wisest not to accept. Instead of deterring Negroes from voting, the parade stepped up the registration and voting on November 2nd.

But in Ocoee, Florida, the Klan did not stop at parades. When Moses Norman, a wealthy Negro who owned a huge and well-tended orange grove and thereby was too prosperous for a Negro, went to the polls to vote a mob beat him severely and ordered him to go home. Instead, he went to the home of July Perry, a Negro friend who, as manager of a large orange grove, was the object of bitter resentment because the whites felt that his was a white man's job. A hooded mob followed Norman to Perry's home, set fire to it and other houses in the colored district, and shot down all colored people who attempted to flee from the burning buildings. Eighteen houses, two churches, a school, and a lodge hall were burned to the ground. The news accounts declared that five Negroes were burned to death, but the actual number was several times greater. Members of the mob eagerly searched the ruins of the burned buildings for charred bones of the victims to be retained as souvenirs, I learned when I went to Ocoee. The facts of the mass lynching along with reports from, and the names of, reputable eyewitnesses, white and Negro, were presented to the Department of Justice, but no punitive action was ever taken.

Week after week and month after month the fight against the Klan was stepped up by the alarming growth of the organization, not only throughout the South but in Northern states such as Indiana, New York, and Massachusetts. Early one Sunday morning I was awakened by an officer of the New York City Police Department Bomb Squad. I had not seen early editions of the *New York World* in which the story of a meeting of Klansmen in the Bronx had been published. A speaker from the Imperial Palace of the Klan at Atlanta had reminded his audience that they had taken an oath to protect the order with their lives. He informed them that a "Negro named Walter White" had come into possession of Klan secrets which they as Klansmen must keep, at any cost, from being made public. The Bomb Squad officer was a gigantic Irish Catholic, over six feet in height. He informed me that detectives were being assigned to protect my family and me and asked for a schedule of our movements so that we would be constantly under protection.

All that morning other volunteer protectors kept our telephone and doorbell ringing. They were Negroes, most of them of modest circumstances, who assured us that "No Kluxer will ever put his hand on you or your family."

In Atlanta, too, friends and neighbors volunteered assistance and saw to it that Mother's and Father's house was carefully guarded. Whether it was due to that protection or the cowardice of the Klan I never knew, but fortunately they were not molested and neither was I.

A triple lynching near Aiken, South Carolina, which I investigated, gave me an unforgettable inside picture of how a movement capitalizing on hate operates at the local level. Three members of a Negro family named Lowman, one of them a young woman, had been lynched after one of them had been freed by the court. Vigorous and courageous defense by a local white lawyer had not only established beyond all doubt that the three Negroes were innocent of the murder for which they had been arrested, but some of the testimony quite clearly showed that the guilty parties were white and prominent in official and business circles. The surest and quickest method of simultaneously shutting off forever embarrassing revelations and of putting fear into the community was lynching the three Negroes. It was established that the triple lynching was handled from its inception by the local Klan.

I don't recall any man so isolated by his community as was the lawyer who had defended the Negroes. His family had been distinguished in social and political life in South Carolina for several generations. As a lawyer he had defended Negroes, sometimes receiving little or no payment for his services, when he was convinced that they were being persecuted because of their color. Such a conviction had caused him to make a gallant and successful fight in defense of the Lowmans. When rumors of the lynching reached him, he had communicated promptly with the governor, judge, and prosecutor, but wholly without results. He told me freely and frankly the names of the ringleaders and, in particular, the name of an individual who lived in a near-by cotton mill town who could give me additional information.

I asked him if he would accompany me to this town if I hired an automobile. His reaction, revealing fear, was startling. He peered out of the window at the descending sun and somewhat anxiously answered, "I will go with you if you will promise to get back to town before sundown."

I asked him why there was need of such caution. "Surely no one would dare harm so well-known and respected a person as yourself," I remarked.

"Those mill hands and Kluxers would harm anybody," he answered with deep conviction.

I promised him that we would get back to town before sundown —because I suddenly found myself as anxious to do so as he. If the Klan would molest him, it did not take much imagination to figure out what they would do to a stranger.

When we reached the little mill town he drove me to a house perched on the side of a hill and introduced me to a man with iron-gray hair and eyes which seemed to bore through us. I told him frankly that I was seeking information about the lynching. He gravely left the room and almost immediately there appeared in the doorway a figure dressed in the full regalia of the Ku Klux Klan. For just a moment I thought that I had walked into a trap, and then the hood was removed, revealing that its wearer was our host.

"I show you this," he said, "so that you will realize I know what I am talking about."

He had been, he told us, the organizer and Kleagle of the local Klan. His activity had been for him, at the outset, an honest though mistaken expression of his desire to clean up corrupt local government and suppress an excess of local criminal activities. But he had not been engaged in Klan activities long before he learned what many others who have entered the movement honestly learned— that the very people whose misdeeds they had hoped to correct had gained control of the organization. He had then resigned and had lived in constant fear of his life ever since. In an adjoining room he showed me a formidable collection of guns and ammunition which he had collected for use, if necessary, in the defense of himself and his family.

Although everything in me hated everything connected with the Ku Klux Klan, I could not help feeling again as I looked at that arsenal in a home the sense of terror which I had known that night in 1906 when my father and I, guns in hand, had knelt in the dark at a window of our house in Atlanta, and I felt a bond of sympathy between this ex-Kluxer and myself. We both knew what it was to be among the hunted.

What he told me that day confirmed all of our former evidence that the Klan had organized and carried out the lynching.

The three victims had been falsely charged with murder and convicted and sentenced to death in a court packed with armed Klansmen. Their case had been appealed to the state supreme court, which promptly reversed the conviction, severely criticized the judge before whom they had been tried, and ordered a new trial. At the new trial (again in a Klan-packed courtroom) the evidence so clearly showed the innocence of one of the defendants that the judge dismissed the case against him. As soon as he was released, however, he was rearrested on a minor charge and again lodged in jail. That night the mob broke into the jail, took the prisoners to the edge of town, told them to run, and shot them down in a fusillade of bullets.

The story came out bit by bit in what the ex-Kluxer told us, and in conversations I had with others during three days of investigation. One of the lynchers told me with sneering contempt and obvious relish, "We had to waste fifty bullets on the wench before one of them stopped her howling." Evidence in affidavit form which could not be doubted indicated clearly that the sheriff, several of his deputies, various jailers and policemen, three relatives of the man who was then governor of the state, a member of the state legislature, and several men prominent in the business, political, and social life of the community, had been members of the mob.

The revelation of these findings after I returned to New York did not add to my popularity in the lynching region. Public sentiment in the state itself, stirred up by several courageous newspapers, began to make it uncomfortable for the lynchers. When the sheriff found things getting a bit too unpleasant, he announced that he was going to ask the grand jury to indict me for "bribery and passing for white."

VIII

Jimcrow in Europe and Harlem

Although it was a brilliant dream that fell short of translation into reality, the Pan-African Congress held in London, Paris, and Geneva in 1921 played a profound role in opening my eyes to the world implications of the race question and the interrelationship between that question and other problems of colonialism, imperialism, markets for manufactured goods made in industrialized regions like the United States and Europe, sources of raw materials for the making of those products, and all the other complex issues facing the modern world, intimately involved with the causes of war and the very bases of civilization. Dr. W. E. B. DuBois, editor of *The Crisis* and creator of the idea of the Congress, and I, sailed in September for England, where the first session was to be held.

We found the British government undergoing a suave case of the jitters because of the meeting. Its colonial peoples in India, Africa, and the West Indies were becoming increasingly resentful and restive because of the meager share they enjoyed of the freedom and opportunity which they had been assured World War One was fought to gain. Marcus Garvey's flamboyant "Back to Africa" movement was at the time in its most gaudy and vocal period. Garvey speeches to the effect that he and his followers were going to oust white people from Africa, bag and baggage, frightened Downing Street even though the government knew there was virtually no likelihood that Garvey would ever be able to gather the money, ships, guns, and supplies necessary to make good on his threats and promises.

The objective of the Pan-African Congress was less specific and dramatic than Garvey's but, in the light of the colonial systems at that time, capable of achieving more peaceable and lasting results. It was believed that regular and frequent meetings on a purely consultative and informative basis would in time acquaint the natives of various colonial areas with the evils of the colonial system, and eventually result in a workable plan to abolish it and to train natives in self-government. Among other objectives of the Congress was the improvement of deplorable educational and health conditions, and the setting up of a united pressure group to force independence, if necessary. Garvey barred from his movement not only all white people but all light-skinned colored people, thus emphasizing a color line within the colored world. The Pan-African Congress, on the other hand, welcomed all those, irrespective of race or nationality, who saw the evils of imperialism.

But despite this more moderate program, there were almost as many secret agents of the British Colonial Office at our sessions as there were delegates, and the same surveillance was encountered in Belgium and France.

Philip Snowden, soon to become one of the top members of Britain's first Labour government, arranged a meeting for Dr. Du Bois and me with the executive committee of the Labour Party, from which I brought away an impression of disappointment. Dr. DuBois tried to obtain some definite statement from Ramsay Mac-Donald as to what the Labour Party proposed to do to correct glaring evils in the colonies, but we received only vague evasions.

This same insularity of interest was again impressed upon me by H. G. Wells, who invited me to luncheon. We plunged into discussion of the race problem as he plied me with questions about lynching in the United States, which aroused in him great indignation. We talked of cruelties and deprivations of opportunity and liberty perpetrated in the German, French, Dutch, Belgian, and Italian colonies, and Wells was unequivocal in his condemnation of imperialism and colonial rule. Feeling certain by then that Wells' condemnation of injustice was universal, I mentioned the recent exposé of slavery in Sierra Leone and other instances of England's guilt. I was brought sharply to attention when Wells interrupted, "Ah, but that is a different situation!" He went on to explain what he conceived to be essential differences between colonial administration in British colonies and mandated areas and that in areas ruled by other European nations. He was not altogether uncritical of British mistakes, I must in fairness report. But it was disappointing to find one I had admired so extravagantly for his erudition and industry afflicted with the "mote and beam" disease. The major ills of colonialism he believed should be corrected, but he envisioned no material change in the system itself.

But nationalism and imperialism, I learned at Paris, were no monopoly of white people. For reasons of self-interest a Senegalese who had been elevated to one of the highest posts in the French government—High Commissioner of Black Troops—was far less critical of his own government than Wells had been of his. M. Blaise Diagne occupied as large and imposing an office and was as carefully protected by as many secretaries and flunkies as was Clemenceau. M. Diagne was militantly critical of the British, German, and Italian colonial policies. But he could see no faintest basis for criticism of the French policy. Diagne went even further; he threatened to withdraw from the Congress and denounce it if there were any condemnation of France. Such action might have meant adjournment of the Congress, and even our expulsion from France, or at least a suggestion that we depart. I was not disturbed and even hoped Diagne would carry out his threat. The publicity would have made it clear, it seemed to me, that our embryonic fight against a dangerous and evil system would be carried on against black as well as white apologists, and perhaps have enlisted the support of persons all over the earth who had not yet heard of the organization.

But Diagne did not resign. One of the speakers at the Paris meeting was an eloquent representative of a French organization for the protection of the *indigènes français*. His indictment of his government's treatment of natives in her colonies was so scathing and meticulously documented that not even Diagne could defend it. André Gide's *Voyage au Congo* was then appearing serially in a popular French magazine and his exposé of what was going on in French Africa aided us in establishing our case and preventing an open break.

Diagne was a man of very considerable executive ability and a perfect example of the canny genius of the French mind. Freer of prejudice than England or the United States, France sought out bright young men in her colonies and brought them to Paris to be educated and indoctrinated with loyalty to France. No objection was ever made to intermarriage, nor was there ever any faintest manifestation of social or other discrimination. Diagne had married into one of France's most distinguished and socially secure families. His beautiful and charming wife had borne him several very attractive children. When boorish Americans had attempted to make trouble for the Diagne family in one of Paris' restaurants, the government had tartly and unequivocally reminded the ill-mannered offenders that they were visitors in France and that if they could not behave themselves and cease trying to impose their prejudices in a country where such stupidities were not welcome, they would be invited to leave. Is there any wonder that men like Diagne felt more loyal to such a government than do citizens of countries like the United States who receive no such protection from their government?

Back in New York a host of activities official and personal awaited me. I was soon plunged into a new fight which demonstrated how the poison of race prejudice, and, even more, of ignorance about the Negro's potentialities, had penetrated the North. Ever since I had arrived in New York I had heard distressing stories about Harlem Hospital. At that time no Negro was permitted in that hospital or any other of the New York City hospital system, except as a patient. This was true despite the fact that there were in New York numbers of Negro doctors and nurses trained in top-flight medical schools such as Harvard, Yale, Pennsylvania, Michigan, Chicago, Columbia, and McGill, as well as some excellent men educated at less well-equipped and well-known medical schools such as Howard University and Meharry Medical College. None of these Negroes was permitted to practice in these tax-supported institutions in New York City.

Negro patients were treated with such scant efficiency at Harlem Hospital that the situation had produced a folk saying: "When any member of your family goes to Harlem Hospital, telephone the undertaker." Dr. Louis T. Wright led the fight to investigate and remedy these conditions. Almost entirely due to his efforts, the North Harlem Medical Association and the NAACP raised enough money to employ William N. Colson, a brilliant graduate of the Columbia University School of Law, to gather the facts. His report confirmed the worst rumors of callous and inadequate treatment and racial discrimination in Harlem Hospital. We presented our findings to Mayor John F. Hylan, who ordered Commissioner of Accounts Hirshfield to investigate the complaints and if necessary to hold public hearings.

We urged upon the City of New York that it not only clear up Harlem Hospital but that it abandon the unwritten law against admission of qualified colored doctors, specialists, and nurses to New York City hospitals. This demand was considered both revolutionary and impossible. A compromise was offered, which some Negroes were eager to accept, to build a two-million dollar hospital to be staffed in its entirety by Negro doctors.

This counterproposal created a situation and forced a decision which has profoundly affected Negro thinking on this issue. Should we accept a jimcrow institution, however deluxe, or should we make the far harder decision of insisting on complete integration?

Louis Wright held out for the maximum program. He contended that the chief advantage to Negro doctors of opportunity to serve in hospitals was that of learning and competing with the best men in the field, and that acceptance of segregated training would fix forever upon the Negro a differential of training and experience. This, in turn, would do harm to the Negro doctors' patients and perpetuate a higher morbidity and mortality rate among Negroes. Second-class status must never be accepted, however long and difficult the attainment of first-class opportunity might be.

The conflict over approach and method of attack on the Negro's health problems was brought more sharply into focus by the Harlem Hospital fight than ever before. And it still rages. But the stand taken for admission of Negroes on the basis of merit and ability has resulted in Negroes serving on the staffs not only of Harlem Hospital, but also of Bellevue, Kings County, Seaview, and other New York municipal and private hospitals.

IX

A Wife, a Book, and a Hospital

In 1922 two things happened to me which have been important factors in everything which has followed. The first and most important was my marriage on February 15th to Leah Gladys Powell, who for two years previous to that had been (from my point of view at least) much the most interesting member of the NAACP staff. The second was Jim Johnson's casual invitation to go along with him to an appointment with H. L. Mencken, then editor of *The Smart Set.*

Shortly after meeting Mencken I received one of his characteristically terse and salty notes asking what I thought of *Birthright,* a novel about the Negro by T. S. Stribling of Tennessee. Flattered, I wrote a lengthy and painfully erudite criticism of the book pointing out that the novel had courage in depicting Negroes as human beings instead of as menials or buffoons, but that it obviously was written from the outside looking in. I said that Stribling's depiction of Negro servants was not too bad, but that he fell down badly in his portrayal of what educated Negroes feel and think. Mencken replied, "Why don't you do the right kind of novel? You could do it, and it would create a sensation."

Such an idea was at first preposterous. I had never even thought of attempting to write fiction. Mencken, Jim, and I talked over the notion as they both tried to convince me that the variety of experiences which my appearance made possible by permitting me to talk with white people as a white man and with my own people as a Negro gave me a unique vantage point. Mary White Ovington generously joined the conspiracy by offering Gladys and me the use of her cottage "Riverbank" at Great Barrington, Massachusetts. We took the train with typewriter, paper, pencils, and little other equipment—and certainly no clearly thought out plot for a novel. I had a rather misty notion of using as my central character a Negro doctor, trained in a first-class Northern medical school and returned to his native Georgia small town, but what would happen to him was not thought out at all.

I started to write and found that many of the characters seemed to rise up begging to be described, and creating their own story. I wrote feverishly and incessantly for twelve days and parts of twelve nights, stopping only when complete fatigue made it physically and mentally impossible to write another word. On the twelfth day the novel was finished and I dropped on a near-by couch and slept for hours.

Back in New York I ran into John Farrar, now a publisher but at that time editor of *The Bookman*, scholarly monthly of the arts published by George H. Doran and Company. In answer to his friendly query as to how I had spent the summer I hesitantly confessed I had written a novel. John asked to see it, but I demurred until I had rewritten it and corrected at least the more glaring deficiencies in writing with which I knew the manuscript was filled.

John insisted that I let him see the novel before it was rewritten: he could determine better if I had any ability as a fiction writer from the first draft, he assured me, than from a later version which might have some of its strength removed by attempts at "elegant writing." Somewhat dubiously, because I had reread parts of the manuscript, I sent the novel to John's office the next morning.

Not long afterward I received from Mr. Doran the most exciting —the most deliriously exciting—letter I had ever received in my life. We like your novel, he wrote, and will publish it after a few changes have been made which we wish to discuss with you.

To say that I walked on air between the receipt of the letter and the day of my appointment with Mr. Doran is a gross understatement. The famous publisher greeted me warmly and introduced me to Eugene Saxton, then one of his associate editors. John Farrar was naturally there too. Mr. Doran warmly congratulated me but I noticed that John and Eugene Saxton appeared to be somewhat uncomfortable. I learned the reason a few minutes later.

"Your novel has great drama and power," Mr. Doran told me. "But there are some changes we want you to make. Your Negro characters—uh, uh—are not what readers expect. I'm sure you will be willing to make the necessary changes," he added somewhat lamely, as he noticed my expression.

We talked for an hour or more, and it became increasingly clear that someone had convinced Mr. Doran that even though there were Negro college graduates who talked correct English instead of dialect, the number of such Negroes was too small to justify their being written of as educated and normal human beings. I learned some time later that Mr. Doran had submitted my novel to Irvin S. Cobb, the Kentucky humorist, who had been so shocked by its outspokenness that he had advised against its publication, fearing that it would cause race riots in the South.

Disheartened and disillusioned, I sent the manuscript to Mencken, who replied almost by return mail, "I have read *The Fire in the Flint*. There is not one episode in it which has not been duplicated in real life over and over again. I suggest that you send it to Alfred Knopf."

Knopf published the novel in 1924, and reaction to it was gratifyingly prompt and vigorous. It told of a Negro doctor who, after graduation from a Northern medical school, returned to his home in Georgia filled with idealistic zeal and determined to devote himself to raising the deplorable health conditions among his people. He was equally determined to avoid involvement in the race question. He soon learned, however, that for a Negro a life devoted to pure science is impossible, and becomes involved more and more in the problems which his people face. Because his medical education is superior to that of any white doctor in the town, he is called upon to operate on and save the life of the daughter of a prominent white citizen. In the meantime he has been active in organizing a cooperative movement among Negroes which brings upon him the organized hostility of local merchants and landlords and of the Ku Klux Klan. The story ends dramatically—perhaps melodramatically would be more accurate—when the doctor is lynched. But while it ends in personal tragedy and death for the hero, one senses that the spirit of revolt against bigotry which he symbolizes will be accelerated rather than diminished by his death.

The first review of the book was written by Laurence Stallings, at that time literary editor of the *New York World*, who, in collaboration with Maxwell Anderson, had achieved phenomenal success as a playwright with the famous play *What Price Glory*. Stallings said that the Central City of *The Fire in the Flint* was the most accurate portrayal of a small town in his native Georgia that he had ever read, and that the characters and plot were the truest of any novel written about the South to date. A columnist, Coleman Hill, on the *Macon Daily Telegraph* in Stallings' home town, reprinted his review and expressed agreement with it. The newspaper was swamped with denunciatory letters, telephone calls, and other expressions of disapproval. To set itself clear with its readers and subscribers, the *Daily Telegraph* published several editorials denouncing Stallings and Hill and, even more vigorously, myself. Heywood Broun took up the cudgels for the three of us in his famous column in the *New York World*. As a result the novel was catapulted into the gratifying position of being a modest best-seller, far beyond its literary merits. The novel went through several editions and was published in England and, in translation, in France, Denmark, Russia, Japan, and Germany. It received the honor of being one of the books burned in Germany after Hitler came into power.

Two interesting experiences attended publication of *The Fire in the Flint* in Russia and Japan. During the height of world-wide agitation over the Scottsboro Case, a newspaper correspondent friend of mine was present at a huge demonstration in a Moscow park at which I was bitterly denounced by the Communists, who had persuaded the Scottsboro defendants to dismiss the NAACP from the case and turn its direction over to the Communists. At the Moscow meeting I was savagely attacked as "a tool of the capitalists" and "an ally of the lyncher forces." Walking away from the meeting, the newspaper correspondent passed the state publishing company, where he saw a display of translations of *The Fire in the Flint* —which, at the time, was enjoying a considerable sale as a picture of what a "capitalist" nation like the United States does to its minorities.

Unwittingly and unwillingly, I was also utilized through the medium of *The Fire in the Flint* in Japan. The novel was first published in translation there under its original title and enjoyed a modest sale. Later, when American indignation over Japan's invasion of China mounted, a new Japanese edition, with the title changed to *Lynching*, was brought out. The new edition sold in fantastic numbers, due to a publicity campaign by the Japanese government pointing out that the novel pictured the kind of barbarities which were tolerated and even encouraged in the democracy which had the temerity to criticize Japan for her acts in China. I am glad to say that I never received royalties from either the Japanese or Russian translations, for I wouldn't have liked that money.

In 1923, the United States Veterans Administration under Brigadier General Frank T. Hines announced that it would establish a segregated hospital for Negro veterans at Tuskegee Institute. The NAACP board of directors had passed a resolution opposing the establishment of a segregated hospital for Negro veterans anywhere in the South. The protest was ignored. Tuskegee Institute welcomed the location of the hospital and gave three hundred acres to the government as a site. Dr. Robert R. Moton, president of Tuskegee, was orally assured that he would be consulted about personnel for the hospital, but that promise was blandly ignored. A bitterly anti-Negro white Alabamian, Colonel Robert H. Stanley, was placed by General Hines in charge of the hospital. Colonel Stanley, backed by the local Ku Klux Klan and businessmen, proceeded immediately to staff the hospital from top to bottom, except in one category of employment, with Southern whites, who were uniformly unsympathetic to Negroes. The single exception made in employment was caused by an Alabama law prohibiting white persons from nursing colored patients. Colonel Stanley adroitly evaded this law by appointment of white nurses at annual salaries ranging from $1,680 to $2,500—considered high wages for nurses in Alabama at that time. To each white nurse was assigned a colored nurse maid who did all the work at a salary of $60.00 a month.

Colonel Stanley's high-handed action created vigorous resentment among Negroes, which was promptly met by a Ku Klux Klan parade through the grounds of Tuskegee Institute culminating in a banquet at United States government expense in the veterans hospital and in threats to kill Dr. Moton.

My brother George happened to be in Alabama at the time in connection with his duties with the American Missionary Association. He rushed, at my request, to Tuskegee and, passing as white, managed to gain the confidence of members of the Ku Klux Klan. They revealed their plan to kill Dr. Moton, if necessary, to burn or blow up buildings on the Tuskegee Institute campus, and to use whatever violent or other means might be necessary to see Stanley's program carried through. George also obtained evidence conclusively establishing that some of the agents of the Department of Justice and the Veterans Administration who had been sent to Alabama were either sympathetic to the Klan or had been intimidated.

Armed with this information, I made several trips to Washington for conferences with John W. Crim, Acting Attorney General, and with top officials of the Veterans Bureau. In the meantime an extraordinary change had been wrought in the attitude of Dr. Moton by the developments. He was a gentle man who hated conflict and violence. Although he had incurred sharp criticism and even bitter resentment for doing so, he had urged upon Negro soldiers in France that they win the war first and then rely on gratitude from their government for the abolition of injustices and indignities. But the brazen attitude of the Ku Klux Klan and the Veterans Administration and the threats to destroy Tuskegee Institute marked a turning point in Dr. Moton's philosophy. I sat with him in his home at Tuskegee during the height of the trouble. He pointed to a rifle and a shotgun, well oiled and grimly businesslike, that stood in the corner of the room. Although his words in cold print may sound overheroic, they did not sound so to me as he said quietly, "I've got only one time to die. If I must die now to save Tuskegee Institute, I'm ready. I've been running long enough."

The break in this situation came when General Hines and other officials of the Veterans Administration were forced, by the gravity of conditions there, to go to Tuskegee. A meeting was arranged between local whites and General Hines, at which the government official was profanely informed that, irrespective of what Washington or the federal government wished or said, the veterans hospital at Tuskegee would be run in the manner determined and desired by the local whites. This was too much for an Army general to take. General Hines peremptorily ordered the staffing of the hospital with a mixed group of Negro and white doctors.

X

A Black Tide Flows Northward

During World War One and the years immediately following there had occurred the greatest migration of Negroes from the South to the North in the history of the United States. The movement of Negroes northward had been accompanied by a considerable migration of Southern whites, both groups having been attracted to Northern industrial centers by high wartime wages. And, inevitably, along with these two parallel migrations there went a third—Southern racist doctrines—which greatly accentuated the race problem as a national, instead of merely a Southern, tragedy.

Drawn to the North by higher wages, as the whites had been, Negroes had also fled from lynching, disfranchisement, inferior schools, confinement to menial and lower-paid employment, and all the other evils from which they had suffered in the South. When the war had ended and wages dropped, Southern whites had returned home in large numbers, but generally speaking the Negro had remained in the North.

Expansion of the Negro population in Northern cities made expansion of the areas in which Negroes lived inevitable, and created a complex problem the solution of which has not yet been found. Some cities, particularly along the border line between the North and South, in efforts to pen Negroes into restricted areas—invariably the least desirable and healthy—had enacted city ordinances to achieve this purpose which the United States Supreme Court in the case of *Buchanan* v. *Warley* [1] held to be invalid.

Those who were determined to make the Negro live in over-

[1] 245 U.S. 60.

crowded, segregated areas were not discouraged but promptly turned to other devices, such as restrictive covenants prohibiting sale or rental to, or occupancy by, Negroes, and pressure of public opinion, including mob violence. In a succession of episodes during the twenties from Los Angeles, California, to Westchester County, New York, there were threats, burning of Ku Klux Klan fiery crosses, and mob violence when Negroes sought to escape the ghetto and move into "white" neighborhoods.

Detroit was the scene of a long succession of such attacks, rivaling Chicago in this respect. Detroit had 8,000 Negro inhabitants in 1915; more than 85,000 in 1925. The tenfold-expanded Negro population was expected to live in the small area bordering on St. Antoine Street where one-tenth of their number had been crowded a decade before, and very few new houses were constructed. Whenever Negroes sought to find breathing space and more decent accommodations outside the ghetto they were met by threats and mobism. Virtually nothing was done by the police authorities to prevent the attacks or to punish the attackers.

It was inevitable that some serious trouble would ensue. This came in 1925 when a Negro physician, Dr. Osian H. Sweet, purchased a home at the corner of Garland and Charlevoix Streets in a middle-class white neighborhood. As soon as it became known that a Negro physician had bought the house, Dr. Sweet was threatened by violence if he attempted to occupy it. He refused to be intimidated. He and his wife and their young child, his brother Henry, a law student, and another brother Otis, a dentist, went ahead with their preparations to occupy their new home. On the 8th of September, 1925, they moved in. They were accompanied by a chauffeur and handyman employed by Dr. Sweet, and two friends of the Sweets, one of them a federal narcotics officer. As soon as darkness fell, crowds began to gather in the streets outside. Later in the evening the mob became so thick that two young women friends of Mrs. Sweet had difficulty getting through to visit the new homeowners. A few stones were thrown at the house during the night, but no other attack was made. Seeing the group gathered outside the darkened house, Dr. Sweet telephoned the police department asking for protection but none was provided.

The next night the crowd was larger and more belligerent. Inside the house Mrs. Sweet had prepared a dinner of roast pork, baked sweet potatoes, mustard greens, ice cream and cake, which they were about to eat when a concerted attack on the house was made. Two Negroes on their way home from work, passing on the outskirts of the mob, were set upon and beaten unmercifully. Policemen stood idly by and raised no hand to check the mob, which was being whipped into a frenzy by several self-appointed leaders.

"Niggers! Niggers! Get them—they're niggers! Get the damn niggers!" the crowd yelled.

Lights were switched off inside the house. Instead of stones and bricks banging against the house, bullets pierced it. The mob began moving in. Suddenly it stopped. The silent house was no longer silent. The fire had been returned. A scream of pain rose over the roar of the mob as one of its members fell. For the first time the police sprang into action. They entered the house and arrested its occupants. One by one they were led through the mob to police cars to be driven away to the county jail. The defendants were cursed and screamed at, but a few of the mob, their hearts apparently touched by the sight of slender, attractive Mrs. Sweet, her face drawn by sleeplessness and terror, cheered when she appeared. All eleven occupants of the house were swiftly arraigned and charged with murder.

At the request of the defendants and our local branch, I went to Detroit and to the county jail directly from the train. The defendants were brought from their cells to a detention pen. When I was admitted and identified myself as assistant secretary of the NAACP, one of the defendants half sobbed and exclaimed, "Thank God! We can now rest easy and get some sleep!"

The importance of the case to the Negro cause was obvious. If the Sweets were not given adequate legal defense, if the ancient Anglo-Saxon principle that "a man's home is his castle" were not made applicable to Negroes as well as to others, we knew that other and even more determined attacks would be made upon the homes of Negroes throughout the country. We were equally convinced that legal affirmation that a Negro had the right to defend his home against mob assault would serve to deter other mobs in Detroit and elsewhere.

It soon became apparent that the task would be terrifically difficult. We sought to employ the ablest lawyers in Detroit for the defense. We wanted attorneys who were not only capable but whose standing in the community would demonstrate to decent people in Detroit and elsewhere that the highly biased stories which had appeared in the newspapers were not correct. In brief, we did not want attorneys who were professionally notorious for their ability to free persons accused of crime no matter how guilty. We wanted instead men whose reputations were established for taking only cases where they were certain that the case of the defendant was just.

With the aid of Judge Ira W. Jayne, a member of the national board of directors of the NAACP, and the late Judge Alfred J. Murphy, I prepared a list of such lawyers and set about consulting them. One after another made some excuse for not taking the case or else frankly told me that public feeling against Dr. Sweet and his fellow defendants was so bitter that they could not afford to accept the case because it would cause them to lose valuable clients. Several other lawyers, somewhat less frank, demanded fees so huge that it was utterly impossible for us to pay them.

I returned to New York to make a very depressing report. It was decided then to telegraph Clarence Darrow in Chicago to ask him if he would head the defense counsel. Mr. Darrow's secretary wired that he was en route to New York and could be reached through Arthur Garfield Hays. Arthur Spingarn, Charles Studin, James Weldon Johnson, and I went to Hays' house to talk with Mr. Darrow. Arthur Spingarn told the tragic story. Mr. Darrow listened with deep sympathy and when Arthur had finished, he said softly, "I understand. I know the suffering your people have endured."

Arthur's naturally dark skin had been deeply tanned during his service in the Army and week ends at his country place in Dutchess County. He informed Mr. Darrow, somewhat to the latter's embarrassment, that, although he was deeply concerned with the Negro question, he himself was not a Negro. Mr. Darrow turned to Charlie Studin, also swarthy-skinned, and said, "Then you understand." Charles laughed and told him that he also was white.

In desperation Mr. Darrow then turned to me. "Well, with your blue eyes and blond hair I could never make the mistake of thinking you colored."

I smiled and told him I *was* colored.

Mr. Darrow agreed to consider entering the case as chief counsel provided it was satisfactory to the defendants and several Negro lawyers who had been engaged by some of them. Although Mr. Darrow was at that time at the very peak of his considerable fame as a lawyer and a champion of human liberty, it was characteristically modest of him to believe that there might possibly be some objection to his appearing as chief counsel for the defense. I already knew the answer, but I went back to Detroit to find unqualified delight on the part of the defendants and approval on the part of all the lawyers already retained, with one exception. That exception dealt with the relative size of the fee to be paid to Mr. Darrow. Suppressing a smile, I asked the attorney who raised the question if he would be willing to accept the same fee we were paying Mr. Darrow, to which there was an instant response in the affirmative.

"Very well. Mr. Darrow is serving without fee in the case," I told him. He did not seem too happy.

In Mr. Darrow's office in Chicago the next morning, he asked many questions.

"Did the defendants shoot into that mob?" he asked.

"I am not sure, particularly as to whether or not one of the defendants fired the shot which killed Leon Breiner, a white man . . ." I mumbled, afraid he might refuse the case if I told him the defendants had also fired.

Mr. Darrow shook his head at me in annoyance. "Don't try to hedge. I know you were not there. But do you *believe* the defendants fired?" he asked me almost angrily.

Meeting the earnest gaze of those intense eyes, I found it impossible to evade their demand.

"I believe they did fire," I said. "And . . ." I was about to add that I thought they were justified in doing so, but he interrupted me.

"Then I'll take the case. If they had not had the courage to shoot back in defense of their own lives, I wouldn't think they were worth defending."

Arthur Garfield Hays also generously offered to serve as associate counsel without compensation. In addition we retained three Detroit colored lawyers, Messrs. Julian W. Perry, Cecil O. Rowlette, and Charles Mahoney, and a Detroit white lawyer, Walter M. Nelson.

Day after day dragged by in the effort to obtain a jury. Sometimes gently, sometimes savagely, Mr. Darrow and his associates pounded away at the prejudices of the prospective jurors until panel after panel of talesmen was exhausted.

Never had a trial been conducted with more scrupulous fairness than it was by Judge Frank Murphy, later destined to become an associate justice of the United States Supreme Court. Little by little the treatment we received in the newspapers began to be transformed into greater impartiality and accuracy as the reporters listened to the development of the case, both as a legal issue and as one of deep human tragedy. I remember particularly a reporter who was assigned by Judge Murphy to take charge of the press·table. He was a slender, blond Southerner with remarkably large ears. When I was introduced to him by Judge Murphy and heard his marked Southern accent, I experienced the first and only doubt of Judge Murphy's assurance of a fair trial. I was soon to learn that I had been guilty of prejudice myself, as Felix Holt soon revealed himself to be the most scrupulously fair reporter on the case. It was not long before he and I together were berating some of the Northern-born reporters for letting prejudice creep into their stories.

A jury obtained, we were three weeks trying the case. Never has there been such unanimity among the prosecution witnesses, particularly policemen, that there had been no mob nor even a crowd anywhere near the Sweet home, despite the inadvertent admission by several of the prosecution witnesses that they had had to detour two blocks from the Sweet home because of the density of the mob.

I remember particularly one witness, whose nervousness very obviously manifested a not too good mind, trying to remember the story he had been coached to tell. He got along all right in his direct examination, but no sooner had Clarence Darrow taken him over for cross-examination with a voice and manner as gentle as any cooing dove than discrepancies appeared in his testimony. He was not stupid enough to be unaware of these contradictions and his nervousness became more and more intense as he twisted his hands, mopped his brow, and stammered out his words. Suddenly Mr. Darrow's manner changed. He roared at the witness, "Just what did you see that night at Garland and Charlevoix?" The thoroughly frightened witness stammered, "I saw a big crowd—I mean a crowd —I mean I saw a few people." Mr. Darrow did not look at the witness but gazed out of the window instead. In a voice returned to his soft gentleness he asked, "You kinda forgot you were told to say that you saw only a few people, didn't you?" The witness answered, "Yes, sir," as the spectators in the courtroom roared with laughter.

At last all the testimony was in. Every available space in the courtroom was jammed with those eager to hear the great lawyer in his summation to the jury. Outside, the corridors were almost as tightly packed by those who stood for hours in the vain hope that someone in the courtroom would leave. The jury leaned forward hour after hour drinking in Darrow's words. It was a magnificent human document which transcended all of the narrow legalism of the law.

There was one man who nodded affirmation as vigorously as a Baptist deacon to his pastor's word. He glared at the prosecutor, energetic Robert M. Toms, now a judge in Detroit. I took comfort in watching this juror. We will at least be assured, I reflected, of a mistrial. The jury retired late on the afternoon of Thanksgiving Eve. We remained in the courtroom until midnight, when Judge Murphy ordered the jury locked up for the night. We returned and sat in the empty courtroom all the next day, our Thanksgiving dinner consisting of two sandwiches and a bottle of skimmed milk so thin that it was blue instead of white. After forty-six hours the jury announced that it was unable to agree, and a mistrial was declared. One of the court attendants told me that the juror on whom I had counted for at least a mistrial because of his apparent agreement with all that Darrow had said in the courtroom angrily shouted, "I don't give a God damn what the facts are. A nigger has killed a white man and I'll be burned in hell before I will ever vote to acquit a nigger who has killed a white man!" Thus it was the incurable prejudice of this one man on whose support I had counted which cost us $21,897.67, the cost of the trial which had gone for nought because of the jury's disagreement.

In the second trial, some months later, we were able to try the defendants separately. The prosecution elected to try first Henry Sweet, then a student at Wilberforce University and planning to be a lawyer. Thomas Chawke, one of the most brilliant lawyers in the state of Michigan, replaced Mr. Hays as Mr. Darrow's chief assistant. By then the passage of time and the effect of the truth as revealed by Mr. Darrow's defense in the first trial had somewhat changed public opinion, though there was still vigorous demand on the part of many Detroiters for a conviction. This time the jury remained out only three hours and twenty-seven minutes before bringing in a verdict of "not guilty." Because the State felt that it had its strongest case against Henry, his acquittal led to the dismissal of the other cases. But it took $37,849 and seven and a half weeks of actual court trial to achieve the victory.

This is but one illustration of what it costs Negroes in dollars and cents, to say nothing of time, physical suffering, and mental and emotional torture, to obtain even elementary justice in many American courts of law. But the nation-wide publicity given the case and the acquittal broke the wave of attacks on the homes of Negroes, and there have fortunately been only a few isolated instances of this type of mob violence in the years since the Sweet case.

But the heaviest price was paid by the Sweet family. Mrs. Gladys Sweet and her brother-in-law Henry contracted heavy colds in the drafty Wayne County Jail. When we were able to effect her release in order to care for her young daughter, she worked tirelessly on the case to help her husband and his fellow defendants. The heavy cold hung on, and this, coupled with the physical and mental strain, so depleted her strength that she contracted tuberculosis and died. Henry was kept in jail much longer, as he was one of the chief defendants. After his acquittal he completed his college and law education and started the practice of law. However, the strain of the trial had taken its toll of him too, and shortly after receiving his law degree he succumbed to tuberculosis.

XI

Gilding the Lily-White Vote

Encouraged by the reception which had been given to *The Fire in the Flint*, I wrote a second novel, *Flight*, the background and writing of which was interesting at least to me. It was published in 1926. It attempted to tell the story of an attractive New Orleans Creole girl who after a variety of personal and racial experiences decided to cross the color line and live as white, but who eventually decided that the benefits thus secured were not worth the price she had to pay. Several critics were generous enough to say that it was a better written novel than *The Fire in the Flint*. But because the story it told was less melodramatic and because it was not as bitterly attacked as my first novel, its sales were small and it was soon forgotten.

The time I took to write *Flight* was a brief respite from the crises to which, it seemed, every mail called our attention. One of these arose when the Mississippi again overflowed its banks in 1927, in what was perhaps the most devastating flood of its history. I was rushed to the scene when reports and rumors reached us that Negro refugees were being treated in some parts of the flooded areas with less consideration than that shown to farm animals. I found the reports incapable of reflecting the horrible truth. In place after place I found Negro refugees penned in concentration camps from which they were not permitted by National Guardsmen to emerge without the consent of their landlords. I found also that Negroes in many instances were being forced to pay for relief which had been supplied gratis by the Red Cross. When they were unable to pay, many of them having lost everything they owned, the "debt" was assumed by the landlord of a near-by plantation, and the Negro taken under guard to the plantation to work out his debt.

Publication of my findings created my first of many bitter clashes with Herbert Hoover, who was in charge of Mississippi flood relief. Mr. Hoover unequivocally and indignantly denied the charges I had made. But the evidence that Mississippi planters were using a terrible disaster to force Negroes into peonage was so irrefutable that Hoover was forced by public indignation to appoint a committee of Negroes, headed by Dr. Robert R. Moton of Tuskegee, to investigate the charges. To Hoover's great disappointment the absolution he manifestly expected did not materialize. The report of the Moton Committee, although more temperate in tone than mine and that of another NAACP investigation made later, confirmed the basic charges we had made. As far as was possible after the passage of so much time, some of the major abuses were corrected.

Several years later we had to make investigation of another flood and the treatment accorded Negroes by Army engineers constructing flood-prevention levees. This investigation, made by Roy Wilkins, assistant secretary of the NAACP, and George S. Schuyler, a well-known Negro writer, was as hazardous as it was successful. The danger and physical discomfort they braved was infinitely greater than any I had ever encountered. Unmistakably Negroes, they could not benefit from the immunity afforded me in investigations by my white skin. Dressed as Negro laborers, they voluntarily risked the suspicions and brutalities the Negro meets in his daily life in states like Mississippi.

They succeeded in visiting twenty levee camps before trouble descended upon them. They found that Negroes, being paid an average of ten cents an hour, were required to purchase all their supplies from commissaries which charged exorbitant prices, and that any Negro who dared protest was beaten unmercifully. Some had been beaten to death and their bodies buried in the levees.

It was not long before their guarded and discreet questions made them the objects of suspicion. One evening George lay reading on the bed in his dingy rooming house in Vicksburg, Mississippi, when two policemen shoved the door open and stuck revolvers into his side. He was ordered to gather up his belongings and was taken, handcuffed, to the police station. Roy Wilkins was fortunately staying in another rooming house and escaped arrest. At the police station they took from George thirty dollars in cash (fortunately not finding some money he had concealed in his shoe), his fountain pen, and his notebooks containing memoranda about the work camps they had visited. He was questioned by various officers and, feeling it would be futile to conceal his mission, since the authorities had the notebooks, he said that he was investigating camps on the Louisiana side of the river for the NAACP and the War Department. He told the questioners that increased wages and improved working conditions would benefit Vicksburg, since the Negro workers, freed of the control of the contractors, would spend their money where they chose. The argument evidently received favorable consideration from officials in the tax-burdened Southern city, for George was released the next morning, although he was wakened several times during the night for further questioning by different police officers to whom the well-informed, unperturbed Negro was a novelty.

His notebooks were returned to him when he was released in the morning, but not the cash or his fountain pen. The detective who took him to the street told him to get out of the state and "don't wait for the train." George thought it wise to take his advice and hired a man—with the money he had concealed in his shoe—to take him to Memphis to catch the train. However, three days later he was back in Mississippi with Roy Wilkins in the northwest section of the state, continuing their investigation.

We tried for a long time to secure the return of George's thirty dollars and fountain pen, but entirely without success. I had lengthy correspondence with Mayor J. C. Hamilton of Vicksburg, who denied that the money had been taken. Mayor Hamilton declared that there had been a holdup near Vicksburg and that the woman who operated the boarding house where George was arrested had "communicated with the Captain of the City Police and informed him that there was a suspicious Negro stopping at her place, whom she suspected was implicated in the holdup," and that after due investigation the county authorities were "satisfied" that Schuyler had no connection with the robbery as suspected by "the darky who reported to the department."

On the basis of the facts uncovered by George and Roy—differentials in wages paid on a basis of race, exploitation at the commissaries, brutalities of all descriptions—we asked Senator Robert F. Wagner of New York to introduce in the United States Senate a resolution for an official investigation. By a fortunate legislative development, in which Huey Long unwittingly aided us, we managed to avert a filibuster and obtain passage of the resolution.

One afternoon Huey Long had virtually emptied the Senate floor by means of one of his filibusters. Senator Wagner was one of only a handful of senators who listened to the Louisiana demagogue. When Long unexpectedly ended his speech and left the floor of the Senate, Senator Wagner looked around him to discover that all the enemies of his resolution and potential filibusterers were absent. He sprang to his feet to ask unanimous consent for passage of the resolution. His motion was carried just as the infuriated Southern senators, having been warned of what was transpiring, came charging into the Senate chamber, too late. The evidence uncovered by the Senate investigation led to sweeping reformation of employment and living conditions among Negroes along the Mississippi.

In 1927, in the *Nixon* v. *Herndon* case, we won in the United States Supreme Court the first of a series of victories in combating disfranchisement by means of the "white Democratic" primary which were destined to revolutionize the political status of the Negro in the South. Although I violate chronology I ask to be forgiven because this long struggle for the ballot for Southern Negroes, culminating in the 1944 *Smith* v. *Allwright* decision, can best be understood if told as a connected series of events. It is an important story, for the issues involved have profoundly affected not only the status and political philosophy of the Negro but also white Americans, and in the years to come the effect will be even greater. Either the Negro must attain full citizenship status with all the rights and obligations thereby involved, even in the most remote sections of Mississippi, or the democratic process for all Americans will be made meaningless.

White America was a long time waking up to one manifestation of this. Busy as it was with its own life, most of the North was indifferent to the fate of the Negro in the South from the Civil War until the late thirties. In the meantime, left to its own devices, the South disfranchised Negroes and in time a large number of the Southern whites. The Negro was denied the right to vote by means of the "grandfather clause" in the constitutions of various Southern states; by "white primaries" which in the one-party South are equivalent to elections; by so-called "understanding clauses" under which a semiliterate white election official could disqualify a Negro Ph.D. from Harvard, and by the poll tax and the terrorism of the lynching mob. Poor whites were disfranchised chiefly by the poll tax and the chicanery of political oligarchists, more ruthless and less benevolent than Tammany Hall at the time of its greatest power and glory. Congressmen and United States senators were regularly elected by as small a proportion of the potential electorate as two to five per cent, in contrast to an average of sixty to eighty per cent in the North. As a result, men not representative of the more educated and decent South were able to build up political machines which made their reelection ridiculously easy and perfunctory. The seniority rule of the Congress elevates these men to the chairmanships of important Senate and House committees and creates a situation which, in the 1940's, enabled the South, with twenty-eight per cent of the nation's population, to hold as many as sixty per cent of the Senate and House chairmanships.

The determination of the anti-Negro element in the South to keep its power no matter what the Constitution or the remainder of the country said can better be understood in the light of these facts.

In 1910 the Oklahoma legislature amended the constitution of the state to prohibit any person from voting unless he was able to read and write, or unless an ancestor had been eligible to vote prior to January 1, 1866, in which case he could vote, even if he was illiterate. Thus the Oklahoma legislature believed that (by not mentioning race or color) it had successfully effected violation of the federal Constitution. Other Southern legislatures followed suit by enacting similar constitutional amendments.

Although the NAACP had not been organized until 1909, one

of its first acts was to urge the Solicitor General of the United States to challenge the constitutionality of the Oklahoma "grandfather clause," as it speedily came to be known.

Moorfield Storey, the first president of the NAACP, and a former president of the American Bar Association, filed a brief *amicus curiae* on behalf of the NAACP and joined in the argument of the Oklahoma case, *Guinn* v. *United States*.[1] Decision in the case (rendered in June 1915) was written and read by Mr. Chief Justice Edward D. White, who, interestingly enough, came from Louisiana. It stated unequivocally that, although the Oklahoma amendment did not, in specific words, deny suffrage to anyone because of "race, color, or previous condition of servitude," its enforcement automatically did so, and so was a violation of the Fifteenth Amendment of the Constitution of the United States.

The Supreme Court's decision stopped other Southern states from enacting discriminatory clauses of this sort. They believed that they could keep Negroes from voting by means of lynchings, which had grown to an average of two hundred annually, and by such devices as the poll tax and understanding clauses.

Oklahoma concocted another device. Immediately after the "grandfather clause" decision, the legislature amended the state constitution to provide that those already registered would remain qualified voters but that all others must register within twelve days or be forever barred from registering. Had this gone unchallenged, the purpose of the "grandfather clause" would have been achieved, since Negroes, having been prevented from registering prior to that time, would forever be barred from voting by the new act. The NAACP crossed swords with Oklahoma over this law when a Negro by the name of I. L. Lane attempted to register in Wagoner County, Oklahoma, was refused, and appealed to us for help. We took the case to the United States Supreme Court. The court, in a decision rendered May 22, 1939, declared the Oklahoma "twelve-day" law a violation of the Fifteenth Amendment.

In the meantime the Seventeenth Amendment, providing for direct elections of United States senators, had been made a part of the federal Constitution. Texas took the initiative in attempting dis-

[1] 238 U.S. 347.

franchisement of Negroes by utilization of the amendment. Its legislature passed a law that "in no event shall a Negro be eligible to participate in a Democratic Party election held in the State of Texas." Other Southern states gleefully prepared to follow the example of Texas by passing similar laws. A successful Negro physician of El Paso, Dr. L. A. Nixon, appealed to the NAACP for assistance in challenging this law. We agreed to enter the case.

Dr. Nixon filed suit for damages against election officials who refused the ballot. The defense promptly moved to dismiss the action on the ground that the subject matter of the suit was "political" and that no violation of the Constitution had been shown. The defendant's motion was sustained and the suit dismissed in the lower courts. We were prepared for this, since in most of these court cases we lost the decisions in the lower courts and won them on appeal to the Supreme Court. We thereupon filed a petition for a writ of error to take the case directly to the United States Supreme Court. Fred C. Knollenberg, our Texas attorney, and Arthur Spingarn pleaded our case, and in spite of obstacles placed in our way by the archconservative and obviously unfriendly Justice Van Devanter, Mr. Justice Oliver Wendell Holmes, on March 7, 1927, handed down the Court's sweeping decision in our favor. Texas political chicanery was scathingly rebuked in these words:

> The objection that the subject matter of the suit is political is little more than a play upon words. Of course the petition concerns political action, but it alleges and seeks to recover for private damages. That private damage may be caused by such political action and may be recovered for in a suit at law hardly has been doubted.

> The statute of Texas in the teeth of the prohibitions referred to assumes to forbid Negroes to take part in a primary election the importance of which we have indicated, discriminating against them by the distinction of color alone. States may do a good deal of classifying that it is difficult to believe rational, but there are limits, and it is too clear for extended argument that color cannot be made the basis of a statutory classification affecting the right set up in this case.

In our jubilation over the victory, we naïvely believed that disfranchisement by means of "white Democratic primaries" was settled. We were soon disillusioned and faced with a new legal stratagem from Texas. Governor Dan Moody of Texas promptly denounced the decision and declared that Texas would not permit Negroes to vote, no matter what the Supreme Court said. The governor boasted that a new and constitutional method would be found to maintain white political control of Texas elections. Moody called a special session of the Texas state legislature to pass a new statute empowering the state Democratic committee to decide its own rule on who would be permitted to vote in primaries. Immediately thereafter the state executive committee of the Democratic Party passed a resolution providing that "all white Democrats who are qualified under the Constitution and laws of Texas and none others are to be allowed to participate in the primary elections."

Dr. Nixon presented himself again for registration and again was refused the right to register. Supported by the NAACP, he sued for damages in the federal courts against the election officials. Again the lower courts dismissed his action and again an appeal was carried to the United States Supreme Court. Mr. Justice Benjamin Cardozo, on May 2, 1932, spoke for the majority of the court in a five-to-four decision, in which Messrs. Justices Van Devanter, Sutherland, McReynolds, and Butler dissented. The decision declared in part:

We do not impugn the competence of the legislature to designate the agencies whereby the party faith shall be declared and the party discipline enforced. The pith of the matter is simply this, that when those agencies are invested with an authority independent of the will of the association in whose name they undertake to speak, they become to that extent the organs of the State itself, the repositories of official power. They are then the governmental instruments whereby parties are organized and regulated to the end that government itself may be established or continued. What they do in that relation, they must do in submission to the mandates of equality and liberty that bind officials everywhere. . . .

Delegates of the State's power have discharged their official functions in such a way as to discriminate invidiously between white citizens and black. The Fourteenth Amendment, adopted as it was with special solicitude for the equal protection of members of the Negro race, lays a duty upon the court to level by its judgment these barriers of color.

Despite the sweeping edict of the Court, Texas legislators and politicians continued to try to find a loophole. They believed that if the state Democratic convention instead of the state executive committee voted to bar all but whites from the primary they would be upheld in such action by the Supreme Court. The state convention thereupon so voted. By this time the two cases involving Dr. Nixon had received such widespread publicity in Texas, and Negroes in that state had been so stirred by the fight for enfranchisement, that they wanted immediately to test this latest subterfuge. A case (*Grovey* v. *Townsend*) was initiated despite the NAACP's advice against bringing it in that form. Our apprehensions, unfortunately, were proved sound. The Supreme Court held that a vote of the state convention of a political party could constitutionally restrict participation in the primary of that party, provided the expenses of such primaries were paid by the party and not by the state.

It should not be difficult to imagine the gloom we all felt. Years of hard work and heavy expense appeared to have gone for naught. But we could not afford to give up in despair. We had to continue the struggle, whatever the cost, to make effective what should have been settled for all time by the Fourteenth and Fifteenth Amendments—the right of every qualified citizen to vote regardless of race.

We searched for the ideal circumstances and litigant to present the issue accurately and overcome the setback we had suffered in *Grovey* v. *Townsend*. In 1941 Dr. Lonnie E. Smith of Houston brought action in the district federal court in Texas for damages and a declaratory judgment against the practice, custom, and usage of refusing to permit qualified Negro electors to vote in Texas Democratic primary elections, and his case was handled at his request by NAACP lawyers.

Thurgood Marshall, special counsel of the Association, and William H. Hastie, former federal judge and later governor of the Virgin Islands, served as chief counsel for Dr. Smith. They contended that the Fourteenth and Fifteenth Amendments, Article I of the United States Constitution, and the Federal Civil Rights Statutes prohibited the denial to Dr. Smith or any other qualified Negro voter of the right to participate in primaries. Again the local federal court ruled against us. Again the case was appealed to the United States Circuit Court of Appeals, which on November 30, 1942, affirmed the decision of the lower court. An appeal for a writ of certiorari was granted by the United States Supreme Court on June 7, 1943.

Again the Supreme Court, in what has come to be known as the *Smith* v. *Allwright* case, decided with us, overruling its former decision in *Grovey* v. *Townsend*. The following paragraph, quoted from the decision (April 3, 1944) states as well as anything I know the basic illegality of denying the vote to any citizen of the United States because of his color:

When primaries become a part of the machinery for choosing officials, state and national, as they have here, the same tests to determine the character of discrimination or abridgment should be applied to the primary as are applied to the general election. . . .

It may now be taken as a postulate that the right to vote in such a primary for the nomination of candidates without discrimination by the State, like the right to vote in a general election, is a right secured by the Constitution. United States vs. Classic, 313 U.S. at 314; Myers vs. Anderson, 238 U.S. 368; Ex parte Yarborough, 110 U.S. 651, 663 et seq. By the terms of the Fifteenth Amendment that right may not be abridged by any state on account of race.

The United States is a constitutional democracy. Its organic law grants to all citizens a right to participate in the choice of elected officials without restriction by any state because of race. This grant to the people of the opportunity for choice is not to be nullified by a state through casting its electoral process in a form which permits a private organization to practice racial discrimination in the election. Constitutional rights would be of little value if they could be thus indirectly denied.

Many Southern states bowed to the inevitable when the United States Supreme Court handed down its decision in *Smith* v. *Allwright*. In the Congressional and other elections of 1946, large numbers of Negroes voted in both primary and general elections in Texas, Georgia, and other Southern states, including Mississippi—despite the scandalous behavior of Senator Bilbo, who advocated mob violence against Negroes who dared to vote.

But South Carolina, one of the more backward states, sought to evade the Supreme Court's decision. George Elmore attempted to vote in the August 13, 1946, Democratic primary in Richland County. He and other Negroes were refused ballots. He appealed to us for aid and we brought action in his behalf in the United States District Court in the Eastern District of South Carolina on the basis of the Supreme Court's decision in *Smith* v. *Allwright*. The case was argued before Judge J. Waties Waring, member of a distinguished South Carolina family. The decision he handed down was prompt, unequivocal, and vigorous.

His opinion quoted at length the address to the state legislature of the then Governer Olin D. Johnston. The latter was elected to the United States Senate as successor to "Cotton Ed" Smith. Governor Johnston's speech had been delivered to a special session of the South Carolina Legislature, after the United States Supreme Court had handed down its decision in *Smith* v. *Allwright*. Johnston had recommended that South Carolina repeal "all primary laws from statute books" as a means of circumventing the higher court's decision, after which action he asserted, "We will have done everything within our power to guarantee white supremacy in our primaries and in our State in so far as legislation is concerned. Should this prove inadequate, we South Carolinians will use the necessary methods to retain white supremacy in our primaries and to safeguard the homes and happiness of our people. White supremacy will be maintained in our primaries. Let the chips fall where they may!" So said Governor Johnston.

Judge Waring coolly and with devastating logic examined this attempted evasion of the Constitution and of the Supreme Court's edicts. Riddling its fallacies with unmerciful accuracy, he declared ironically that the state's proposals were utterly unconstitutional and worthless:

For too many years the people of this Country and perhaps particularly of this State have evaded realistic issues. In these days when this nation and the nations of the world are forced to face facts in a realistic manner and when this country is taking the lead in maintaining the democratic process and attempting to show to the world that the American Government and the American way of life is the fairest and best that has yet been suggested, it is time for us to take stock of our internal affairs . . . it is time for South Carolina to rejoin the Union. It is time to fall in step with the other States and to adopt the American way of conducting elections. . . . Racial distinctions cannot exist in the machinery that selects the officers and law-makers of the United States; and all citizens of this State and Country are entitled to cast a free and untrammelled ballot in our elections, and if the only material and realistic elections are clothed with the name primary, they are equally entitled to vote there.

An appeal was taken to the United States Circuit Court of Appeals, which, six weeks after argument in that Court, affirmed on December 30, 1947, Judge Waring's vigorous and uncompromising decision. The opinion of the Circuit Court of Appeals was written and delivered by Judge John J. Parker:

An essential feature of our form of government is the right of the citizen to participate in the governmental process. The political philosophy of the Declaration of Independence is that governments derive their just powers from the consent of the governed; and the right to a voice in the selection of officers of government on the part of all citizens is important not only as a means of insuring that government shall have the strength of popular support but also as a means of securing to the individual citizen proper consideration of his rights by those in power. The disfranchised can never speak with the same force as those who are able to vote. . . . Denial to the Negro of the right to participate in the primary denies him of effective voice in the government of his Country. There can be no question that such denial amounts to the denial of the constitutional rights to the Negro; and we think it equally clear that those who participate in the denial are exercising state power to that end, since the primary is used in connection with the general election in the selection of state officers.

But even these two sweeping decisions do not seem at the time of writing to end the matter. The advocates of white supremacy and disfranchisement have announced that they will appeal to the United States Supreme Court!

We will, of course, meet them there.

In many Southern states Negroes today vote with complete freedom and their votes are eagerly sought by rival factions of the Democratic Party. The entire nation is the beneficiary. Now that Negroes vote more widely in the South, fewer bigots whose sole appeal is anti-Negroism will be elected to office to disgrace the nation in the eyes of the world. Although the poll tax and the dishonest use of understanding clauses continue to act as barriers to full enfranchisement, they too are on their way out. The fight has been long and expensive, but it has accomplished a great deal. It has been well worth making.

XII

Villa Sweet'um

When, in 1926, I received a Guggenheim Fellowship Grant for creative writing in any foreign country to which I chose to go, Gladys and I had a fascinating time considering the relative advantages of the far places of the earth. Our second child was scheduled to arrive in June 1927. We had to find a place where the cost of living was low because the $2,500 fellowship, though ample for a single person, would not go far for a family of four. The decision was made for us by Rebecca West and G. B. Stern, then on a visit to the United States. At a party at Carl and Fania Van Vechten's house they told us one evening that a furnished house could be rented for fifty dollars a year at Villefranche-sur-Mer on the French Riviera. "It's the one place worth living in which British and American tourists haven't invaded," they told us, "and it's the most beautiful place in southern France." After weeks of frenzied flesh- and spirit-wearying packing and arranging for a year's absence, we sailed late in July aboard a one-class ship.

We went first to Paris, where one night William Aspenwall Bradley took us to a superb dinner at his favorite *rendezvous des cochers* and afterward to his lovely apartment to meet Isadora Duncan and to hear Paul Robeson's first phonograph records. As "Go Down, Moses" in Paul's magnificent voice filled the room, Miss Duncan rose and began to dance. As though she had shed a robe she had been wearing, her weight and age seemed to disappear. The song finished, we all sat there mute, too deeply moved by the music and dance to speak. The dancer sank to the floor, exhausted by the emotional experience she had undergone. Lines of age and weariness again etched her face. It seemed utterly incongruous that this aging woman had but a few seconds before been the lithe, graceful figure which had so deeply moved us all.

From Paris we went to Villefranche, the rugged beauty of which magnificently lived up to its advance billing by Rebecca West and G. B. Stern. Jean Cocteau and his *Bœuf sur le Toit* following had not yet "discovered" Villefranche despite its proximity to Nice, Mentone, Monte Carlo, and Cannes. The only other English-speaking residents then were Glenway Wescott and Monroe Wheeler, whom we seldom saw.

M. Lassablière, the one local real estate agent, having tried first to rent us châteaux far beyond our means, finally clapped his hand on his forehead and exclaimed, "*Sacré bleu!* Why have I not thought of Villa Sweet'um?" (At least that is what we thought he said.) Off we went up the winding road called the Moyen Corniche, to arrive at the house we had dreamed of. Smoky pink walls and red tile roof gleamed in the warm Mediterranean sunlight. Eight large rooms furnished in rococo but not too garish style, brand-new silver and china and glassware, "*chauffrage central*" for coolish nights, electric lights, running water, bathtub and hot-water heaters for bathroom and kitchen, garage with servants' quarters—everything one could desire was there. And the rent only two hundred and fifty dollars a year! The name, which had been given the villa by a romantic Parisian woman, was "Home, Sweet Home!"

The fellowship had been granted to write a three-generation novel of Negro life. It yet remains to be written. I had thought that, far away from the American scene, I would be able, in the absence of the daily fare of lynching and injustice with which the NAACP constantly dealt, to devote myself to leisurely pursuit of belles-lettres. But distance, strangely enough, seemed to accentuate rather than diminish concern with what was happening back home to those who could do so little to help themselves. Perhaps it was due to the fact that in the midst of such idyllic beauty there was leisure to think about the content of letters from James Weldon Johnson and others in the Association about this lynching or that one; this fight in Congress or the other; the difficulty of raising money as America pulled itself slowly out of one depression and, unwittingly, headed for another destined to be the worst of all. Or perhaps it was because the Nice and Paris newspapers, which then published only occasional items about the United States, invariably featured news of lynchings and race riots.

Under these influences I found myself writing, instead of a novel, a study of the complex influences—economic, political, social, religious, sexual—behind the gruesome, and too little understood, phenomenon of lynching, under the title *Rope and Faggot*.

The Sacco-Vanzetti case, then approaching its tragic climax, added measurably to the local feeling against the United States. We seldom went into town. But we knew what was going on far better than we could have learned ourselves, thanks to our *bonne à tout faire*, Victoria. Looking somewhat like a gargoyle, she could cook like an angel. But she was far more than a servant. Being part Italian and part French, she had a passionate interest in the rise of Mussolini, then being extolled by Americans because he had caused the trains to run on time and cleaned up the sections of Italian cities likely to be explored by tourists. It was from Victoria that we learned, after she had worked for us long enough to find out where our sympathies lay, that her house on the waterfront was one of the stations of a latter-day Underground Railroad similar to those in the United States prior to the Civil War. Villefranche is only a few kilometers from the Italian border. Night after night Italians fled Mussoliniland under protection of darkness. Many of them hid during the day in Victoria's modest home, to take off again at nightfall to lose themselves deeper in France. Occasionally she would permit us to talk with some of the refugees from fascism.

The rapidity with which days passed at Villefranche as noted in the datelines of the Nice *l'Eclaireur* was a constant source of astonishment. To be able to sit on the terrace and look down on the lovely bay of Villefranche and off in the distance at the constantly changing, colorful beauty of the tiny peninsula which formed the left arm of the harbor made the first leisure I had ever known in adult life a never-ending peace and happiness.

But that idyllic experience was rudely ended when the opening of the fashionable season brought its influx of tourists—whereas before one seldom heard any language but French. We could not emerge from our villa except to run into tourists rushing madly from Cannes or Nice to Monte Carlo and back again. With painful frequency the noisiest, most drunken, and most unpleasant tourists were Americans, many of whom freely expressed their low opinion of "foreigners" oblivious to whether or not English, as they spoke it, was understood by the natives. Prices skyrocketed. The most painful economy was insufficient to meet the tremendously increased cost of living. What had been an ideal existence was speedily converted into a nightmare. M. Lassablière was frugally sympathetic when we told him we would have to go elsewhere. We knew as well as he that he would have no difficulty renting our villa for as much for the season as we were paying for the year. He was generous enough, therefore, to release us from the lease for one half the balance of the rent for the year. Half the town came down to the tiny railroad station to bid us good-by when we left for Avignon.

Again good luck attended our househunting. We rented the second-floor apartment belonging to M. Jules Pochy, a dealer in Provençal furniture, which was then coming into vogue with American tourists. M. Pochy's mother and father lived on the third floor, while his shop filled the street floor.

Thanks to the Pochys, we were soon accepted. Of an afternoon, after writing during the earlier part of the day, I used to sit at a sidewalk café at the Place d'Horloge with my friend Henri, who was a guide at the Palais des Papes. Henri must have been one of the handsomest Frenchmen who ever lived. No small part of his income must have been expended on pomades for his beard and mustache. He had once gone as far from Avignon as Paris, but had not liked the experience. He had so steeped himself in the history, folklore, and beauty of Provence that for him the sum and summation of all human experience was concentrated there. One day we talked, for some inexplicable reason, of echoes. Henri's shoulders squared themselves and he tossed his head proudly in a manner to which I was now becoming accustomed.

"I shall demonstrate to you, m'sieu, the most beautiful echo in the world. Come with me!"

Making sure to drain the last drop of his drink before leaving, he rose, and we trudged up the hill to the Palais des Papes. With a flourish he ushered me into the hall of Clement VI. The only object in the room was the chalky white sarcophagus of the long-dead pope. The late-afternoon golden sunlight streaming in through tall, narrow slits of windows marked off the grayish-white floors and walls like the lines on a football field. Henri guided me to one of the corners of the huge room, where he began to sing parts of a Mass in what had once been an excellent baritone and in which even then his age was noticeable only in the higher notes.

Like a response from a far-off invisible choir the sound came back to us. It was a moment of complete beauty.

We trudged down the hill in silence, and no word was spoken even when we touched hands in parting.

Before returning to America I went to England and Scotland under the auspices of the English Society of Friends to lecture on various aspects of the race question in the United States. The people I met in the homes in which I was entertained came so dangerously close to making me an anglophile that one of my hosts, an elderly and kindly Quaker, admonished me with pardonable pride, "Don't judge all of England by the people you are meeting—we have some bad ones in England too."

I was fortunate enough to participate in one of the fights for principle of the English Quakers. Lady Simon, wife of Lord John Simon who later became Chancellor of the Exchequer, was responsible for the revelation that many thousands of natives were being held in slavery in the African territory of Sierra Leone, which was administered by the British under a mandate from the League of Nations. Despite the exposure and debate of the facts in Parliament, there seemed to be considerable doubt that any corrective action would be taken. The Quakers swung into action immediately and arranged a huge meeting of protest in the Guild Hall of Hull, at which I was asked to speak.

The speaker who immediately preceded me was John H. Harris, member of Parliament and director of the Anti-Slavery and Aborigines Protection Society. Mr. Harris was earnest and eloquent, but addicted to nationalist clichés similar to those which Americans are accustomed to hear at Fourth of July celebrations.

"No injustice is ever permitted to exist under the Union Jack!" he orated, ignoring the frowns of doubt on the faces of many of his audience. He went on to speak of "our distinguished visitor from overseas" as preface to excoriation of the United States for permitting lynching to continue, which crime, he alleged, would be impossible anywhere within the British Empire.

I was faced with a dilemma. As a guest in England, should I ignore the speaker's remarks or take issue with them? I determined to do the latter, even at the risk of being guilty of bad taste. For the first time in my life I found myself being dangerously close to a "one hundred per cent American." Angrily I abandoned the manuscript I had carefully prepared and pointed out that the British government had sided with and greatly aided the South in our American Civil War, and that British ships had earned huge sums by the slave trade. I went on to declare that much of the wealth of near-by Liverpool had been derived from cheap American cotton produced by slaves. I freely admitted the shame of lynching in my own country and pointed out that neither nation had much to be proud of as to the slave trade and the theft of property and labor from colored peoples under imperialism.

I did not know and, in my annoyance, did not particularly care, what the reaction of the audience would be. To my surprise an ovation followed my speech, many of the audience coming to me afterward to express agreement with what I had said and admiration that I had pulled no punches.

I gained far more knowledge on this trip than I imparted. But I did tell audiences not only the grim facts about lynching and peonage and disfranchisement in the United States, but also of the fight being waged by Negroes and whites to implement the ideals of democracy. I read James Weldon Johnson's extraordinary *God's Trombones—Seven Negro Sermons in Verse*. Although I did not read them very well, the imaginative poetry of the old-time Negro preacher who had taken, in Jim's words, the imagery and "the sublime phraseology of the Hebrew prophet" which were "steeped in the idioms of King James English" and transformed them into figures of speech and experience familiar to his audience, was loved by my audiences.

I move ahead of my story slightly here to tell of the product of my Guggenheim year.

Rope and Faggot, ironically subtitled "The Biography of Judge Lynch," was published in 1929 and was cordially received by reviewers, including many in the South, as the first attempt to analyze the causative factors of lynchings. I was immensely pleased that a number of colleges, universities, and high schools included the book in their required reading or reference lists. And I was flattered that several writers and columnists chose to refer to the "Rope and Faggot Line" as a new synonym for Mason and Dixon's line.

XIII

Al Smith and the Negro Vote

In the late spring of 1928 I received a cablegram in Avignon from my friend Charles H. Studin asking whether I could return to the United States for a conference on a very important matter. Charlie Studin is a distinguished and successful New York lawyer with a magnificent talent for friendship who has for many years served as a member of the board of directors and of the national legal committee of the NAACP. His cable was so cryptic that I cabled him in return that unless it were a matter of life or death which no one else could handle I would prefer not to leave France at that time.

Charlie replied, still somewhat mysteriously, that Alfred E. Smith, New York's Governor, wanted my advice on an important matter. He assured me that I could return to France almost immediately without the loss of more than two or three weeks. He asked me as a special favor to him to make the trip. I sailed for New York a few days later.

When I reached New York, Charlie introduced me to one of the most colorful and forceful individuals I have ever known—Mrs. Belle Moskowitz. I had known her husband, Dr. Henry Moskowitz, who had been working for years to improve living and working conditions in New York City, particularly among immigrants on the Lower East Side. Dr. Moskowitz had been one of the signers of the call to the organization meeting of the NAACP.

Mrs. Moskowitz told me that Al Smith and his advisers had decided to make the first open and aggressive campaign to win the support of the Negro vote for the Democratic ticket in the presidential election. The Governor planned, if elected president, to extend to the nation the benefits of the social legislation New York state enjoyed because of the pioneer work by Governor Smith, Senator Robert F. Wagner, and Franklin D. Roosevelt. She told me that Charlie Studin had explained to her that the NAACP was a nonpolitical organization and that none of its paid executives were permitted to engage in partisan political activity. She asked me if I would consider taking a leave of absence from the Association to direct a campaign on Governor Smith's behalf among Negroes. I told her that I would not do so and that furthermore I opposed the setting up of a racially segregated campaign bureau.

She voiced her disappointment but made no further attempt to persuade me. She then asked me if I would be willing to talk with Governor Smith at Albany and advise him on what Negroes were demanding and thinking. This I agreed to do if it were made clear that I was not to be a participant in his campaign.

The Governor greeted me cordially enough but I had a strangely uncomfortable feeling, which was confirmed when he offered me a good job, if elected, in return for my support among Negroes. When, to his surprise, I had finally convinced him that no inducement would persuade me to enter a political campaign, our conversation became constructive. He told me of his ambition to see Congress enact legislation to wipe out the vast inequalities in income and status among the American people, which, he feared, would inevitably lead to conflict which would destroy America if not resolved.

He then came to the reasons for wanting to talk with me. "I know Negroes distrust the Democratic Party, and I can't blame them. But I want to show them that the old Democratic Party, ruled entirely by the South, is on its way out, and that we Northern Democrats have a totally different approach to the Negro."

I asked him how he proposed to demonstrate this conversion, to which he replied that he had asked me to come in to help him plan a program.

One of my suggestions was that he issue a detailed and unequivocal statement making it clear to the Negro and to the country generally that, if elected, he would be president of all the people and would not be ruled by the anti-Negro South. He assured me that he would do this and he asked me if I would draft the statement.

Days and then weeks passed without a word from Albany after I had sent him the statement. Mrs. Moskowitz told me one day that Senator Joseph T. Robinson of Arkansas, Smith's choice as candidate for vice-president, and Senator Pat Harrison had bitterly opposed the issuance of any statement, however mild, by Governor Smith, and that Judge Joseph Proskauer, close personal friend and adviser of Smith, believed that such a statement would too greatly antagonize the South. I found myself sorry for Mrs. Moskowitz at being assigned the unpleasant job of telling me this. Almost plaintively she asked, "Can't you—won't you take the Governor on faith as we have?"

I explained why I could not, telling her that any usefulness I might have would be ended if I supported Governor Smith and he were then elected and forced by the ruthless and dominant Southern wing of the Democratic Party to do things which would be against the best interests of the Negro.

Because Herbert Hoover demonstrated an even greater unwillingness to show in any fashion that he regarded Negroes as citizens and human beings, and because of Al Smith's record in New York state, many Negroes voted for Smith, despite his silence.

Shortly before her death, Mrs. Moskowitz told me that, after his defeat, Al Smith had told her that he wished he had signed the statement and made an all-out bid for the Negro vote. He was convinced that he would thereby have won enough votes in pivotal Northern and border states, which he had lost by narrow margins, to elect him.

XIV

The Man in the Lily-White House

My return to France was postponed several times at the insistence of Mrs. Moskowitz and Charlie Studin until the imminent expiration of my leave of absence from the Association made needlessly expensive the return trip. Gladys and the children remained in Paris, to return in the fall, while I resumed my work with the NAACP.

The second Texas primary case, already described, was on its way to the United States Supreme Court. Our unrelenting campaign against lynching and the increasing public condemnation of the crime had begun to show effect. The annual number of lynchings had declined from an average of two hundred to eleven in 1929. But we found that the improvement was more apparent than real. The South was becoming almost pathologically sensitive on the subject and resentful of "outside interference." The practice was developing, we learned, of suppressing the news of lynchings or reporting such mob murders as instances of criminals being killed by "posses." This new strategy required increased alertness and considerably more effort to ferret out the crimes and establish their authenticity. In this we were tremendously aided by the steady growth of NAACP branches in Southern states and by friends, both white and Negro, who kept us informed, often at danger of reprisals from the mobs for doing so.

The situation was accented by an event in our World War One jimcrow army. A twelve-year campaign on behalf of members of the all-Negro 24th Infantry Regiment was ending. In 1917 these Negro soldiers, goaded to desperation by repeated acts of hostility at Brownsville, Texas, and the failure of the War Department and other branches of the federal government to protect them, had resisted with arms. In the riot which followed a number of both Negroes and whites were injured, and some were killed. Immediately the machinery of the law swung into action—against the Negroes. No charges were made against whites.

The NAACP had investigated the riot, engaged a local white attorney to defend the men in courts-martial, and had publicized the facts throughout the country. Despite the maximum efforts which the then small Association could muster, thirteen members of the 24th Infantry were executed on December 11, 1917, and six others subsequently. The Association had gathered twelve thousand signatures to a petition which was presented to President Wilson in 1918, and fifty thousand signatures to another presented to President Harding in 1921. A number of death sentences had been commuted to life imprisonment as a result, and later there were further reductions and the eventual release of men whose martyrdom forms a tragic page in American history.

The success, though limited, of the fight for the 24th Infantry, and the demonstration of dogged determination which went into it, played a decisive role in preventing outbreaks of such major proportions during World War Two. Both at home and overseas there were a tragically large number of injustices perpetrated upon Negroes due to segregation in the armed services, as I was destined to learn in the years 1943 to 1945 in the European and Pacific theaters of war. But in World War Two there was a notable advance in the active opposition by military and naval leaders to mistreatment of colored soldiers and sailors. Outstanding were General Eisenhower, Admiral Nimitz, Secretary of War Patterson, and President Roosevelt.

Greatly increased work and responsibility were added in 1929 when Jim was granted a year's leave of absence to serve as a member of the American delegation to the Institute of Pacific Relations, held that year at Kyoto, Japan, and to accept a fellowship from the Julius Rosenwald Fund for creative writing. I blithely accepted the responsibility of acting secretary, wholly unaware of the difficult days immediately ahead. The stock market was climbing to dizzier heights than ever before in history. The unemployment and apprehension of the early twenties were disappearing, even for Negroes, as millions of Americans dreamed of becoming millionaires by stock market speculation, and the psychology of unending and unlimited prosperity and peace created a fool's paradise.

But our already precarious financial situation became desperate soon after the stock market crash in October 1929. As business firms and factories failed, Negroes began to lose many of the skilled and semiskilled jobs they had gained with such difficulty during and immediately after the war. The grim years were upon us, and interracial tensions began to mount too. The "Great Engineer" sat stolidly in the White House, refusing bluntly to receive Negro citizens who wished to lay before him the facts of their steadily worsening plight or to consider any remedial legislation or governmental action. His attitude to Negroes caused me to coin a phrase which gained considerable currency, particularly in the Negro world, in which I described Hoover as "the man in the lily-White House."

Hoover's attitude toward Negroes and minorities generally was made dramatically evident in 1930 when Supreme Court Justice Sanford died and the President sent to the Senate the name of John J. Parker of North Carolina in nomination for the seat. Parker was then a judge of the United States Circuit Court whose record was almost totally unknown. As the Senate might vote on the nomination at any time, it was imperative that we move with the utmost speed. Long distance telephone calls and telegrams were sent to key Negro and white friends for information on Judge Parker's attitude on the Negro and related questions.

The first replies from North Carolina reported that the senders knew little or nothing about him. And then came a telegram which galvanized us into action. It stated that Judge Parker, as a candidate on the Republican ticket for governor of North Carolina in 1920, had advocated continuation of disfranchisement of Negro citizens. We telephoned the sender of this message asking him to get us proof, through newspaper clippings, affidavits, or other irrefutable material. The following morning we received a yellowed newspaper clipping from the *Greensboro Daily News* of April 19, 1920, in which Judge Parker was quoted directly in approval of a 1900 amendment to the constitution of North Carolina which provided for the payment of a poll tax, for literacy tests of voters, and for the inclusion of a grandfather clause despite the fact that the United States Supreme Court in the case of *Guinn and Beale* v. *United States* [1] handed down a decision in 1915 holding grandfather clauses to be unconstitutional. In addition, Judge Parker had said:

The participation of the Negro in politics is a source of evil and danger to both races and is not desired by the wise men in either race or by the Republican Party of North Carolina.

Plainly this attitude would constitute a grave threat to the future of the Negro and to the work in the Negro's behalf by the NAACP if he became a part of the Supreme Court, which at that time was distinctly conservative and almost invariably more concerned with property rights than with human rights.

It was decided, therefore, to make inquiry of Judge Parker by wire, first, as to whether or not he had been correctly quoted by the *Greensboro Daily News* in the decade-old clipping, and second, whether, even if he had made such a statement as a candidate for governor in 1920, he still held such beliefs in 1930. To make sure that Judge Parker had received the telegram we asked Western Union to deliver it to him only and report on its delivery.

A few hours later Western Union advised us that the telegram had been delivered to and signed for personally by Judge Parker.

In the meantime, the Senate Judiciary Committee had appointed a subcommittee to hold hearings on the nomination. The consensus of Washington opinion was that the inquiry would be a matter of form and that confirmation was inevitable. We waited seventy-two hours for Judge Parker's reply. None came. I presented the facts to the NAACP board of directors and it was agreed that we should protest and oppose as vigorously as possible Judge Parker's confirmation.

Hoover was asked to withdraw the Parker nomination. We cited as precedent President Taft's withdrawal of his nomination of Judge Hook in 1912 after protest by the NAACP on Hook's anti-Negro record. This request was angrily refused by Hoover.

It was then voted that I, as acting secretary, should appear before

[1] 238 U.S. 347.

the Senate subcommittee of the Judiciary Committee in opposition to Parker's confirmation. I did so, but scant attention was paid to the memorandum I presented. The American Federation of Labor had also protested Parker's confirmation because of decisions he had rendered in upholding so-called "yellow-dog" contracts. But Parker and his friends had defended themselves by pointing out that he had merely followed the precedent of the United States Supreme Court in the Hitchman case.

It was a strange and uncomfortable situation which I found. The American Federation of Labor was exceedingly anxious to prevent identification of its opposition against Parker with that of Negroes. Throughout the fight, the AFL statements abstemiously refrained from mentioning Parker's anti-Negro stand. William Green, president of the AFL, and I entered the hearings room at the same time. Although I had met him on several occasions before that day, he appeared conspicuously to avoid speaking lest senators on the committee, newspapermen, or spectators believe that we were fighting as allies in a common battle. I was not called upon by Senator Overman of North Carolina, chairman of the subcommittee, until the very end of the hearing.

When I did speak, both Senators Borah and Overman, particularly the latter, became incensed at the temerity of a Negro organization presuming to voice an opinion on a nomination to the Supreme Court. Overman angrily asked me if I did not know that "niggras vote freely throughout North Carolina." I informed Mr. Overman that I did not know this to be true and neither did he, and that there was ample proof to the contrary. Senator Borah attempted to put me on the defensive by asking involved questions about legal decisions which, not being a lawyer, it would have been most foolish for me to attempt to answer. I refused to be drawn into such a trap and insisted on confining my testimony to the incontrovertible fact that Judge Parker, though he had been given an opportunity to do so, had not denied having advocated the disfranchisement of Negro American citizens despite the explicit provisions of the Fourteenth and Fifteenth Amendments.

After the hearing, we telegraphed every branch of the NAACP, particularly those in Northern and border states where Negroes voted, urging telegraphic protests by themselves and by church, fraternal, labor, civic, educational, and other bodies to be directed to senators from those states, urging that they vote against Parker's confirmation. Mass meetings were arranged and addressed by various officers of the national office of the Association, including Arthur B. Spingarn, W. E. B. DuBois, and William Pickens. Telegraph blanks were supplied, already addressed to the United States senators from each state, for the convenience of the audiences in making their protests. Newspaper editors were kept supplied with the facts as the campaign developed.

At first a trickle, the telegrams, letters, petitions, long distance telephone calls, and personal visits to senators in Washington grew to an avalanche. Two newspaper correspondent friends in Washington kept us advised of what was going on behind the scenes. Senators who at first had been apathetic or contemptuous began to pay attention to the unprecedented articulateness of Negroes.

As the fight waxed hotter, virtually every trick of legislative maneuvering, fair or foul, was utilized. One of the very first was a brazen and unequivocal denial that Parker had ever made such a statement or that the *Greensboro Daily News* had ever published the now-famous clipping quoting Judge Parker's anti-Negro speech. This charge was made on the floor of the Senate about two P.M. The following day at nine A.M. a photostatic copy of the *Greensboro Daily News* clipping was on the desk of each member of the Senate, on President Hoover's desk, and in the hands of every newspaper correspondent in Washington.

The next charge was that the clipping had been illegally taken from the files of the *Greensboro Daily News*. This charge, because it was true, threatened disaster. The North Carolina citizen who had sent us the clipping was a Negro whose skin color clearly proved his race. Wise in the ways of Dixie, he had known that there would have been difficulty in examining ten-year-old files of the newspaper had he gone himself to look up the clipping. He had, therefore, sent a young Negro who looked white to get the facts, instructing him to copy the clipping. But the young Negro had been disinclined to copy the lengthy clipping and had used his penknife to cut it from the bound file. One of the photostats we had sent to Washington had been rushed to Greensboro. It had fitted precisely into the mutilated copy of the paper. Fortunately, the episode was soon forgotten.

Another crisis arose when the sectional issue was raised by Parker's supporters. Lobbyists with thick Southern accents buttonholed Cole Blease of South Carolina, Pat Harrison of Mississippi, Carter Glass of Virginia, and "Cotton Ed" Smith of South Carolina, asking contemptuously whether they were going to bow to the "dictation" of a "nigger advancement society." Our friends in Washington reported that this campaign was having effect. It would have been futile for us to have approached men like Blease, Smith, and Harrison. Coming from states where Negroes were totally disfranchised, we would have had no influence and probably would have strengthened their determination to vote for Parker because he was a Southerner. Another approach was necessary. We were successful in arranging to have fellow senators and other white persons of influence with the Southern senators ask if they proposed to vote for Parker and thus "help Hoover reward North Carolina for going Republican in the 1928 elections"? The stratagem worked even on those so notoriously opposed to equal rights for Negroes as "Tom-Tom" Heflin of Alabama, Tom Connally of Texas, Joseph T. Robinson of Arkansas, and Kenneth McKellar of Tennessee.

The next trick pulled on us was pressure on "Negro leaders" of North Carolina to issue statements in support of Parker and in repudiation of the NAACP. But despite threats of physical violence and of economic reprisals, this campaign was an almost total failure. Only two "Negro leaders" in North Carolina could be induced to endorse Parker, and their endorsements were exceedingly temperate. One of the two "leaders" was the president of a state school for Negroes who was thereby dependent upon the legislature for appropriations. The other was an almost completely unknown individual with a most unimpressive record. Facts concerning these men were promptly broadcast to the press, white and colored, by the NAACP.

The vigor of the campaign and the importance of the fight made the issue front-page news and the subject of editorial comment of varying attitudes in newspapers throughout the United States. The

Scripps-Howard chain of newspapers, at that time liberal in policy, Heywood Broun in his widely syndicated column, and many individual newspapers in Northern and border states vigorously supported the fight against Parker.

However, the *New York Times* was grievously disappointing in its attitude, and most of the Southern newspapers were exceedingly vicious. In many of them facts were brazenly distorted. False stories deliberately designed to becloud the issue and to play on race prejudice were circulated to the effect that the opposition to Parker's confirmation was based on his refusal to "dine with Negroes." Other papers stated that he was being fought only because he did not believe that Negroes had "yet developed enough intelligence to vote." Many of the Southern papers and a few in the North scurrilously attacked the NAACP, declaring that the charge against Parker, despite the incontrovertible proof which had been presented, was a "vicious falsehood," "disreputable politics," "garbage," "a low publicity stunt," and other epithets. Vehemently and frequently the charge was made that if Parker's nomination were defeated, thereafter no Southerner could hope to sit on the Supreme Court bench or occupy other federal office until he had been approved by the "National Association for the Advancement of Colored People and Walter White."

The galleries were packed on May 7th, the day agreed upon for a vote on the nomination. We had difficulty in refraining from applause when blind Senator Thomas D. Schall of Minnesota entered the Senate chamber. He had been dangerously ill but had returned to Washington at our urging, although there were very few Negro votes in his state.

The Senate debate was spirited, at times vicious. Its highest note came when Senator Wagner, the only member of the upper house who dared mention the Negro angle of the opposition although it was the one issue in the mind of every senator, rose to speak. He minced no words and declared:

I see a deep and fundamental consistency between his view of labor relations and his reported attitude toward colored people of the United States. They both spring from a single trait of character. Judged by the available record, he is obviously incapable of viewing with sympathy the aspirations of those who are aiming for a higher and better place in the world. His sympathies naturally flow out to those who are already on top and he has used the authority of his office and the influence of his opinion to keep them on top whether they be an exploited economic group or a minority racial group.

The "ayes and nays" were called for, and anxious hands, none more so than my own, checked the tally as the tide swung from rejection to confirmation and back again. As the clerk droned on toward the end of the alphabetical roll, our hopes sank as four senators who had pledged to vote against confirmation switched their votes under pressure from the White House. But hope, somewhat bedraggled, revived slightly as several doubtful senators whose votes we had not counted on voted "nay."

Feverishly we rechecked the tallies we had kept and breathlessly awaited, fearing an error on our part, the announcement by the tally clerk of the Senate.

He announced, "For confirmation—39. Against confirmation—41." The shift of one vote to create a tie would have been a disaster.

Immediately the opposition newspapers attacked the decision. Notable among them were the *Montgomery Advertiser*, the *Norfolk Ledger-Dispatch*, and the *Macon Telegraph*. They furiously condemned the senators who had voted against confirmation, somberly bemoaned the state of a nation in which Negroes were allowed to "dictate" to its president and legislative body, and direly predicted that (in the words of the *Macon Telegraph*) "no President will dare in the future to appoint a man whose views on the Negro question are not entirely satisfactory to the Association for the Advancement of Colored People. . . . In the future the man who is appointed to the Supreme Court must pass in review before Walter White." Even the *New York Times*, choosing to ignore the facts, and as unfair in its opinion as many papers in the deep South, said, "No principle is at stake. Only a political self-interest is driving on these Republican senators (to vote against Parker). . . . Compared with them the Negro agitators hot on their trail are straightforward and honorable."

But, fortunately, many other newspapers, notable among which was the *Washington Post*, reported the facts with accuracy and without bias. The Parker fight was recognized as the political coming of age of the hitherto-ignored Negro voters. The *Post* published a lengthy feature in its issue of May 18, 1930, by one of its star correspondents, A. H. Ulm, in which the new significance of the Negro vote and the importance of the NAACP were recognized.

Dire predictions made by some Southern newspapers and even a few Northern ones that Negro opposition to Judge Parker would result in race riots happily proved bad prophecy. Equally false has been proved the assertion that no Southerner would be confirmed for the Supreme Court after Parker's defeat, as has been proved by the confirmation, which Negroes approved or did not oppose, of Southerners like Hugo Black of Alabama and Stanley Reed, Fred Vinson, and Wiley Rutledge, all of Kentucky. Negro approval or disapproval of Supreme Court nominees has been strictly confined to consideration of a man's public and private record on vital issues and not of the place of his birth.

The question presented itself immediately upon the rejection of Parker as to what position the NAACP would take on the senators who had voted for confirmation. Up to that time we had neither endorsed nor opposed political candidates. *The Crisis*, official publication of the NAACP, listed such senators whose terms expired in 1930, 1932, and 1934, with the prefatory statement: "The following Senators have Negro constituents in considerable, if not large numbers, and against the expressed wishes of these constituents, they voted for the confirmation of Judge Parker. . . . Paste this in your hat and keep it there until November, 1934."

There were influential Negroes like the beloved Dean Kelly Miller of Howard University who publicly urged that Negroes and their friends should be content with Parker's rejection and take no further steps such as opposition to the reelection of senators who had flouted the pleas of Negro and labor voters in their states. However, there were others who were equally convinced that, Negro voters having served notice during the fight upon their senators that those voters would not vote for reelection of any member of the Senate who had voted to place a man with Parker's views on the Supreme Court, those threats had to be implemented or else Negro voters would be laughed at the next time they appealed to their elected representatives.

The extent and nature of the participation of the Association in such campaigns was debated lengthily and with great care. Decision was finally reached that the unfinished job had to be completed. McCulloch of Ohio, Baird of New Jersey, Gillette of Massachusetts, Hastings of Delaware, Grundy of Pennsylvania, Goff of West Virginia, had voted for confirmation and were candidates for re-election in the fall of 1930. Ohio was overwhelmingly Republican. The stock market crash of 1929 had not yet lessened the flow of campaign funds for Republican candidates. I was instructed by the NAACP board of directors to campaign only through meetings arranged by the NAACP branches in Ohio and not through any political organization against McCulloch on the basis of his Parker vote. I learned the facts of life about politics in extraordinary fashion as a result.

Despite the defeat of Parker, the Negro was still the object of derogation almost to the point of contempt on the part of politicians. Understandably basing their judgment on contacts with a handful of Negro politicians who made a living convincing white political bosses that these Negroes could "deliver the Negro vote," a number of Republican leaders believed that they could buy the Negro vote. Money was poured lavishly into such purchases, with almost complete lack of success because Negro voters had been so stirred by the Parker fight that even a hitherto respected Negro minister who attempted to defend McCulloch was laughed out of Ohio.

And then the mysterious forces resorted to attempts to impugn the characters of those who were opposing McCulloch, and to utilize money, liquor, and women to discredit them. Arriving in an Ohio city on a speaking tour, I had just reached the home at which I was to stay when the telephone rang and a seductive female voice invited me to come to her house to permit her to tell me the facts about a case in which the NAACP would be interested. When I informed her that I would talk with her only in the presence of witnesses and at the place where I was staying, the conversation abruptly ended. I resented most the obvious intimation that I would be so easily tricked.

In another city I was scheduled to speak at a mass meeting which was held in the largest auditorium available because of the feverish interest in the campaign. So dense was the crowd that I had to alight from my taxicab a block away from the auditorium to wedge my way through the crowd. I hung my topcoat and hat in an anteroom off the platform. After the meeting I found that the topcoat seemed somewhat heavier. In the right-hand pocket someone had placed a whisky bottle. As the platform party and I emerged from the anteroom into the auditorium, a number of persons fastened eagle eyes not on us, but on the right-hand pocket of my coat, and seemed somewhat disappointed to see nothing there.

McCulloch of Ohio, Baird of New Jersey, and Allen of Kansas went down in defeat in 1930, followed in subsequent years by Shortridge of California, Patterson of Maryland, Watson of Indiana, Fess of Ohio, Reed of Pennsylvania, Hatfield of West Virginia, Wolcott of Connecticut, and Hebert of Rhode Island, all of them, in large measure, because of the implacable and effective opposition of Negro voters.

"Hastings of Delaware and one or two Senators from far north New England States escaped," wryly commented *The Crisis* in December 1934.

Out of these effective hard-hitting and uncompromising campaigns two changed political attitudes came. White politicians, Republican and Democratic, did not like the new situation, but were forced to recognize that the Negro voter no longer was gullible, purchasable, or complacent as before and would have to be recognized as an increasingly potent force in the American political scene.

As for Negroes, they found new hope and dignity. Hitherto their efforts had been crowned at best with purely "moral" victories. Even the most philosophical among them, who recognized that such moral victories were part of the maturing of a minority group, had found difficulty in acceptance of defeat. But in the Parker fight victory had been achieved and a philosophy and aura of success had replaced the purely protest values of preceding battles. One of the most gratifying developments of the Parker fight was the editorial reaction of the constantly growing Negro press which had backed the fight for principle. It was inevitable that jubilation should permeate the editorial comment. However, there was sober realization that the rejection of the North Carolina jurist was but a stage in a long and difficult struggle.

In Judge Parker's behalf, I should like to add this postscript: Since his rejection, his decisions on both Negro and labor cases which have come before him have been above reproach in their strict adherence not only to the law but to the spirit of the Constitution.

In 1940 there came before the three justices of the Circuit Court of Appeals, of whom Judge Parker was one, the case of Melvin O. Alston against the School Board of Norfolk, Virginia. Mr. Alston, the plaintiff, on behalf of himself and other Negro teachers in the segregated school system of Norfolk, had brought action against the gross differential between salaries paid to white teachers and those paid to Negro teachers, who were nevertheless required to meet the same standards of education and experience. The case, which had been carried through the lower courts by NAACP attorneys Oliver W. Hill of Richmond, William H. Hastie, and Dr. L. A. Ransom—chairman and member, respectively, of the national legal committee—and Special Counsel Thurgood Marshall, had been decided against Alston in the Federal District Court. Appeal had been taken to the Circuit Court of Appeals. It had been urged upon me that I should be present in the courtroom when the appeal was argued. But because of the Senate fight over the confirmation of Judge Parker, it seemed to the NAACP attorneys and myself that my appearance in the court would have been distinctly bad taste. At the conclusion of the argument, Judge Parker congratulated William H. Hastie and Thurgood Marshall on the presentation of their case, doing so wholly on the basis of the facts. Shortly thereafter Judge Parker wrote and read for the Court a sweeping decision reversing the Federal District Court in behalf of Mr. Alston and other Negro teachers of Norfolk. That decision wiped out an annual differential of $129,000, between the salaries of white and Negro school teachers in Norfolk.

And one final postscript. Hoover's intransigeance in the Parker case permanently alienated Negroes. The Negro vote played a very considerable part in the overwhelming rejection of the Republican candidate in favor of Franklin D. Roosevelt in the 1932 presidential election.

At the end of his year's leave of absence Jim's doctors forbade him to return to the heavy program of work he had been carrying as secretary of the NAACP, and he resigned. His resignation was accepted with very great reluctance and sorrow by the board of directors. We arranged a dinner in his honor at the Pennsylvania Hotel which was attended by one of the most distinguished audiences I have ever seen in New York or anywhere else. Rosamond Johnson set the tone of gaiety and reminiscence for the evening by playing and singing some of the songs he and Jim had written for Marie Cahill, Lillian Held, Bert Williams, Sophie Tucker, and Ernest Hogan—"Under the Bamboo Tree," "The Maiden With the Dreamy Eyes," "Congo Love Song," and "Lift Ev'ry Voice and Sing." Heywood Broun, Carl Van Doren, Dantes Bellegarde, Haitian Minister to the United States, Arthur Spingarn, and several others paid heartfelt tributes to Jim, all of them deserved and more, until Jim's eyes were misty when he rose to speak.

I was promoted from acting secretary to secretary, and wondered what troubles lay ahead.

Opportunity was afforded us in 1931 to learn another phase of the international picture of the race question when Gladys and I visited Haiti, on a trip on which I combined a vacation with the task of carrying on an NAACP investigation.

The investigation that Jim and Herbert Seligmann had made in 1920 of the ruthlessness of the American occupation of that small Caribbean country had become an issue in the presidential campaign of that year because the occupation had been a constant source of criticism in Latin America of "Yanqui" imperialism. The NAACP exposé had resulted in withdrawal of the United States Marines and in the softening of the treatment of the hapless country. But the American Financial Adviser, acting as much for the National City Bank of New York as for the United States government, continued to exercise dictatorial power over the finances of Haiti, a condition which continues in only slightly modified fashion to this day. Jim had been instrumental in forming the Union Patriotique d'Haiti to work for the restoration of independence, and the Haitian president at the time of our visit, M. Stenio Vincent, had served as president of the patriotic society, using our offices in New York as the headquarters on his visits to the United States.

Gladys and I had hoped to slip away from the United States and arrive in Haiti without advance publicity. We were both tired from the long ordeal of the Parker and other Association struggles. We were anxious also to avoid having any official significance attached to our visit, so that we could wander about and see and talk to whomever we pleased without interference. Unfortunately for our plans, a newspaper reporter spied our luggage-laden taxicab crossing the Brooklyn Bridge to the pier. He followed us, blandly ignored our evasions, and, noting that the ship we boarded would stop at Port-au-Prince, correctly assumed that lovely capital to be our destination.

No sooner had we reached our hotel—even before we had time to start unpacking—than a captain of Marines knocked at our door to tell us that he had been assigned to be our guide while in Haiti. A sleek and luxurious black limousine, belonging to the Bishop of Haiti, stood at the door awaiting us. From the crack of dawn to late in the evening when weariness drove us to bed, Captain Faustin Wirkus, the Marine who wrote "The White King of LaGonave," was constantly with us. We were shown roads, schools, and other improvements which he attributed to the Americans. All our efforts to get in touch with our Haitian friends were adroitly blocked by Wirkus's telling us that he had arranged a trip to some point of interest, usually a day's drive distant, or luncheon with the American Minister or some other United States official.

Wirkus was so delightful a person that we were reluctant to offend him by telling him we wished to have at least a part of the time to ourselves. He eventually saved us this embarrassment by telling us frankly that, at the request of American governmental authorities, he had been assigned the duty of monopolizing our time to leave us as little as possible for talk with Haitians, and that we should not hesitate to tell him to go away when we did not wish to be bothered with him—a decision we had already made.

Gladys and I were the only Americans at the Hotel Bellevue on the Champs de Mars facing the presidential palace who were not connected with the occupation government. Some of the other guests constantly embarrassed us by their prejudice-ridden and rude statements about the Haitians. Because prices and wages were low, particularly personal service (maids could be employed for six dollars a month), most of the Americans were living at a luxury level infinitely higher than they had ever enjoyed in the States. Many of them came from the South and made no attempt whatever to conceal their antipathy for dark-skinned people. Apparently they believed that the difference of language kept the French-speaking Haitians from understanding what was being said, which was absurd, since many Haitians have learned to speak English or at least to understand it. Often we wondered why our country should be so foolish as to send bigoted American whites to the Caribbean and South America on the fantastic theory that only they "understood Negroes."

Our fellow guests at the Bellevue were startled one day when President Vincent's official car arrived to take Gladys and me to the Palace for a formal dinner in our honor. We could hear the tongues clattering as we drove out of the courtyard. But at the dazzlingly white palace modeled after the Petit Trianon and set down in the midst of intoxicatingly colorful and fragrant tropical flowers, we soon forgot the gaucheries and prejudices we had left behind us at the hotel. President Vincent had assembled his cabinet and their wives and other distinguished Haitians. We have never before nor since heard the French language spoken with such precision or beauty, not even among educated Parisians. Many of the Haitians had been educated at the Sorbonne. They and those who had not enjoyed such training were proud of the purity of the French they spoke and scrupulously but not ostentatiously kept free of idiomatic and colloquial usages.

The conversation at first was somewhat stilted and formal as we talked of somber matters like crops and Haitian-American relations. Suddenly, as though someone had applied a match to resinous pine knots, the talk came to life when one of the guests, to illustrate a point, quoted an obscure sixteenth-century poet with whose work, much less his name, Gladys and I were totally unfamiliar. The quotation was instantly challenged by his opponent, who animatedly quoted another poet, equally unknown to us, who had said it better, the second speaker was certain. Mundane matters like trade balances and taxes were totally forgotten as Gladys and I frantically attempted with our inadequate French to follow the conversation which exploded throughout the huge and ornate dining room like firecrackers on the Fourth of July.

On our way home we laughed as we tried to imagine a similar conversation springing up at the White House back home with the humorless Hoover and his sobersides cabinet. Probably, Gladys was sure, such an interest in culture instead of profits would promptly be considered a proof of Haitian "inferiority."

The scholarly Dr. Dantes Bellegarde, later the Haitian Ambassador to the United States, the brilliant Dr. Joseph Price-Mars, whose books have circulated widely in Europe as well as in Haiti, President Vincent, and other Haitians supplied answers to our numerous questions. The country was poor then and is still poor today. But we were ashamed that a nation which has contributed as much to the present power and wealth of the United States as has Haiti should be so shabbily treated by us.

It was the revolt of the Haitian slaves under Toussaint l'Ouverture, Dessalines, and Pétion, and their crushing defeat of the pick of France's troops under General LeClerc which smashed Napoleon's dreams of a vast empire in the Americas and forced him to sell the Louisiana Territory to the United States during the presidency of Thomas Jefferson. Without the vast expanse of territory extending from the Gulf of Mexico to Canada and embracing most of our great Middle West, the United States would have been restricted to the Atlantic seaboard. But we have never demonstrated any gratitude to Haiti, and our history textbooks ignore this epic chapter in our national history.

My deep concern with the American treatment of Haiti has been kept alive through the years, not only because of its great physical beauty and the charm of its people, but also by the continuation of our cavalier treatment of that country. A few years after our visit, Haiti guaranteed a loan of $5,500,000 to an American engineering company for the building of roads, sanitation facilities, and other needed improvements. Most of the construction was wiped out by the first heavy rain, but Haiti has had to pay the bill with interest. She guaranteed another loan from the Export-Import Bank for agricultural development, which was taken over as a war emergency project to raise rubber from the cryptostegia plant—a project carried on wholly under the direction of American "experts," and which was a total failure. One hundred thousand acres of the best farming land, from which its owners derived at prewar prices an income of $50,000,000, was expropriated for the futile experiment. Houses, fences, and vines and trees which had been years in the growing, were destroyed by bulldozers. The owners were given compensation averaging three dollars per acre for nearly three years' use of the land. But when a delegation headed by Dr. Joseph Price-Mars came to the United States in 1947 to seek a loan from the Export-Import Bank to renegotiate and consolidate previous loans on which interest rates far higher than the current market were being paid, and to restore Haiti's shattered economy, Washington gave the delegation a curt brushoff, announcing that no further loans were being made —even as astronomical sums were being loaned or given outright to England, Italy, and virtually every other country on earth, except black Haiti.

XV

The Civil War in Washington

The Parker fight had demonstrated that Negroes when united could win important victories and enlist in their aid many fair-minded whites who both respected fighting ability and were aware that the struggle for democracy was an indivisible one in which their interests were closely involved with those of Negroes. It had also made clear that so long as the overwhelming majority of both white and Negro voters in the South were denied the vote, the sole avenue of legislative remedy was the Congress. Many of us did not want to see centralization of too much power in Washington nor in the hands of any man or group. The prospect of an American Hitler or Mussolini was not one to be viewed with comfort. But at the same time it was crystal-clear that a dangerous form of dictatorship already existed, and had been in existence unnoticed for many years, in the growing power of the Southern oligarchy. That group of dictatorial legislators were more and more voting and working with the archconservatives of the Republican Party. We were forced therefore to choose the lesser of two evils—to work for federal action against lynching, disfranchisement, unequal apportionment of school and other tax moneys, and thereby concentrate more authority in Washington, or to let such dangerous practices continue and spread to the rest of the nation.

Choice of the former course caused me to spend more and more time in Washington. What I saw and heard there has frequently been a severe tax on my faith in the democratic process.

There was, for example, a letter I wrote Gladys late one night after an eighteen-hour day of frustration and double-dealing at the hands of congressmen and senators who were trying to evade iron-clad promises which had been made to enact a federal anti-lynching bill. I wrote: "Democracy must be tough-fibered to survive practice of it by democrats."

My low spirits that evening had been induced by an experience which revealed the methods which some lobbyists were using successfully to obtain passage of favored bills. A high-salaried, assertive representative of a pressure group which was demanding huge sums of money from the public treasury—which they got—came over to where I was sitting in the reception room of the Senate chamber.

"I have been watching you for a long time," he began, "working around here trying to get your anti-lynching bill passed. You haven't a ghost of a chance as long as you operate as you do. I don't favor the bill, but I can't help but admire the way you are working on a shoestring, appealing to the 'better nature' of politicians."

He bit off the end of a cigar and spat it out on the immaculate tile floor.

"The only way you can move most of these bastards is by getting something on them and threatening to expose it. I am going to help you pass your anti-lynching bill by letting you have what we have dug up!"

A faint nausea came over me.

"What sort of stuff have you got?" I asked.

He asked me to meet him at his office after dinner that evening. There he opened a sturdy safe and took out file after file, each labeled with the name of a member of the United States Senate. Some were thin—these were the files of new or relatively new senators. Others were fat and their contents filthy. Affidavits, photostats, reports of private detectives, newspaper clippings, court records, and unsavory revelations in letters which might well make a normal human being afraid to sit on the floor of the United States Senate.

I asked to see folders on several senators whom I knew from many years of firsthand observation and acquaintance to be men of complete integrity. The dossiers of these men were even more revolting. Trumped-up charges by neurotic women, which even an amateur psychiatrist would have recognized as either fantastic or purchased, were included in the files. Of one of the episodes I had firsthand knowledge. I had been in the office of this senator one day several years before when an expensively dressed woman had been ushered in. She had a shade too much makeup on her face. Her clothes, though expensive and in reasonably good taste, verged on the flashy. She moved into the room exuding the aroma of perfume which must have cost fifty dollars an ounce. It was obvious that she was annoyed at the presence of a third person, so I went into another room. When she had gone, my friend the senator told me that his visitor had invited him to her "cozy little apartment when the cares of state became so burdensome that he needed relaxation." I would make any wager, such is my confidence in the character and discretion of that particular senator, that he never accepted the invitation nor of his own choice saw the woman again. He was far too experienced in the ways of Washington and the world to miss seeing that the woman had been employed to compromise him. But in the dossier was an account of the visit of the woman, with highly suggestive and derogatory implications against the senator.

After I had examined a half dozen or so of the "records" I felt an overwhelming urge to wash my hands with carbolic acid soap to rid them of the filth they had touched. I told the lobbyist that I did not care to take advantage of his offer. He looked at me as though I were mentally deranged.

"It won't cost you a penny—I am giving it to you," he told me. "You'd be a fool not to use it. You will never get your bill through otherwise." I told him that we were fighting for a principle and that we would under no circumstance use unprincipled methods to achieve passage of the bill. To this day he looks at me whenever I encounter him as though he is now convinced that Negroes have no brains.

Year after year and session after session of Congress we have fought with meager resources and often in the face of indifference, chicanery, and even sometimes contempt for our efforts by members of the Congress. Time and again we have succeeded in achieving passage of the anti-lynching bills in the House only to see them die at the hands of filibusterers in the Senate. But we also saw signs that our efforts, fruitless as far as legislation was concerned, were not without effect. The increasing independence of Negro voters played a considerable part in achieving this change. Exposure by debate on the floor of the Senate and the House of Representatives of the sadism of lynching and the not infrequent innocence of the victims steadily increased public sentiment against lynching.

I shall never forget a dramatic experience in 1937 as Southern congressmen like Rankin of Mississippi and Hatton W. Sumners of Texas bombastically orated about "states' rights" and declared that the South itself would stop lynching if only it were let alone. As the Civil War was being fought again on the floor of the House, I was summoned hastily from my seat in the gallery. A friendly newspaperman had snatched from the news ticker an Associated Press dispatch telling of the blowtorch lynching of two Negroes at Duck Hill, Mississippi. It was one of the most unbelievable barbarities in human history. I sent the clipping in to Congressman Joseph A. Gavagan of New York, who was leading the fight for the anti-lynching bill. The startling dispatch was read quietly but with terribly dramatic impact. One would have thought that such a revelation would have silenced, at least temporarily, the congressional defenders of lynching. It did not. After the gasp of horror which swept the House had subsided, the Southern orators resumed their onslaught as though nothing had happened.

But not all of the Southern congressmen, even those who fought anti-lynching legislation, were as convinced that federal legislation was either unnecessary or unconstitutional as their speeches proclaimed. One day Congressman Hatton W. Sumners, an able lawyer and eloquent orator who had achieved chairmanship of the House Judiciary Committee by the seniority rule, received an ovation after a long denunciation of the anti-lynching bill. Upon encountering me in the corridor of the Capitol a few minutes later he jubilantly demanded, flushed with his triumph: "How do the chances for your anti-lynching bill look now?" I assured him, not without some misgivings, that he had changed not a single vote.

He hastily changed the conversation by asking if there had been any arrests or indictments of the Mississippi blowtorch lynchers.

I told him that I was sure he knew as well as I that there had been no arrests, nor would there be any as long as the present regime based on disfranchisement and mob violence continued to control Mississippi. Half to himself and half to me he remarked, "Maybe you are right—maybe we will have to have an anti-lynching bill after all."

XVI

Jimcrow on a Freight Car

In March of 1931 I received early one morning on arrival at the
office a long-distance telephone call from Dr. P. H. Stephens, a
practicing physician in Chattanooga, Tennessee, and president of the
NAACP branch in that city. That was the first news we received of
a tragedy which was to become known throughout the world as
the Scottsboro Case. Nine whites had clambered aboard a freight
train at Chattanooga about noon on a day late in March to hobo
their way home to Huntsville, Alabama. To escape being seen by
railroad detectives, the nine huddled in a gondola—a freight car with
sides but no top—which was filled to two thirds of its capacity with
crushed rock.

When the train reached Stevenson, Alabama, a group of Negroes,
numbering between twenty and thirty, climbed aboard. One of
the white men, thoroughly impregnated with jimcrowism, even on
freight cars, angrily shouted, "You niggers get out of here!" Some
of the whites later alleged that a fight ensued and the Negroes by
their superior number had overpowered seven of the nine white men
and thrown them from the train. However, one of the men later
admitted that seven of them had hastily quit the train. The man who
told this story revealed that as he was trying to climb down he fell
between two cars and would have been killed had not two of the
Negroes caught him in time and pulled him back safely to the car.
The white men who quit the train sped to a telephone to call the
sheriff at Paint Rock, the next town through which the train would
pass, and asked that he arrest the Negroes. The sheriff obliged,
arresting nine Negroes and three whites found on the train.

Examination revealed that two of the three white "men" were women; tough, hard-boiled Victoria Price, a cottonmill worker and part-time prostitute, and a younger mill worker, also free with her favors for a price, Ruby Bates.

News of the discovery of the sex of two of the whites instantaneously put a new and more sinister interpretation on what ordinarily would have been an interracial clash of no uniqueness. The two women were grilled by the sheriff and his deputies for hours as to whether or not sex offenses had been committed on them by the Negroes. In their early testimony both girls said that the Negroes had made no suggestions of intimacy with them.

News of the episode spread throughout the community, and a potential mob gathered around the jail, making threats of a wholesale lynching. When the two white women continued to maintain that there had been no sexual intercourse aboard the train, two local white physicians were summoned to examine them, Doctors Lynch and Bridges. The doctors testified that they had found the girls in "normal condition, mentally and physically." The only physical injury found was slight abrasion on the buttocks of one of the girls, which, the doctors testified, might have been caused by sitting on crushed gravel in a gondola freight car for fifty miles. Further examination disclosed that both girls had had recent sexual intercourse but that it had occurred twelve or more hours previously. Both girls admitted that they had had intercourse with white men in the freight yards at Chattanooga the night before. There was no evidence of criminal assault, according to the doctors.

Outside the jail the mob grew in size and vociferousness, as it worked itself up to a lynching pitch. Each telling of the story added new details to the unbelievable sexual atrocities which had been perpetrated upon the two white girls. And their reputations for unblemished purity grew steadily. Finally Victoria Price, reveling in the unaccustomed spotlight playing upon her, changed her story. She alleged that in the time it took the train to travel the thirty-eight miles from Stevenson to Paint Rock she and Ruby Bates had each been assaulted six times by the Negroes, each of whom, with extraordinary agility, had held a long, sharp knife at the girls' throats during the process. By nightfall the mob had grown to such size and ferocity, especially after news of Victoria Price's "confession," that the nine terrified Negro boys, one of them only thirteen years of age, were speedily taken from the jail by the back door and hurried to the stronger jail at Gadsden.

Dr. Stephens told me of the efforts of Chattanooga Negroes, faced with the emergency, to provide legal defense for the accused Negroes. The local branch of the NAACP and the colored inter-denominational ministerial alliance had hastily raised a hundred dollars to employ a lawyer. A committee had been appointed which had retained Stephen R. Roddy, the only white lawyer in Chatta-nooga who, as far as they knew, dared to face the hostile atmosphere of the impending trial at Scottsboro. Dr. Stephens implored the national office to give assistance and asked that a national officer be sent to Tennessee at once. I was chosen to go.

Seldom have I seen an atmosphere so charged with racial hatred and the lynching spirit. We knew that the conviction in the lower court of the nine Negro boys was inevitable in such an atmosphere. The most we could hope to accomplish would be inclusion in the record of as much evidence of the innocence of the defendants as was possible, and the notation of violations by the Court of the constitutional rights of the defendants' due process protection as the basis of appeal from the inevitable guilty verdict.

Our worst fears were confirmed. A few days after the arrest the defendants were returned to Scottsboro, indicted on charges of rape, and in the minimum time allowed under the law were placed on trial. National Guardsmen with drawn bayonets, tear-gas bombs, and machine guns made the antiquated Jackson County courthouse appear like a fortified position in an advanced battle zone. More than ten thousand whites, many of them making no effort to conceal weapons, jammed the courthouse grounds and the streets of the sleepy little town of fifteen hundred population.

As the defendants were penniless, Judge A. J. Hawkins assigned the entire Jackson County bar, consisting of seven lawyers, to the defense. Six of them hastily requested the court to be excused and their requests were granted, Only one lawyer dared face the diffi-cult case—elderly Milo Moody. At this point Stephen Roddy asked the court for permission to associate himself with Mr. Moody. An ominous murmur swept the courtroom at the injection of a "foreign" lawyer into the case, Mr. Roddy's foreignness consisting of his coming from just across the state line, not more than a hundred miles away. After some discussion permission was granted.

Victoria Price was put on the stand. Jauntily she told in great detail, obviously loving every minute of the rapt attention accorded her, of the six mythical criminal assaults she had undergone. Ruby Bates followed her on the stand. Less of an extrovert and obviously more reluctant to tell the lies she had been coached to tell, she however corroborated sufficiently the lurid recital of the flamboyant Victoria Price to insure the sentencing to death of eight of the defendants and to life imprisonment of the ninth. The prosecutor asked only for life imprisonment for him because he had "celebrated" his fourteenth birthday in jail as he awaited trial.

It is certain that convictions were inevitable in that atmosphere. But if there had been any slightest chance of a fair trial, that chance went glimmering when Judge Hawkins revealed that he had received a telegram from a Communist organization in New York City, the International Labor Defense, asserting that he as presiding judge would be held personally responsible unless the nine defendants were immediately released.

The condemned defendants were spirited to the Kilby State Prison near Montgomery to await execution. Simultaneously the NAACP appealed the convictions to the Alabama State Supreme Court. The trial had so flagrantly violated virtually every principle of law that we were confident the Alabama State Supreme Court would reverse the Jackson County court's verdict; and, if it did not do so, the United States Supreme Court would assuredly do so on the basis of the decision in the Phillips County, Arkansas, riot cases in which it had held that a mob-dominated trial violated due process and a conviction in such circumstances must be set aside and a new trial ordered.

We appealed to Clarence Darrow, who promptly agreed to act as chief counsel in the appeal and in any subsequent trials. Arthur Garfield Hays of New York joined him as associate counsel. But it was imperative also that the very best Alabama counsel obtainable be retained. I was sent to Alabama and retained Roderick Beddow

of the firm of Fort, Beddow, and Ray of Birmingham, reputed to
be the ablest trial lawyer of the state. Mr. Darrow and Mr. Hays
joined me in Birmingham for a conference with Mr. Beddow and
his associate to prepare the appeal to the Alabama Supreme Court.

Our task was enormous. In addition to the usual difficulties involved in defense of Negroes charged with rape in the South, we
had to cope with the multiplied antagonism caused by the inept
tactics of the Communist ILD. The governor, the warden of Kilby
Prison, and virtually every other state official even remotely connected with the case were being bombarded with telegrams from
Northern cities and later with cablegrams from other parts of the
world "demanding" immediate release of the nine Scottsboro boys.
Most of the telegrams declared that the official addressed would be
"held personally accountable" if the boys were not released. Along
with this mass pressure campaign, Roddy had been approached by
representatives of the International Labor Defense with the propo-
sition that he renounce his employment by the NAACP and switch
to the International Labor Defense.

When Roddy refused, he immediately became the target of abuse.
He was accused in the *Daily Worker* of being a member of the
Ku Klux Klan. He was charged with having conspired with the
prosecutor to electrocute the defendants. It was alleged that he
had been the inmate of an insane asylum. Later a story was published
that Roddy had gone violently insane and had attempted to kill his
wife with an ax and had been placed by his father in an insane
asylum.

On the day after Mr. Darrow and Mr. Hays arrived in Birmingham, a telegram signed by all nine of the defendants was received
by Mr. Darrow demanding that he withdraw from the NAACP and
accept employment from the International Labor Defense. Let Mr.
Darrow tell the story of what happened. He wrote in *The Crisis*
of March 1932 that, on receipt of the telegram—

We immediately got in touch with the representatives of the I.L.D.
and asked them to come to Birmingham for a consultation. When they
arrived we at once told them that we could not go into a contest to
procure clients. We then stated to them, orally and in writing, that we
were willing to go into the case with the I.L.D. attorneys provided that

each organization was a party to the record, and asked that all lawyers appear for the defendants alone.

After waiting for more than a day, while the agents and attorneys for the I.L.D. telephoned to New York and Chattanooga, they announced that we must withdraw from any connection with the N.A.A.C.P. and come in with them under the I.L.D. This, of course, we refused to do. . . .

Neither Mr. Hays nor I could possibly forsake the N.A.A.C.P. whose long and devoted services to the colored people are well-known in every state in the Union. No more could we give out that we were representing the I.L.D. I am sure that we could have done nothing else than take this stand. . . .

William Pickens, at the time field secretary of the NAACP, went to Alabama and with Mr. Beddow interviewed the defendants and their parents and guardians, and was assured by the boys that they wished the NAACP to defend them. But some of the parents had been convinced that the Communists and no one else could save the lives of the boys. A mother of one of the defendants had become so convinced of this that she was reported to have expressed vigorously the opinion that "the NAACP is trying to get my boy electrocuted."

The defendants and their parents and guardians together presented one of the most damning indications of Southern race prejudice I have ever seen—all of them had been given little education and had been ground by poverty and bigotry all their lives. It was an exciting new experience for them to be addressed as "Mister" or "Missus" and to be treated by white people as human beings on a plane of equality which they had never known before from the "good, white, hundred per cent Americans" of their native South.

When, by various means, the defendants and their parents and guardians became convinced that the ILD was the organization which they wished to defend them, there was no alternative left except for the NAACP to withdraw from the case, making public its reasons for so doing, with an itemized accounting of moneys raised and expended in the case.

In control of the case, the Communists proceeded to publicize and agitate it in every part of the world. Public meetings of the NAACP were particularly the target of the campaign. A favorite device was to announce in such a meeting that one of the Scottsboro mothers was present and demanded the right to speak. If permission was granted, a Communist would make a lengthy introduction expounding the merits of communism. If permission were denied, at a pre-arranged signal Communists in the audience or their sympathizers would join in a shout demanding that the mother be heard. There were only five living "mothers" of the nine defendants, but many more than five "mothers" were produced in various parts of the country at public gatherings. In one instance a colored woman presented as a Scottsboro mother had lived for more than twenty years in the Northern city in which she spoke. All this apparently was based upon strategy at that time being followed by Communists throughout the world, namely, to attempt to organize with greatest vigor among the most exploited and oppressed group in each "capitalist" country as the most fertile soil for revolutionary propaganda. It will be remembered that the Scottsboro case came two years after the stock market collapse of 1929 and as America moved into the most serious economic depression it had ever known.

The story of all the appeals to the supreme court of Alabama and the United States Supreme Court is too long and dreary to tell here. But time and again various lawyers, including Samuel S. Leibowitz, Joseph R. Brodsky, Walter H. Pollak, Osmond K. Fraenkel, George W. Chamlee of Chattanooga, and others appeared in the case. Four years later, in 1935, Ruby Bates repudiated her previous testimony and declared that neither she nor Victoria Price had been raped or otherwise molested in any fashion. But Victoria Price continued to stick to her lurid story despite analysis and repudiation of her every statement in an opinion by Judge James E. Horton of the Alabama Circuit Court. Eventually it became clear, even to the ILD, that the combination of prejudices against the defendants, because they were Negroes charged with the rape of white women and because of the adamant resistance of Alabama to the Communist campaign, was so great that no further progress could be made nor hope maintained of eventual freedom for the defendants.

I wrote an article for *Harper's*, "The Negro and the Communists," telling the story of the Scottsboro case, which opened the eyes of a great many people, according to the letters I received. I sought to be scrupulously fair and to understate instead of emphasizing the drama and political chicanery of the case. As I had expected, publication of the article brought down upon me abuse from both the extreme right and the extreme left of political and economic thinking. The former element, particularly in the South, bitterly resented my emphasizing that miscarriages of justice of this character were more effective propaganda for communism than all the revolutionary efforts the Communists could possibly produce. The Communists themselves, of course, did not like the exposure of their methods and tactics. But many of the great and growing number of honest and troubled Americans who were genuinely concerned about the fissures in the democratic structure welcomed the revelation of the truth.

Samuel Leibowitz invited me one day to attend a conference in his office. Mr. Leibowitz informed me that he could no longer work with the Communists, that the nine defendants would do whatever he wished them to do, and that if I would promise him the support of the NAACP, he would advise the nine boys to request in writing that the NAACP take over their case. I refused to be a party to such an arrangement.

Shortly afterward another request was made to the NAACP to reenter the case. We were reluctant to undertake again the responsibility involved, particularly because by that time the outlook appeared even more hopeless than it had in 1931. But there was no choice. If the boys were allowed to die without our having made every effort to save them, we would have felt that we ourselves had been passive allies of the exponents of race prejudice. Victory for the Alabama bigots would have served as a green light to other mobs to do as they wished with Negroes, and the Communists would have proclaimed throughout the world that the nine boys were the victims of "capitalist" justice.

It was imperative that organizations representing various races, creeds, and economic circumstances be brought into a coalition for the defense. It was also imperative that this new Scottsboro Defense Committee should be officered by men of such probity that neither their motives nor political beliefs could be brought into question. Dr. Allan Knight Chalmers, pastor of the Broadway Tabernacle in New York City, was persuaded to accept the chairmanship despite a load of work which was already so heavy that it would have broken the body and spirit of a lesser man. I spent an afternoon with Dr. Chalmers in his study pointing out all the difficulties. I shall never forget that the argument which eventually persuaded him to accept the thankless and difficult task was one to the effect that the outlook for success was so bleak that I would not for a moment blame him if he refused to serve. For eleven years now Dr. Chalmers has worked skillfully. To him more than to any other individual goes the credit for the freeing of seven of the nine defendants to date. Even as this is written Dr. Chalmers is continuing his efforts to free the two defendants who remain in jail.

With Dr. Chalmers on the Scottsboro Defense Committee were appointed Colonel William Jay Schieffelin, president of the Schieffelin Pharmaceutical Company of New York and Trustee of Tuskegee Institute, who served as treasurer, and Bishop Scarlett of St. Louis, Dean Elbert Russell of Durham, North Carolina, and the late James Weldon Johnson, then of Fisk University, who served as vice-chairmen.

But the Communists did not lose interest when we again took over the case. Over and over again, in world-wide publicity, they have called attention to the miserable failure of the legal processes and the pall of prejudice which hangs eternally over a case of this character as evidences of "capitalist society decadence."

In the intervening years it had become increasingly clear that the tragedy of a Scottsboro lies, not only in the bitterly cruel injustice which it works upon its immediate victims, but also, and perhaps even more, in the cynical use of human misery by Communists in propagandizing for communism, and in the complacency with which a democratic government views the basic evils from which such a case arises. A majority of Americans still ignore, even after World War Two has demonstrated that the problem of race is a world-wide one, the plain implications in similar tragedies.

XVII

Death of a Citizen

Father retired from the post office in 1921 after forty-three years of delivering and collecting mail. They gave him a testimonial banquet at the colored YMCA and presented him with a gold watch as token of his faithfulness as a public servant and a citizen. I always regretted I could not be present at the banquet, although it would have been painful to watch him squirm as the usual lavish and tender exaggerations of testimonials were heaped upon his shy person.

But I would have liked saying a few things myself—none of them exaggerated—of his pride, for example, in having been tardy at work only once in forty-three years and that during the blizzard of 1888 which struck even as far south as Atlanta. In spite of the difficulties that morning, Father had fought his way in the early morning hours through the snowdrifts and had been only twelve minutes late when he reported at 5:42 A.M. He was one of only two or three postal employees who showed up for work at all that day. I would have liked paying tribute to him and mother for performance of a financial miracle in establishing a comfortable home which was tax and mortgage free, in giving college educations to seven children, and in helping others on a salary which never exceeded a hundred and fifty dollars a month.

Father had worked too long and too hard to be content with idleness. Nor could he afford it, so meager was the government pension even when supplemented by rent money from the old house on the back of the lot. Mornings he devoted to searching the public market for bargains in food. Afternoons he gave to puttering around the place, patching and mending. Sundays were, of course, given to church and the quiet regimen of a Sabbath as rigid as any Puritan's in abstention from worldly deeds and thoughts. Tuesdays he spent with my sister Helen, playing with the grandchildren. Thursdays were devoted to Olive and her family.

On one of these Thursdays in 1931 Father was returning home just before dusk, carrying a lemon meringue pie which Olive had made for Madeline. He stopped, as was his cautious custom, at the corner of Houston Street and Piedmont Avenue to look through his bifocals for traffic and to wait for the light to change. When the crosstown light turned, he stepped from the curb just in time to be struck by an automobile speeding recklessly to beat the light. The driver of the car was a doctor at the Henry W. Grady City Hospital. He helped lift Father into the automobile and sped him to the Grady Hospital.

Grady Hospital is on Butler Street. On one side are modern, sanitary, beautifully equipped buildings. This side is for whites. Across the street is the Negro building. For many years it had been occupied by the Atlanta College of Physicians and Surgeons for the education and training of white doctors. Eventually deterioration from age had made the place so antiquated that more modern quarters were built elsewhere for the medical school. The old buildings were considered good enough for the Negro wards of the Municipal Hospital.

Because of his light-colored skin, Father's unconscious body was taken to the white side of the street, where the best doctors in the hospital worked feverishly to save his life.

Father had no identification papers on him, but neighbors who had seen the accident telephoned my brother-in-law, who rushed to the hospital. Inquiry at the colored ward revealed no trace of Father. Wise in the ways of the South, my brother-in-law went across the street and asked for the injured man.

"Do you know who this man is?" he was asked.

"He is my father-in-law," my brother-in-law, whose skin is brown, replied.

"Have we put a nigger in the white ward?" they asked, horrified. Father was snatched from the examination table lest he contaminate the "white" air, and taken hurriedly across the street in a driving downpour of rain to the "Negro" ward.

He had regained consciousness when I reached Atlanta a few hours later.

"I feel like a watermelon that has been dropped from a wagon— all squashed up inside," he told me.

Overworked Negro nurses and orderlies scrubbed and swept incessantly, but with dismal failure, to keep the closely packed wards reasonably clean. The obsolescent building and facilities had too great a head start. Dinginess, misery, and poverty pressed so hard on one from every side that even a well person could not avoid feeling a little sick in those surroundings. Father's injuries were such that no hope was held out for his recovery. Since the end might come at any time, my brother and I took turns around the clock to be with him. We became as philosophical about the sordid surroundings as we could. There were numerous private hospitals in Atlanta maintained by churches, Protestant and Catholic, but they were all for whites. Ninety thousand Negroes needing hospitalization had only a single choice—either Grady Hospital or a private sanitarium of about a dozen beds which had little modern equipment.

The vigil during the day was not too trying because there were diversions to keep one's mind from the inadequacy and sordidness of the hospital. But night was unmitigated horror as Father's life slowly ebbed away. With the dimming of the light and the cessation of movement, the quiet was broken only by the slight stir when a new patient was brought in or when one of those already there' died or called out for the nurse. Huge cockroaches came out of hiding places and scampered about the wards and corridors. The pattern of nocturnal nausea they made was occasionally varied by the appearance of a rat. George and I instinctively kept our feet off the floor on the rungs of the chair to avoid the vermin.

One human being helped to relieve the agony and horror of the vigil as Father, to the amazement of the doctors, fought desperately for his life despite his advanced age and the gravity of his injuries. That human being was a young white intern who came from Scottsboro, Alabama, where a short time before the famous Scottsboro case had originated. It was his plan to go to China as a medical missionary when he had completed his internship. After a working day of twelve hours and despite the jeers of his fellow interns for associating with "niggers," this young doctor sat night after night with George and me talking softly in the darkened corridor. We talked of many things—of war, peace, and human nature, and of his dreams of service to the physical needs of the Chinese. But, as is invariably true in the South, the Negro question colored all that we discussed.

Once George asked him gently, "Why do you go to China to do missionary work? Don't you think there is great need for it in your home town of Scottsboro?"

The young doctor hung his head and remained silent for a full minute before replying, "Yes. I know. But it will be easier in China."

Sixteen days and nights passed. The seventeenth was a Sunday. When daybreak came I went to Father's bedside. The ward was even more crowded because of the usual Saturday night cuttings and shootings. In the bed next to Father a Negro who had been shot by a policeman was dying. Only enough strength was left to Father to open his eyes and to ask feebly if we had been there all night. When we told him we had, he chided us, still completely forgetful of himself, saying, "You shouldn't have done that. You should have been home getting your rest."

Around nightfall they put the grim screen around his bed. Father had lapsed into a coma from which even the strength born of abstemious living and the determination to live could not rouse him. As we stood by his bed the ward filled suddenly with raucous sounds. A band of white men and women screeched hymns about Jesus's love and God, the Father of us all. I suppose I should have been more tolerant and perhaps even grateful that they had deigned to cross the color line to sing for black Americans as well as white ones. But the strain and bitterness were too great. I suspect my own voice was as harsh as theirs and I told them to go away and at least let my father die in peace.

And then Father died.

For seventy years he had in his quiet way done all he could to make Atlanta a more decent and Christian place. If he ever broke even the most minor law of man or God, we never knew of it. He had faithfully paid city, county, state, real estate, and every other kind of tax on the days such taxes were due, if not before the due date. He had, in the truest sense of the word, been always a good citizen.

But when death had come, he had been ushered out of life in the meanest circumstances an implacable color line had decreed for all Negroes, whatever their character or circumstances might be.

XVIII

Ada Sipuel and Others "Similarly Situated"

1932 marked the emergence of the Negro voter as a force which no political party could longer ignore or flout. We drafted a questionnaire which was sent to Herbert Hoover and Franklin D. Roosevelt, asking for a "plain and unequivocal declaration on the subject of race relations," which, though unanswered by either candidate, served an important purpose in establishing a yardstick by which Negro voters could measure the records of both candidates. We did not want to create a "Negro bloc," and I was particularly opposed to such a development.

There are Negro capitalists and Negro paupers; Negro Republicans, Democrats, Socialists, and Communists; there are Negro internationalists and Negro chauvinists. I have always strongly advocated that in a democracy Negroes should function as members of a democratic society and not as a segregated bloc. But circumstances over which we had no control decreed otherwise, and this condition continues to exist, although fortunately to a lesser degree than in the thirties. As long as lynching continues, and especially when Negroes are the chief victims of that practice, a senator's or congressman's attitude toward race relations, and his vote on such legislation as federal anti-lynching bills, anti-poll tax bills, fair employment practices, enfranchisement, etc., are inevitably important determinants of the attitude of Negro voters toward him.

In the questionnaire sent to Hoover and Roosevelt we bluntly asked for statements of their position on eleven of these issues, which included disfranchisement, discrimination in the civil service, appointment of Negroes based on ability, racial segregation in Washington, abolition of segregation in the armed forces, positive action to eliminate discrimination in the use of federal funds for educational purposes, federal support of higher education for Negroes—particularly in the professions; abolition of color discrimination on relief and public works projects, restoration of self-government and independence to Liberia and Haiti, and general establishment of the full citizenship rights of Negroes.

It was gratifying to find during these trying days that the position we took was slowly and steadily adding to the number of white adherents of the principles we espoused. The annual conferences of the NAACP, usually held during the last week in June, were addressed by more distinguished Americans each year, which marked a decided change in attitude from the early days of the Association when only a handful of supercourageous white Americans—like Mary White Ovington, Moorfield Storey, Joel and Arthur Spingarn, Charles Edward Russell, Oswald Garrison Villard, and Jane Addams—dared speak out boldly for unqualified freedom for Negro Americans.

Toward the mid-thirties we even found federal and state officials willing to take such a stand, although they risked political obliteration by doing so.

A sensational example of this occurred during the hearings before the Senate Judiciary Committee on the Costigan-Wagner Anti-Lynching Bill, when W. Preston Lane, Attorney General of Maryland, appeared before the committee to testify for federal legislation and to relate the circumstances of the burning alive of George Armwood, a Negro, at Princess Anne, Maryland, on October 18, 1933. No state official within my experience ever attempted so sincerely to bring lynchers to justice as did Mr. Lane in this case. When he went to the scene of the lynching, a mob attempted to lynch him also, and was prevented from doing so only by state troopers. Threats were made to kill Governor Ritchie, and editors and reporters of the *Baltimore Sun*, which exposed and excoriated the lynchers. An interesting evidence of the growth of decent public opinion, as a result of relentless campaigning against lynching, is probably to be seen in the fact that, although he was bitterly denounced and threatened with political extermination at the time, Mr. Lane was later elected governor of the State of Maryland.

The dismal decade of the thirties grew more and more dismal. I found myself with less and less time for the theater, baseball, parties, writing, or any of the other diversions which had formerly lightened the load of problems and hard work.

We saw the percentage of Negroes on relief rolls mounting far beyond their proportion in the national population; their meager savings accumulated during the flush days dwindled and disappeared. Wherever I went I found a deepening despair despite the aid unemployed Negroes received from federal and state governments and through agencies like FERA, WPA, and PWA. Negroes became increasingly morose as they repeatedly saw the few jobs which were available during the economic crisis given to others, even when Negro applicants were more experienced or better prepared. We knew that trouble was ahead and worked night and day to ameliorate conditions as far as was possible and to do such long-range planning as our slender resources permitted.

The picture was not all dark, however. A grant of one hundred thousand dollars—which unfortunately dropped to a third of that amount because of shrinkage of assets due to the stock market crash—was made to the Association by the American Fund for Public Service.

This was made possible by the generosity of an idealistic young American by the name of Charles Garland, who had inherited an estate in excess of one million dollars from his father. Mr. Garland believed both before and after he received his inheritance that no man had the right to enjoy and spend money unless he himself had earned it. He had turned over a small amount of his bequest to his divorced wife for the support of herself and their child, and the balance was used to establish the American Fund for Public Service. Mr. Garland's interest in the NAACP had been aroused and stimulated by James Weldon Johnson. At Mr. Garland's request, Mr. Johnson had become a member of the American Fund Board, and—with characteristic impartiality—had suggested contributions not only to the NAACP but also to other organizations working in the field of race relations. Among these were the National Urban League and the Brotherhood of Sleeping Car Porters, which was then struggling—under the able and unselfish leadership of A. Philip Randolph—to establish itself to battle for decent wages and working conditions from the multimillionaire Pullman Company.

The American Fund grant permitted a change in the approach to the Negro's handicaps—especially in the field of law—which we had long desired but had been prevented from undertaking by poverty. From its inception the Association had followed a policy, to which it still adheres, of applying two tests to every appeal for legal aid made to it. We examine each case to determine, first, whether it is a case in which injustice has been done or is threatened because of race and color, and, second, whether entrance of the Association will establish a precedent which will affect the basic citizenship rights of Negroes and other Americans.

Limited resources and the constant succession of cases which the Association had to handle on an emergency basis had confined us to action on crises as they arose. The grant from the Garland Fund permitted us to alter our entire method of operation. First, it enabled us to make the most complete and authoritative study of the legal status of the Negro which had even been conceived or executed. We were fortunate in being able to employ Nathan R. Margold, who had made an extraordinary record as an assistant United States attorney in New York and as legal adviser on Indian Affairs in the Institute for Government Research.

Mr. Margold did a brilliant job of research, covering all known court decisions on unequal apportionment of school funds, property holders' covenants, disfranchisement, civil liberties defense (including lynching), job discrimination, jimcrow travel, and denial of other citizenship rights.

On the basis of Margold's study we mapped out a broad frontal attack on the basic causes of discrimination instead of waiting to handle the manifestations. Charles H. Houston of Washington was added to our staff as the first full-time lawyer to head our legal department.

For twenty-seven years Arthur B. Spingarn had served as volunteer chairman of our national legal committee, and had given so generously of his time to supervision and handling of most of the Association's legal work that it was a kind of a joke between him and ourselves that he handled his own private law practice during such brief periods as he was not engaged in working without compensation for the NAACP.

Charlie Houston had made a record at Amherst and Harvard Law School which few men have equaled and almost none have surpassed at either of these educational institutions. He had been elected to Phi Beta Kappa at Amherst, and at the Harvard Law School he was the first Negro to be elected editor of the *Harvard Law Review,* a record which has been equaled and duplicated only by his cousin, William H. Hastie, now Governor of the Virgin Islands.

Charlie's first job with us was the legal attack on one of the most grievous handicaps from which the Negro suffers—the gross inequalities in the expenditure of public moneys for education of whites and Negroes in those states where nine thirteenths of Negroes live and where segregated schools are required by law and custom. The United States Bureau of Education had estimated conservatively that it would take twenty-six million dollars annually to equalize education of Negroes and whites in those states. The United States Supreme Court had on several occasions ruled that there was no discrimination per se in forcing Negroes to attend segregated schools as long as the facilities were equal. However, such equality was notoriously a figment of the legal imagination. The average per capita expenditure for whites in these states was around forty-five dollars a year and that for Negroes twelve dollars.

I was particularly concerned with this matter of education because it was a continuation of the struggle we had begun in Atlanta two decades before—the first to be carried out in a determined and organized fashion, and one which had met with at least partial success. More than a decade later we are still engaged in that struggle, but much progress has been made during the past fifteen years.

In a case arising in Missouri where a young Negro by the name of Lloyd Gaines brought suit, with the aid of the NAACP, to obtain a legal education on the same basis as was provided for white Missourians, the United States Supreme Court ruled in 1938 that the state must either supply a law school for Negroes substantially equal to that supplied for whites, or else must admit Negro applicants to the already existing "white" law school of the University of Missouri.

Although the Gaines decision was handed down only a few years ago, enormous changes in public opinion and that of state officials has taken place. The ultimate objective of the NAACP, which we have stated without equivocation, is the total abolition of every form of segregated education in tax-supported institutions. The record has established beyond all doubt that for economic and other reasons it is wholly impossible for even the wealthiest states to pay for duplication of schools of law, medicine, engineering, and other professional and graduate subjects. The states which are backward enough to require such segregation are, in addition, the poorest states in the Union.

There were many persons, including some of our friends and supporters, who questioned the wisdom of our all-out campaign against educational inequalities, even against inequalities in teachers' salaries. We were not at all certain ourselves that there might not be disturbances in some of the states of the deeper South. We therefor planned our campaign carefully to fight such cases not only in courts of law, but in those of public opinion as well. We stressed the cost to society as a whole of such discrimination. The results have been gratifying and in some instances startling. Each year we have found more newspapers, public officials, and others admitting the justice of our contentions and frequently supporting them.

Two of the most exciting cases in which we have played a part are those of Ada Lois Sipuel and Hemon Marion Sweatt.

Miss Sipuel, an honor graduate from the State College for Negroes at Langston, Oklahoma, is an attractive young colored woman who yearned for a legal education such as was available to her white fellow Oklahomans. Unable to afford the much higher cost of going North for training as a lawyer, she appealed to the NAACP for aid in her effort to enter the University of Oklahoma after she had been refused admittance because she was a Negro. Miss Sipuel's case reached the Supreme Court of the United States for argument almost two years after the date of filing of the first suit in her behalf on

April 6, 1946. But long before it reached that tribunal, it had become apparent in Oklahoma that a new South was being born. When Miss Sipuel had applied in person to the University for admission to the law school, she was greeted on the campus, to the amazement of herself and her attorneys, by a sizable number of students who welcomed her and took her to luncheon after the ordeal of refusal of admission was over. This revolutionary change was most noticeable among students who were veterans of World War Two.

The insecurity which defenders of the old order experienced at this change of attitude on the part of many students was apparent in the attitude of the white Oklahoma attorneys when they sought to defend the University's action before the Supreme Court. Cross-examination by the Court was almost savage as the flaws in the argument of the Oklahoma attorneys were pointed out by the Supreme Court justices. Mr. Justice Jackson, for example, implacably pursued his questioning of the attorneys as to what the State of Oklahoma had done to comply with the lower court's order that the State had to admit Miss Sipuel to the existing law school or to provide a "substantially equal" but segregated law school for Negroes. Attempts to evade a direct answer were futile. Eventually the lawyer, Mac Q. Williamson, admitted that, although two years had passed, nothing had been done to comply with the court's mandate. Mr. Justice Jackson snorted that at that rate of speed of compliance Miss Sipuel would be "an old lady" before she became a lawyer.

We were jubilant when the Supreme Court five days after argument of the case (one of the shortest periods between argument and decision in the history of the Supreme Court) unanimously ordered Oklahoma to supply *forthwith* a legal education to Miss Sipuel. Although the Court evaded a specific ruling on the issue of segregation, as had been characteristic of the Court's decisions to date, the forthwith order could mean only one thing—admission of Miss Sipuel to the already existing law school, since it would be impossible to create a separate "Negro" school overnight. Our jubilation was short-lived.

The Supreme Court decision handed down on January 12, 1948, had unequivocally held that

The petitioner is entitled to secure legal education afforded by a state institution. To this time, it has been denied her although during the same period many white applicants have been afforded legal education by the State. The State must provide it for her in conformity with the equal-protection clause of the Fourteenth Amendment and provide it as soon as it does for applicants of any other group. *Missouri ex rel. Gaines* versus *Canada,* 305 U.S. 337 (1938).

The Board of Regents of the University of Oklahoma had voted seven to one to admit Miss Sipuel and all other qualified Negroes to professional schools at the University which were not duplicated at the State College for Negroes at Langston. Their action was based not only on respect for the United States Supreme Court but also on the very practical circumstance that the cost of duplicate, and substantially equal, professional and graduate schools for Negroes would be fantastically prohibitive. President George L. Cross of the University of Oklahoma was quoted as saying realistically, "You can't build a cyclotron for one student!"

The reaction of a majority of the students at the University of Oklahoma was more vigorous and direct. They staged a dramatic demonstration in front of the administration building of the University when the State Attorney General issued an indignant opinion to the effect that Oklahoma laws prohibiting white and Negro students from attending the same schools took precedence over the mandate of the United States Supreme Court. The Supreme Court of Oklahoma on January 17, 1948, ordered the Board of Regents "to afford the plaintiff, and all others similarly situated, an opportunity to commence the study of law at a state institution as soon as citizens of other groups are afforded such opportunity." On the basis of this decision the District Court of Cleveland County of Oklahoma five days later directed the Oklahoma State Regents for Higher Education to enroll plaintiff or not enroll "any applicant of any group in said class [first-year class of the School of Law of the University of Oklahoma] until said separate school is established and ready to function."

With haste which was ludicrous had not its implications of evasion of the United States Supreme Court edict been so tragic, the Board of Regents roped off a space in the State Capitol as a "law school" for Miss Sipuel "and others similarly situated," assigning three teachers to the makeshift school. Because the subterfuge came nowhere near to meeting the most minimum requirements of the American Bar Association and the Association of American Law Schools, Miss Sipuel refused to enroll in the "law school."

Again the white students at the University of Oklahoma sprang into action. More than one thousand of them attended the mass meeting already mentioned in front of the administration building of the University on January 29, 1948. Speaker after speaker asserted that the overwhelming majority of the students not only did not object to the admission of Negro graduate and professional students but insisted that they be admitted. At the conclusion of the meeting a solemn and melodramatic rite was performed—a copy of the Fourteenth Amendment to the United States Constitution was burned as a youthful speaker eloquently asserted that "This amendment has been nullified by the Board of Regents." The ashes were carefully placed in an envelope addressed to the President of the United States. A delegation of one hundred students marched solemnly to the post office to mail the letter to the White House.

To our surprise and chagrin, the Court turned down by a seven-to-two vote the petition for a writ of mandamus which we filed in Miss Sipuel's behalf. The majority of the Court held that its mandate had not been violated, despite the incontrovertible facts which were apparent even to the layman: that Miss Sipuel was not being given a legal education on the same basis as that which was being provided for white applicants. Mr. Justice Wiley B. Rutledge vigorously and bluntly dissented. The Supreme Court's decision, he asserted, could not be complied with "by establishing overnight a separate law school for Negroes." Technical compliance could have been effected by excluding *all* applicants for admission to the first-year class of the State University Law School after the date of the order or, depending upon the meaning of that order, by excluding such applicants and asking all first-year students enrolled prior to that order's date to withdraw from school.

But neither of those courses would comply with the Supreme Court's mandate, Mr. Justice Rutledge declared. That mandate meant to him that

Oklahoma should end the discrimination practiced against petitioner at once, not at some later time, near or remote . . . in my comprehension the quality required was equality in fact, not in legal fiction.

Obviously no separate law school could be established elsewhere overnight capable of giving petitioner a legal education equal to that afforded by the state's long-established and well-known state university law school. Nor could the necessary time be taken to create such facilities, while continuing to deny them to petitioner, without incurring the delay which would continue the discrimination our mandate required to end at once. Neither would the state comply with it by continuing to deny the required legal education to petitioner while affording it to any other student, as it could do by excluding only students in the first-year class from the state university law school.

Since the state court's orders allow the state authorities at their election to pursue alternative courses, some of which do not comply with our mandate, I think those orders inconsistent with it. Accordingly I dissent from the Court's opinion and decision in this case.

Mr. Justice Frank Murphy wrote no formal dissent but was reported as holding the opinion that a hearing should be granted by the Supreme Court to determine "whether the action of the Oklahoma courts subsequent to the issuance of this Court's mandate constitutes an evasion of that mandate."

But what had been accepted by the country at large and particularly by a sizable segment of the people of Oklahoma to be a final determination of the issue of segregation or denial of professional or graduate training for Negroes was deferred. Wearily, we had once again to recommence action in the Oklahoma court, at considerable expense of time, money, and energy, to attain for Negro citizens the elemental privileges which the authors of the Fourteenth Amendment believed they were assuring when they wrote that historic document.

Miss Sipuel's legal action for legal education was commenced April 6, 1946. Approximately five weeks later, on May 15th, a similar action was commenced in Houston, Texas, on behalf of Hemon Marion Sweatt, a young Negro mail carrier who also wanted to become a lawyer. It was possible in Mr. Sweatt's case, for a variety of reasons, to raise even more explicitly than in Miss Sipuel's the basic issue as to whether or not there could ever be real equality of opportunity in a racially segregated pattern of education.

To avoid boring the reader with dry recitals of legal procedures, I shall very briefly summarize the steps in the long legal battle whose end is not yet in sight as I write. But although the writing of briefs and the filing of motions of appeal from unfavorable decisions in lower courts may sound uninteresting, Mr. Sweatt's case, like those of countless others for whom we have interceded, was packed tight with drama as gripping as that of most novels and plays. Because we were fighting for basic human rights, courtrooms were invariably packed to capacity with auditors both white and Negro, even when some of the most routine legal procedures were being argued.

One month after filing of the case, the One Hundred and Twenty-sixth District Court of Travis County, Texas, granted the application for a writ of mandamus against the members of the Board of Regents and officials of the University of Texas, to which Mr. Sweatt had applied for entrance. The court's decision held that Sweatt was fully qualified for admission to the law school and had been denied admission solely because of his race and had thereby been denied his constitutional right to the equal protection of the laws. But issuance of the writ was stayed for six months to permit Texas to establish a "separate law school for Negroes substantially equal to the one at the University of Texas." Six months later, on December 17, 1946, no substantially equivalent or any other kind of law school having been established, another petition for mandamus was filed. Despite the obvious and easily provable fact that Texas had totally failed to obey the court's order except in setting up a "law school" in the basement of a building in Houston which Sweatt, upon our advice, ignored, the petition for mandamus was dismissed and an appeal taken to the Court of Civil Appeals of Texas. This appeal was argued on March 5, 1947, and the lower court as the result was ordered to rehear the case. It was obvious that every stratagem which could be devised was being utilized to keep the law school of the University of Texas "white." But those who were doing this ran into opposition from quarters which had not been anticipated—the student body and a number of faculty members of the University.

As in the Sipuel case in Oklahoma, the new South began to be heard. Conservative newspapers, organizations like the Klan, and elderly members of the Board of Trustees asserted that admission of Negroes to the "white" university would result immediately in riots of protest by the student body. The least ominous development, they asserted, would be ostracism of Sweatt and other Negro students by the students themselves.

The instant reaction of students and many other white Texans was most heartening. Led by a popular young war veteran, Jim Smith, whose leadership qualities had caused him to be elected president of the student body, a mass meeting was staged by University of Texas students at Austin during the trial of the case. More than two thousand persons packed the hall and filled near-by corridors. Smith told the audience—and Texas—that he did not presume to speak for all of the students at the University, but that he did voice the convictions of a majority of the white students who believed that democracy and Christianity should be practiced as well as preached. As for the reports that Sweatt would be manhandled or ostracized if he were admitted to the University, Smith, with quiet but moving sincerity, declared, "Hemon Sweatt is my friend now—and he will be my friend after he is admitted to the University of Texas!"

The revered and famous Professor J. Frank Dobie, at that time head of the Department of English at the University of Texas, was also a speaker at the meeting. "If Texas establishes a genuinely equal school of law," he declared, "I shall say no more. But if it does not do so, I favor the admission of Mr. Sweatt and all other similarly situated to the law school of the University now." It took courage to make such a statement. Homer Rainey, president of the University and former head of the U. S. Department of Education, had been summarily dismissed from his post not long before for making statements favoring more adequate educational opportunities for Negroes which were considerably less forthright than were Professor Dobie's. He knew that he risked the same fate as that which had befallen President Rainey. But his own personal integrity made him incapable of silence, whatever the cost. Professor Dobie's courageous action, however, revealed an interesting and significant development of public opinion. Despite the bluster of its politicians, Texas demonstrated that it was not as incapable of growth as the professional

Southerners declared, nor as insensitive to outside criticism. Unlike President Rainey, who had found little support in Texas outside of the University for his more moderate position, Professor Dobie was widely commended for his stand. But the bigots were not finished. The Board of Trustees decided shortly afterward that it would not renew Professor Dobie's contract, on the ground that he did not teach as many hours per week as other professors, conveniently ignoring the fact that Professor Dobie's literary reputation as historian, poet, and distinguished authority on Americana exceeded that of any other living Texas writer.

But the students refused to stop with the holding of a mass protest meeting. A college chapter of the National Association for the Advancement of Colored People was organized on the campus of the University—the only all-white unit of the NAACP. We were assured that as soon as Mr. Sweatt's fight was won he and other Negro students would join the college chapter and thereby cure its involuntary all-whiteness. Members of the college chapter launched a vigorous campaign in the city of Austin for funds to assist the NAACP in fighting the Sweatt case.

This revealed a most amazing fissure in the wall, apparently impenetrable, of nonstudent Texas opposition to the breaking down of educational segregation. A policeman had harried the students as they solicited passers-by for contributions, demanding repeatedly that they move to another spot because in the one they occupied they were "obstructing traffic." Toward the end of the day, the officer sidled up to one of the students and asked, "You fellows seem to believe in what you are doing, don't you?" Assuming the policeman to be hostile, one of the students assured him somewhat belligerently that they did indeed believe in equality. Surreptitiously the policeman handed the student a piece of paper, looking about him at the same time somewhat apprehensively to see if his action was being observed. It turned out to be a five-dollar bill to help in the fight.

Thurgood Marshall and W. J. Durham of Dallas argued the Sweatt case again in the Court of Civil Appeals early in 1948, and again the higher court affirmed the trial court's refusal to order Sweatt admitted to the law school. Hemon Sweatt continues to deliver mail

Houston to earn a living for himself and his family. The years pass for him and Ada Sipuel and others "similarly situated"—taxed to support "public" institutions of learning from which no circumstance other than color bars them. But they and others know that they fight not only for themselves, nor even exclusively for Negroes, but to cure a disease which threatens to rot the very roots of democracy.

But I am getting ahead of the story. During the thirties, at Middleburg, Virginia, a Negro named George Crawford was charged with the murder of a socially prominent white woman and her maid in that exclusive fox-hunting area. Crawford was arrested in Massachusetts, where he stoutly maintained he was at the time of the murder. Posses had combed the countryside, and had the murderer been apprehended at the time, a prominent citizen of Loudoun County told me afterward, he would have been burned at the stake. The leader of one of the posses was the famous General "Billy" Mitchell.

We hurried a young white woman investigator to the scene and she reported that as far as she was able to determine, Crawford was telling the truth. We therefore decided to oppose extradition of Crawford from Massachusetts to Virginia. J. Weston Allen, former Attorney General of Massachusetts, and Butler R. Wilson, a prominent Negro lawyer and president of our Boston branch, fought extradition and sued for a writ of habeas corpus in the United States District Court, which was granted by Judge James A. Lowell. Judge Lowell's action became a nation-wide issue when Southern congressmen demanded his impeachment for action on the law as he interpreted it. Actual impeachment proceedings were begun against him and were pending at the time of his death. The Circuit Court of Appeals reversed Judge Lowell, and Crawford was returned to Virginia for trial in an atmosphere which was so explosive that both Crawford and his counsel were openly threatened with death.

Charlie Houston and I talked long and often over the strategy to be used in Crawford's defense. Up to that time Negro lawyers, particularly in the South, were seldom employed even by their own people, on the grounds that they lacked, among other things, experience. But these same lawyers could not obtain experience for reasons of nonemployment. An increasing number of brilliant lawyers like Charlie Houston himself were graduating from first-class Northern law schools. These men were needed in the South particularly, as well as in Northern cities, to handle the many thousands of cases of individual litigation or issues affecting the basic rights of Negroes and other minorities. At the same time we were experiencing difficulty in obtaining the services of top white lawyers because of the bitter feeling surrounding the Crawford case. We decided that the die must be cast sometime soon on the issue of the use of Negro lawyers in important cases. We knew that for many years to come there would be certain types of cases in which there would be an advantage in having a white lawyer in preference to a Negro attorney, but our real objective was to hasten the time when an attorney's color in a court of law would be of no importance and where the only criterion would be his ability. We therefore decided that Charlie should serve as chief counsel and that Leon A. Ransom, Edward P. Lovett, and James B. Tysson, young colored attorney of Washington, should assist him.

Just as we were about to go to trial, the already explosive situation threatened full conflagration through a viciously garbled account of a speech made by Charlie at a mass meeting in Washington. As counsel for Crawford, Charlie of course refrained from discussing the details of the case, but as one of the most distinguished Negro citizens of the nation's capital he excoriated the indifference there to the conditions to which less fortunate Negroes were subjected. "Negro Washington boasts of more college degrees and a higher average income than any other city in the country," he declared. "But what happens to your 'security' when you cross the Potomac River? It matters not how many college degrees or how large a bank account you possess—so long as your skin is dark you will be as quickly a victim of prejudice as the most illiterate and impoverished Negro."

Then came the paragraph which was later so distorted as to endanger our safety.

"You've got to be willing to make every sacrifice, even to the point of having your own heads cracked, until no Negro can be mistreated solely because he is a Negro, anywhere in the United States."

A small country newspaper in Loudoun County published an inflammatory front-page story the following day headed: LAWYER ADVISES NEGROES TO CRACK HEADS IN LOUDOUN COUNTY. The apprehension caused by this headline in an already overwrought situation caused Douglas Southall Freeman, editor of the *Richmond News Leader* and Pulitzer Prize–winning author of a biography of General Robert E. Lee, and Virginius Dabney, editor of the *Richmond Times-Dispatch*, to request the governor to furnish protection by state troopers for Charlie and the other counsel and myself and to prevent disorder at the trial itself.

Another indication of the tension was found in the refusal of any Negro in Loudoun County to give food and shelter to us during the trial. They understandably feared attacks upon their homes if we stayed there. It was therefore necessary for us to drive the thirty-five miles from Washington to Leesburg each morning and return to Washington each night to find a place to sleep. For the first week we had to take box lunches to Leesburg because both whites and Negroes were afraid to feed us, although a courageous colored woman later prepared delicious hot meals for us. Both the judge and the state police insisted during the first few days of the trial on adjournment in time to permit us to reach the District of Columbia line before nightfall.

The feeling in the community was such that we were in complete agreement with this plan.

Each night during the trial the lawyers worked late in the library of the Howard University Law School. There was a lanky, brash young senior law student who was always present. I used to wonder at his presence and sometimes was amazed at his assertiveness in challenging positions taken by Charlie and the other lawyers. But I soon learned of his great value to the case in doing everything he was asked, from research on obscure legal opinions to foraging for coffee and sandwiches. The law student was Thurgood Marshall, who later became special counsel of the Association and one whose arguments were listened to with respect by the United States Supreme Court.

A minor miracle occurred as the trial progressed. The prosecutor, though steeped in Southern tradition, had shared with us on the day we went to trial some of the information he had gathered. To our dismay, we learned that our investigators had not secured all the facts and that Crawford had lied about not having left Massachusetts from the day he had gone there from Virginia and the day that he was brought back a prisoner. Lonesome for his wife, he had returned to Virginia and there encountered a Negro who had proposed that they rob the Ilsley home that night. Crawford had agreed, but, because he was a timorous person, mortally afraid of the law and of "white folks," he had remained outside as a lookout while the other man had entered to commit the robbery. His accomplice had committed the murders when the two women, aroused from sleep, attempted to attack him.

Such a revelation would have disheartened less interested or skilled lawyers. The judge who presided over the trial shared the paternalistic attitude of many Southerners toward Negroes. But the brilliance of the defense by Houston, Ransom, Lovett, and Tyson and their obvious superiority to the local lawyers drew respect from the Court, jury, and spectators which was reluctant at first, but eventually was almost without reservation. One day I sat near a lanky Virginia farmer clad in overalls and manifestly in need of a shave and bath. A spirited passage at arms over a legal technicality was being waged between the prosecutor and Houston. The latter's greater familiarity with the law was so obvious that the Court ruled in his favor. The Virginia farmer turned to his companion, nodding his head admiringly, and declared, "You got to give it to him. He knows what he's talking about even if he is a nigger."

The turning point of the case rested on the acceptance or rejection by the jury of the testimony of a pathologist from Washington on whether or not bits of skin found under the fingernails of Mrs. Ilsley were Crawford's. Andy Ransom had spent many days and nights steeping himself in facts gleaned from interviews with scientists and reading books on the subject of identification of such tissues. His cross-examination of the pathologist was so well-informed and unrelenting that even the jury, which was none too sympathetic, refused to accept the pathologist's confident statements. Ransom's cross-examination and Houston's summation to the jury resulted in a sentence of life imprisonment instead of the death chair. Negro and white Virginians, as well as those in other states, learned from the Crawford case that there were Negro lawyers, given an opportunity to prove their mettle and ability, who were equal to lawyers of any other race, even in cases involving racial tension as deep as that of the Crawford case.

Early in 1933 Thomas Hocutt, a young graduate of the North Carolina State College for Negroes at Durham, wrote me of his ambition to study pharmacy. His white fellow North Carolinians were able to secure such education at little cost in the excellent School of Pharmacy of the University of North Carolina, but Hocutt, because he was a Negro, was barred. Faced with the choice of abandoning his dream or finding the money somewhere for travel and tuition at a school of pharmacy in the North, he asked our advice and assistance. His letter was responsible for my meeting one of the ablest men I have ever known and the enlistment of his great ability in the work of the NAACP.

Two years earlier Felix Frankfurter had told me at his home in Cambridge to "keep your eye on a young man named Hastie who will graduate in June from the Harvard Law School—he is one of the finest students who has ever studied at Harvard during my time."

Charlie Houston was engrossed in preparation for the George Crawford trial when Hocutt's appeal reached us. Charlie suggested that we enlist the services of William H. Hastie, who at the time was back at Harvard for his degree of Doctor of Juridical Science. Hastie immediately agreed to go to North Carolina without fee to join the two local attorneys, Conrad O. Pearson and Cecil A. McCoy, in a hearing on a writ of mandamus in Hocutt's behalf to test the constitutionality of the law excluding Negroes from the tax-supported professional schools of the University of North Carolina.

Filing of the suit created a sensation, as it was the first of its kind. North Carolina newspapers played up the statement that the same NAACP which had defeated North Carolina's John J. Parker for the Supreme Court had at its beck and call the most distinguished constitutional lawyers in the United States. It was predicted that a whole battery of such lawyers would be sent south to force Hocutt's entrance into the state university. These threats apparently were taken at full face value, because there were assigned to defend the University the Attorney General of the state, Dennis Brummitt; the First Assistant Attorney General, A. A. F. Seawell, and Victor Bryant, one of the leading white members of the North Carolina bar. They were assisted by the Dean and Assistant Dean of the University Law School.

We purposely made no announcement of Hocutt's counsel until the day of the trial. The Southern courtroom gasped when it learned that we had assigned two young North Carolina Negro lawyers and Mr. Hastie to oppose the distinguished battery of defense counsel for the state. Attorney General Brummitt was a lawyer of the old school, addicted to flamboyant oratory. Whatever apprehension he might have experienced prior to the trial appeared to vanish when he looked across the room and saw that his opposition consisted of Negroes. His self-assurance, however, was short-lived. He began an impassioned harangue that the legal action in Hocutt's behalf had been brought solely to promote "social equality" and "intermarriage." He flailed his arms as he shouted that for one hundred and forty-four years the University had been operated exclusively for whites and that "I think there is a deep motive behind this suit and I think that motive is that this niggra wants to associate with white people."

But each time the Attorney General dragged in extraneous issues in waving the bloody shirt and refighting the Civil War, Hastie quietly called the attention of the Court to violations of correct legal procedure and noted exceptions for the record, which increasingly discomfited the bombastic Attorney General. The courtroom was crowded to utmost capacity, and contained a large number of students of the University of North Carolina and of near-by Duke University. Soon derisive laughter began to greet each deflation of the Attorney General as Judge M. V. Barnhill impartially ruled in Hastie's favor. Overnight the case became even more a *cause célèbre*. Lawyers and other citizens from all over the state came to Durham as news of the exciting exchanges in the courtroom were published by the press. We saw a new development in the South when young white students from Duke and North Carolina University surrounded Hastie and his fellow counsel for Hocutt to congratulate them, much to the annoyance of the Attorney General.

The case exhibited an amusing trait of those older Southerners who found their concepts of Negroes upset by the manner in which the colored lawyers, and particularly Hastie, were handling themselves. Stories began to spread over the state that any Negro as able as Hastie was atypical. One story was circulated that Hastie was a federal judge (which he was later to become); another, that he was an assistant United States attorney general. To support old concepts of Negro inferiority, Hastie had to be proved a biological and racial exception.

Negroes, on hearing the stories, concocted their own—that Hastie was neither a judge nor an attorney general, but only a law student, whom the NAACP thought good enough to handle the Attorney General of North Carolina.

Judge Barnhill told me after the case was finished that it had been one of the most brilliantly argued trials in his experience of twenty-two years on the bench. He ruled against us on a technicality, and that technicality is an interesting revelation of the moral effect on some Negro educators of segregation. The regulations of the University of North Carolina required an applicant to attach a transcript of his scholastic record at the school he had previously attended, but Hocutt was unable to attach his record to his application because of the refusal of the president of the North Carolina College for Negroes to supply him with it. The president had refused Hocutt his transcript—although he was legally entitled to it upon request—when he learned that Hocutt intended to apply to the University of North Carolina. The president of the Negro college feared that he would be charged with complicity in the case when next he applied to the state legislature for funds for the Negro school.

Judge Barnhill ruled that Hocutt had not fully complied with the admission requirements by writing on his application that the University could obtain his scholastic record from the North Carolina College for Negroes.

But in denying the writ of mandamus, Judge Barnhill stated unequivocally that in his judgment Hocutt had been denied admission solely on the ground that he was a person of African descent. He held that the State of North Carolina must comply with the United States Supreme Court ruling that "substantially equal" facilities must be supplied to Negro citizens.

Although we lost the case legally, we won it in extraordinary fashion in the court of public opinion. Students of the University of North Carolina were polled by *The Daily Tarheel*, and a surprisingly large percentage favored immediate admission of qualified Negroes at least to the graduate schools of the University. Even those students who favored continuation of segregation voted their belief that nonsegregated tax-supported schools were inevitable. The state legislature was asked to appropriate funds for education of Negro students in professional schools "where they may be lawfully admitted," but the state senate killed the bill after it had been passed by the house of representatives. But even in that development a new South made its appearance.

Angered by the Hocutt suit, some of the legislators, particularly those from the more backward rural areas, demanded decrease instead of increase in funds for the education of Negroes.

One legislator, Deacon Barden of Craven, was so stirred by the proposal that he was moved to declare, as quoted in the *Greensboro Daily News* of March 18, 1933:

"Mr. Speaker, I have sat here and watched this house today. I know there is nothing I can say that will stop what you are doing. But I tremble when I think of its consequences. Here you have voted to decrease all the appropriations and God knows they are small enough, at best, to the Negro institutions, and you give the Cherokee Indian school nearly fifty percent more than the gentleman from Ashe had allowed it. Mr. Speaker, I wonder by what process you increase the appropriation to the Indians who scalped our forefathers and take from the Negroes who slaved for us?

"I came to this general assembly as honestly and as reverently as I went to my church. I wanted to do the fair thing by everybody in North Carolina. This thing affects me deeply. I am a freshman here, and maybe I am not yet callous to such injustice as this. I am apprehensive of what is going on here. I know it's pleasant to be in the majority but there are things that ring louder in my ears than the shouts of majorities. Mr. Speaker, the gentleman from Durham introduced an amendment here to lift the appropriations of the North Carolina College for Negroes from $18,130 to $24,170 recommended by the Appropriations Committee. I would like to know why you voted this down."

Mr. Cherry replied: "Because we thought they could live on it."

Mr. Barden went back at him. "Does the gentleman mean then, that in making other recommendations for increases, or decreases, he did not know what he was doing? . . . The original appropriation in all conscience is small enough."

Mr. Bowie, who had kept still nearly all the day, rose to enlighten Judge Barden.

"Doesn't the gentleman know that this Negro college in Durham is doing classical work?" Mr. Bowie asked.

"I do, and hasn't it the right to do that kind of work?" Mr. Barden replied spiritedly.

"Well, at a time like this I don't think so," Mr. Bowie continued.

"Your son got a classical education, didn't he?" Mr. Barden asked.

"Yes, but my son and a Negro are different," Mr. Bowie said with manifest resentment.

"They are both citizens of North Carolina, aren't they?" Mr. Barden shot back.

Chairman Murphy rapped for order, but said: "The chair wishes to say that it agrees heartily with the gentleman from Craven."

Exposure of the complete failure of Southern states to provide graduate and professional training shocked a great many white Americans, though the fact had long been known to Negro Americans. The directing head of one of the large educational foundations who had contributed generously to Negro education admitted afterward that his fears that the bringing of legal action would result in race riots had proved wholly unfounded. As for Negroes themselves, they were determined to make similar tests in other states and to continue the fight no matter how numerous the setbacks or how great the difficulty.

In 1935 Donald Murray applied to us for aid when refused admission to the University of Maryland School of Law. When the University authorities stood adamant in their refusal to admit him to the law school or to provide "substantially equal" facilities for a legal education elsewhere, we brought a mandamus action in his behalf. As the case progressed, public sentiment developed against unnecessary expenditure of money to establish a separate law school for

Murray. When we won the case in the Court of Appeals, the University of Maryland admitted him to its law school. There were a few threats of violence against Murray, most of them from individuals who had no connection with the University, but the atmosphere was supercharged the day he reported for classes. One of the faculty suggested to us that Murray take the most inconspicuous seat in the rear of the classroom to demonstrate that he was not "forcing himself" upon the other students. This did not seem to us any more sound psychologically than it would have been for him to march in and take the most conspicuous seat. It was, therefore, agreed that he should come into the classroom like any other student, take a seat—neither conspicuous nor inconspicuous—and permit his fellow students to sit either as close to or as far away from him as the room would permit.

Whatever potential crisis may have existed was dissolved when a white student from a town on the Eastern Shore of Maryland, where a Negro had been burned alive by a mob a short while before, and who was the most popular man in the class, entered the room, marched directly to where Murray was sitting, shook hands with him, and sat down beside him. There was no more trouble. Donald Murray graduated after having made an excellent record and today practices law successfully in Baltimore.

Despite the growing willingness and even eagerness of white students at state universities to see Negroes admitted, these struggles are often like beachhead invasions. Even after clear-cut legal victories are won and Negro students admitted, counterassaults are often made which necessitate a continuous struggle, and occasionally the necessity of fighting to regain ground already won.

Twelve years after Donald Murray was admitted to the University of Maryland the same school refused to admit a Negro ex-Army officer, Wilmore B. Leonard, to a postgraduate course in chemistry, on the ground that formal notice in writing of his acceptance as a student had been "a mistake." But the principle established in the Murray case serves as legal basis for Captain Leonard and other qualified Negroes, and keeps their hope alive. For years we have been swamped with appeals from ambitious young Negroes in virtually every Southern state who want training in law, medicine, dentistry, journalism, and other professions. The campaign in their behalf has been materially hampered by the series of events which followed the United States Supreme Court's decision in the Lloyd Gaines case.

Despite the decision, Missouri stubbornly refused to admit Gaines to the law school. As we were preparing to require the State of Missouri to prove in the federal courts that it had complied with the Court's mandate by establishing a two-room law school in the basement of a St. Louis building, Gaines disappeared. To this day we have never located him. He has been variously reported in Mexico, apparently supplied with ample funds, and in other parts of North America.

But when the University learned that other Negroes were planning to apply for admission to the law school, the state legislature hastily appropriated funds totaling more than half a million dollars to establish a law school at the all-Negro Lincoln University in Jefferson City. In the meantime, militant Negroes picketed the jim-crow law school in St. Louis. To the considerable discomfort of the University and the legislature, they were joined in the picketing by white students from the University of Missouri, carrying signs reading: WHO OBJECTS TO NEGROES AT THE UNIVERSITY OF MISSOURI? WE CERTAINLY DO NOT!

Shortly after this, in 1942, a brilliant young colored woman, Lucille Bluford of the *Kansas City Call*, applied for graduate education in journalism at the University of Missouri. When she went to Columbia to make formal application, a large body of students met her in welcome to a town where only a few years earlier a lynching had taken place. Relentless fighting of Miss Bluford's case caused the legislature again to act on this issue in appropriating funds at considerable cost to the state to establish a school of journalism at Lincoln University. Whatever the cost to the taxpayer, most of the Southern states were determined to maintain segregation even if it bankrupted the state. One notable exception was West Virginia, which quietly admitted qualified Negroes to its graduate schools. The experiment has been carried out without difficulty.

We commenced our battle against educational discrimination at the graduate and professional level because here not even a feeble pretense of supplying "equal but separate" facilities was being offered by Southern states. But shortly afterward we struck the first of many blows at the practice of paying Negro teachers far lower salaries than was paid to whites. In its total this difference accounted for a large part of the twenty-five million dollars annually which authorities estimated would be necessary to bring schools for Negroes up to the level of schools for whites in the South.

We encountered extraordinary though not unexpected difficulties among some Negro teachers themselves. These were chiefly of the older generation who feared to antagonize white school boards. But eventually the more militant and younger teachers insisted on action. At the request of the Maryland State Colored Teachers Association we supplied legal aid to William F. Gibbs, Jr., an elementary school principal who brought suit to wipe out the considerable difference between his salary and the salaries paid to white principals who had the same qualifications and did identical work. It was developed during the trial of this case that the differentials in a single Maryland county exceeded thirty thousand dollars annually and that typically a white janitor in a white school received $339.00 per year more than a Negro elementary school teacher and $101.00 more than a Negro high school teacher. The facts were so incontrovertible and shocking that the Court decided in our favor and ordered equalization within a two-year period. Similar actions were brought in other counties, until eventually in 1941 the Maryland General Assembly enacted a bill which wiped out differentials totaling more than five hundred thousand dollars.

The long and successful struggle in Maryland gave courage to teachers in states farther south, and we were increasingly implored to give legal aid during this period to fight differentials in other states. The Alston case, in which Judge John J. Parker abolished $129,000 in differentials between white and Negro teachers' salaries in Norfolk, Virginia, has already been mentioned. Judge Parker's characterization that such differentials were "as clearly discrimination on the ground of race as can be imagined and [that they fell] squarely within the inhibition of both the due process and the equal protection clauses of the Fourteenth Amendment" was of immeasurable value to our campaign. An action on behalf of Negro teachers in Louisville, Kentucky, which resulted in the wiping out of a $59,000 annual differential in that city, contributed, interestingly enough, to the abolition of pay differentials between white male and female teachers, for which the latter had been unsuccessfully fighting for many years, at considerable expense.

But if I give the impression that these gains were won with ease, it would be grossly incorrect. We had to meet all kinds of legal trickery. Various states, particularly in the Deep South, sought to evade the issue by abolishing ratings and tenure of teachers. Others attempted to put all teachers, white and Negro, on a year-to-year basis which would have given school boards the power of life and death over jobs of all teachers. The school superintendents of Kentucky sought to justify the inequality of salaries paid Negro and white teachers on the grounds that (1) the standards of living of Negroes in the South are lower than those of whites, therefore the cost of living is less for Negroes than for whites, (2) traditionally Negroes are paid less than whites, and public sentiment will not support equality in the salaries of white and Negro teachers, and (3) the quality of instruction of Negro teachers is generally inferior to that of white teachers with equal training.

This is an example of the "which comes first—the chicken or the egg" type of reasoning which we constantly had to combat. We still must·do so, though fortunately to a lesser extent each year. Taking Negroes in the South as a whole and contrasting the cost of living for them with whites as a whole is manifestly fallacious. The necessity of restricting one's expenditures to his income rating is not confined to any one race, creed, or color. The cost of living for well-to-do Negroes is much higher than that of poor whites. Because whites have greater opportunity in business and the professions than Negroes in the South and in the country as a whole, they have larger incomes, can afford to buy better houses and goods, and thus naturally have a higher cost of living. Our contention has been that one should be paid what he is capable of earning, with no differential based on race. Lower salaries paid to Negro teachers mean that they cannot afford as good houses, food, clothing, medical treatment, and recreation. It gives them less money to subscribe to technical and other journals. Teachers' salaries as low as twenty dollars per month in Mississippi do not permit teachers to take summer courses in institutions like Teachers College in New York or at the University of Chicago. It does not even permit them to attend the few training institutions for teachers which exist in Southern states.

But already we feel greatly heartened by the fact that since 1935 the successful termination of a good many legal actions brought to equalize teachers' salaries has resulted in wiping out approximately three million dollars of the twenty-five-million-dollar annual racial differential. More Negro teachers are going to summer schools and in other ways making themselves better teachers. But we have a long path yet to travel in wiping out the handicaps and deficiencies which have been three centuries in the making.

XIX

Not Content with Preaching

As the depression deepened and unemployment caused increasing competition for jobs, the annual number of lynchings steadily rose. In 1933 twenty-eight lynchings occurred, twenty-four of the victims being Negroes and four of them whites. One of the victims was a young Negro boy who was lynched at Columbia, Tennessee, after having been acquitted on a charge of "molesting" a young white girl. At Princess Anne, Maryland, a Negro was burned at the stake. Two white men were lynched in San Jose, California. A statement by Governor Rolph of California attempting to justify the lynchers so shocked the nation that many organizations and individuals which had hitherto been indifferent were roused to action.

I had unsuccessfully urged President Roosevelt on several occasions to speak out against lynching and to give his support to federal anti-lynching legislation. He finally did speak out on the occasion of the San Jose lynching. Addressing the annual conference of the Federal Council of the Churches of Christ in America over a nation-wide radio hookup, he declared: "This new generation, for example, is not content with preaching against that vile form of collective murder, lynch law, which has broken out in our midst anew. We know that it is murder, and a deliberate and definite disobedience of the commandment 'Thou shalt not kill.' We do not excuse those in high places or in low who condone lynch law."

The San Jose lynchings brought valuable allies to our cause. Lewis Gannett of the *New York Herald Tribune*, Helen Woodward, Benjamin Stolberg, and I joined in signing a telegram to one hundred leading writers, editors, and publishers asking if they would join us in forming a Writers' League Against Lynching. Eighty-one of the one hundred responded affirmatively and promptly, expressing their eagerness to join in using their talents against the crime. Within a fortnight the number had grown to two hundred. Harry Hansen of the *New York World-Telegram* was elected chairman and Lenore Marshall treasurer. Suzanne La Follette served as secretary and Nella Larsen as assistant secretary. The committee kept writers supplied with carefully checked facts about lynchings and there has been ever since a continuing concern which has been reflected in articles, fiction, plays and other writings.

The Writers' League Against Lynching brought me into the first of an unbroken series of clashes and unpleasant experiences with Westbrook Pegler. Pegler had been a sports writer but had been suddenly promoted to columnist on the *New York World-Telegram* by Roy Howard as a possible replacement for Heywood Broun.

Following the San Jose lynchings he wrote an article defending the lynchers and Governor Rolph which the Writers' League Against Lynching vigorously protested. Pegler promptly began a long series of columns attacking the Writers' League in general and myself in particular.

But the Peglers and the Rolphs were increasingly becoming a minority in public opinion. When we renewed and stepped up our fight for the Costigan-Wagner Anti-Lynching Bill, we found the opposition no less determined, but at the same time we found support for the legislation from some who would have been most unlikely to give support even a few years before. The state legislatures of California, Colorado, Kansas, Minnesota, New Jersey, and Pennsylvania; the state assemblies of Indiana, New York, and Illinois; the Massachusetts state senate, and the city councils of several cities, passed resolutions endorsing the bill. Church, labor, women's, civil rights, fraternal, professional, and other groups, with a total membership of 53,720,593, were lined up in behalf of the legislation. But the archaic Senate rules which permit any senator to filibuster by speaking twice on any bill and on each amendment thereto for as long as he wishes again stymied our efforts. We were unable to get the Senate to consider the bill in 1934, despite a favorable report on it by the Senate Judiciary Committee and a tremendous volume of public opinion in its support.

But in 1935 the filibusterers could not prevent its consideration. It was taken up by the Senate on April 16th, and immediately the late Senator "Cotton Ed" Smith of South Carolina launched a venomous attack on the bill and a defense of lynching as necessary "to protect the fair womanhood of the South from beasts." Time and again the bill's opponents attempted to dislodge it from the Senate calendar by motion to adjourn, but we were able to muster votes to defeat the motion each legislative day until May 1st. In the meantime before packed galleries the dismal tragicomedy was played with cynical skill by Southern senators, aided by Senator William E. Borah of Idaho.

It was during this fight that I sought, for a long time unsuccessfully, to obtain an appointment with President Roosevelt to urge him to take a definite stand on the anti-lynching bill. The lean and saturnine Marvin McIntyre, I learned later, had intercepted my letters and telegrams, showing none of them to the President. When the situation became so critical that the fate of the bill hung in the balance from hour to hour I turned in desperation to Mrs. Roosevelt. I explained the situation over the long-distance telephone and she promptly promised to give the facts I had told her to the President.

The interview thus arranged was a most interesting revelation to me. I had known Mr. Roosevelt as Governor of New York state, but not too well. What I did know of his abilities during that period had caused me to be greatly surprised at the vigor and resourcefulness he had exhibited on becoming President. Since he had entered the White House my contacts with him had been few, but at the conference arranged by his wife on the anti-lynching bill there developed between us a closer relationship, which was destined to last to the day of his death.

The scene of the conference was the south portico of the White House on a warm spring Sunday in 1935. I found Mrs. Sara Delano Roosevelt and the President's wife on the porch, but the President had been delayed in returning from a cruise on the Potomac River.

While waiting, Mrs. Eleanor Roosevelt and I discussed some of the arguments being made against the anti-lynching bill. Shortly afterward the President arrived in exuberant good spirits. As was his custom when he wished to avoid discussing a subject, he told many gay and amusing anecdotes to postpone an anticipated ordeal. But finally I was able to bring the conversation to the pending filibuster.

"But Joe Robinson [at the time Senate majority leader] tells me the bill is unconstitutional," the President remarked.

Having heard from Mrs. Roosevelt some of the arguments on this point which had been presented to the President by the bill's opponents, I was ready with the opinions of prominent lawyers who had declared the bill constitutional.

The President then told me of another argument which one of the filibusterers had made and I was able to present facts in refutation. When this had happened three or four times, the President turned sharply and declared, "Somebody's been priming you. Was it my wife?"

I smiled and suggested that we stick to our discussion of the bill.

The President then asked Mrs. Roosevelt if she had coached me, and she too smiled and suggested that the President stick to the subject.

Laughing, the President turned to his mother to say, "Well, at least I know you'll be on my side."

The President's mother shook her head and expressed the opinion that she agreed with Mr. White.

Being a good loser, the President roared with laughter and confessed defeat.

But I gained from the visit only a moral victory, because the President was frankly unwilling to challenge the Southern leadership of his party.

"I did not choose the tools with which I must work," he told me. "Had I been permitted to choose them I would have selected quite different ones. But I've got to get legislation passed by Congress to save America. The Southerners by reason of the seniority rule in Congress are chairmen or occupy strategic places on most of the Senate and House committees. If I come out for the anti-lynching bill now, they will block every bill I ask Congress to pass to keep America from collapsing. I just can't take that risk."

On another occasion I had to contend with the President's predilection for telling lengthy and amusing stories to consume time and thereby shorten the opportunity for discussion of subjects he did not want to discuss.

I had been informed by McIntyre that I had been allowed fifteen minutes and must not stay longer because the President had a very important engagement to follow mine. When I entered the President's office he greeted me warmly and said, "I've got a perfectly corking story for you which I have been saving because I know you will enjoy it."

My heart sank, because I knew I would have to talk very fast to get in the facts even in fifteen minutes. However pleasant the President's story might be, I preferred to waste none of the time allotted me. Ignoring protocol, I broke in to say, "Mac has told me that I have just fifteen minutes. If you start spinning yarns, Mac will reappear to announce the British Ambassador or the Secretary of State and I will not have had time to tell you what I came to say and which you need to hear. So let me talk first."

The President was startled at my temerity, but if he was annoyed by it, he concealed it completely. Instead he laughed and said, "All right, go ahead. But save me two minutes, because it's a darned good story."

I talked as rapidly as I could, because I was very annoyed at the President's failure to take a more forthright stand against the Southern filibusterers and the steadily increasing wave of lynching. At the end of thirteen minutes I looked at my watch and informed the President that two minutes remained for his story.

Again the President laughed and said, "No story could be good under these circumstances, but I'll tell it to you anyhow." Unfortunately the story was not as good as those he usually told, but because he had been a good sport I simulated as hearty laughter as was possible under the circumstances.

One of the most inexplicable but interesting phenomena to me has been the extraordinary attitudes of several Western senators who were regarded as liberals on economic questions but who have been among the most injurious to the Negroes' cause. Chief among the latter number was the late Senator William E. Borah of Idaho, who persistently and consistently used his oratory and reputation as an authority on constitutional law to oppose federal anti-lynching laws and other legislation of that character.

During the famous seven-week filibuster of 1938, which incidentally cost the United States over half a million dollars for the operation of a Senate which did no work, Senator Borah spoke at length to crowded galleries. Charlie Houston and I happened to encounter one of the senators who supported the bill—and who possessed an excellent legal mind—as he was leaving the Senate chamber. When I asked him why he was leaving, he replied that Borah's arguments were so profound that he was unable to follow them.

Charlie and I asked him why he did not remain on the floor to analyze the arguments of the senator from Idaho, several of which were exceedingly fallacious. Charlie went on to point out that Borah had just been guilty of a dishonest statement in quoting a minority opinion of the Supreme Court as the majority opinion. The senator was startled at this revelation of the feet of clay of the popular Borah. He asked Charlie to prepare a memorandum brief for use in answering Borah which was done. The following day when the senator devastatingly demolished Borah's argument, the "lion of Idaho" with crimson face fled from the Senate chamber.

Borah's persistent enmity to the Negro cost him dearly when he sought the Republican nomination for president in 1936. Louis L. Redding of Wilmington, Delaware, who had made a brilliant record at the Harvard Law School, wrote a devastating analysis of Borah's record which we published in *The Crisis*. It exposed the succession of instances in which Borah had voted on a variety of issues in direct opposition to the stand he had taken on the same issues in public speeches. The article caused such widespread comment that we were forced to reprint it in large quantities.

The Idaho senator's campaign for the nomination opened in Brooklyn on the bitterly cold night of January 28th. Icy winds from the East River cut like jagged knives through the clothing of fifty pickets carrying signs attacking Borah for his stand on the Costigan-

Wagner Anti-Lynching Bill. Borah's face blanched as he stepped from the automobile which had brought him to the meeting and his shoulders seemed to shrink as with lowered head against the cold blasts of weather and disapproval he entered the building. Instead of the vigor and boldness which had characterized his speeches in the Senate, he faltered and fumbled his words to such an extent that the audience and newspapermen looked at one another in amazement. Borah's campaign ended the night it opened. Opposition of the solid Negro Republican vote in the Ohio primary shortly afterward wrecked his presidential aspirations and his campaign died a-borning.

In 1937 we had to face Negro, as well as white, opposition to a measure which we felt strong enough to be effective. A doughty Irishman, Congressman Joseph A. Gavagan, had introduced the bill which we supported. Congressman Hatton W. Sumners of Texas, chairman of the House Judiciary Committee, stubbornly and without apology had refused even to permit hearings on the measure. Congressman Gavagan placed a discharge petition on the speaker's desk, and we went at the task of securing the necessary two hundred and eighteen signatures to bring the bill to the floor of the House for debate and vote. When one hundred and seventy signatures were obtained Congressman Sumners and his fellow Southerners became alarmed and hastily reported out favorably a much weaker bill which had been introduced by Arthur W. Mitchell, Negro congressman from Chicago. Sumners later told me quite frankly that he had not believed that the National Association for the Advancement of Colored People would have the nerve to oppose passage of a bill introduced by the one Negro member of Congress.

He was wrong. The provisions of the Mitchell Bill were so innocuous that we were convinced that it would do little if anything toward eradicating lynchings or punishing lynchers. We marshaled our forces and defeated the Mitchell Bill by a vote of 257 to 122. The house passed the Gavagan Bill a week later by a vote of 277 to 119—aided by the Duck Hill, Mississippi, blowtorch lynchings.

We found that the long struggle to arouse public opinion had penetrated areas and created support where a decade before we would never have dreamed of receiving such support. Southern newspapers like the *Richmond Times-Dispatch*, the *Greensboro Daily News*, the *Danville Register*, and other leading newspapers vigorously and unequivocally urged passage of the bill. Southern church, labor, and student bodies, particularly the women of the Methodist Episcopal Church South, were equally outspoken. But the stronger the Southern and national support became, the more vindictive were the filibustering tactics of senators like Connally of Texas, Smith of South Carolina, Bilbo of Mississippi, Russell and George of Georgia, and McKellar of Tennessee, aided openly by Borah and less openly by some of the conservative Republican senators. A seven-week filibuster in 1938 was finally successful when an emergency relief appropriation bill to feed the unemployed was used to displace the anti-lynching bill in the Senate.

XX

Handshake from a Son

In 1937 I was honored by being chosen as the twenty-third recipient of the Spingarn Medal. The award was made for the work I had done in investigating lynchings, lobbying for federal legislation against that crime, and for the books and articles which I had written.

The Spingarn Medal was initiated in 1914 by Joel E. Spingarn, at that time treasurer and later president of the NAACP. It is awarded annually to the American Negro who, in the opinion of an independent award committee, contributed most in the year or years preceding his selection in any elevated field of human endeavor. The medal is designed, in the words of Mr. Spingarn, to stimulate distinguished achievement by Negroes and to call attention of the world to such achievement.

There were several individuals who, in my opinion, were more deserving of the award in 1937 than myself. But I was flattered that the Award Committee saw fit to include me among that distinguished group of Negro Americans who have received the medal. They include the biologist Ernest E. Just; Dr. Louis T. Wright, for his work in brain surgery; the distinguished musicians Harry T. Burleigh, Roland Hayes, Marian Anderson, and Paul Robeson; educators including Dr. John Hope, Mrs. Mary McLeod Bethune, Dr. Henry A. Hunt, and Dr. Robert R. Moton; the sociologists and writers Dr. W. E. B. DuBois and James Weldon Johnson; the novelist Richard Wright; Dr. Percy Julian, the biochemist, who originated a method of extracting hormones from soy beans and the foam method of extinguishing fire which saved many lives during the war; William H. Hastie and Thurgood Marshall for their leadership in the legal battle for constitutional rights; and others who have made notable contributions to society.

The formal presentation of the medal was made by Governor Frank Murphy of Michigan, who today is a distinguished member of the United States Supreme Court. He almost made Mother faint in astonishment when he wound up his address with the statement "and above all else, Walter is a true Christian gentleman."

George, as the first-born, was Mother's favorite, we used to tease her, and he in her sight could do no wrong. Because Mother and I were both quite strong-willed, we occasionally disagreed, and usually such disagreements ended with Mother speculating as to whether or not I, of all the children, would wind up less respectable than any others of the family. Thus my being publicly extolled as "a true Christian gentleman" by a distinguished public figure like Frank Murphy seemed to come as a great and pleasant surprise to her.

The other formal address that evening was delivered by James Weldon Johnson, and I shall always be deeply moved by memory of it, for two reasons. Jim saved me the embarrassment characteristic of such occasions by devoting very little of his speech to laudation of the recipient. He discussed instead the philosophy which lay behind the frequent libel that there are no "leaders" among Negroes. Jim pointed out that a single individual could lead an entire race in the relatively simple days when that race was seeking to achieve a place in an uncomplicated society. He cited Frederick Douglass and Booker T. Washington as men who in their day could be the final authority for the Negro on questions about all phases of his life.

But, Jim pointed out, the greater the progress of a minority like the Negro and the more complex society itself became, the more necessary became the needs for a variety of leaders, each trained and gifted in his particular field. A decade later it is still necessary that Jim's wise words be considered by Negroes themselves and by non-Negroes in thinking about the Negro.

Gladys, Mother, Jane, and Walter sat on the platform that evening, and it meant a great deal to me to have them there. Walter, whose nickname is "Pidge" from the affectionate *le petit pigeon* which a French painter and his wife used to call him when he was an infant in Villefranche-sur-Mer, wore that evening his first pair of long trousers. They were white duck and I am told he concentrated as much on keeping the crease in them as on the presentation of the medal. After the award had been made and Governor Murphy had shaken my hand in congratulation, Walter also rose from his seat, carefully adjusted the crease in his trousers, and with solemn face walked across the platform to shake hands gravely with me. I was as pleased with his doing so as I had been by Frank's and Jim's speeches of praise.

Although, quite understandably, he completely overshadowed me as far as the audience was concerned, I was delighted that my friend Joe Louis was present that evening and also attended a party given for Gladys and me later by the John Roxboroughs.

I am glad that we did not know that evening that Jim's speech was the last he was to make to an NAACP audience. The following year while driving in Maine he was killed instantly, and Grace was gravely injured, when their automobile was struck by a speeding train.

XXI

Hugo Black and the NAACP

In 1937 Senator Hugo L. Black of Alabama was nominated by President Roosevelt to fill a vacancy on the United States Supreme Court. The position which I took in that bitterly contested case brought down upon me a considerable deluge of criticism, the most acrimonious of it coming from a Negro politician who declared to an annual convention of the Negro Elks that "Walter White has sold out his race and ought to be driven out of the race."

Senator Black had joined with other Southern senators in fighting anti-lynching bills and had participated in filibusters. He had never descended, however, to the cruel and cheap vilification of the Negro of which most of his Dixie colleagues were guilty. He opposed federal laws against lynching on the grounds that, first, such measures were unconstitutional and, second (by somewhat invo'ved reasoning), that they might be used against labor unions. Although we did not agree with either of Senator Black's arguments, I was convinced that he believed what he said. His superiority of intellect and character over most of his colleagues from the South, such as Senators Bilbo, Tom Connally of Texas, "Cotton Ed" Smith of South Carolina, and Kenneth McKellar of Tennessee, was so apparent that he seemed to me to be an advance guard of the new South we dreamed of and hoped for when that section of the country emancipated itself from the racial, economic, and political bondage which fear, prejudice, and a regional inferiority complex had created.

In discussing with Senator Black the federal aid to education bill which he had introduced I had learned that he was not only capable of intellectual growth but was one of the ablest men in the Senate. The dead hand of tradition was anathema to him, although he combined a very shrewd and realistic expediency with his belief that many American concepts had to be revised because of changing world conditions. Charles Houston and I talked at length one day with him about an amendment we had drafted to the education bill to guarantee that moneys so appropriated by the federal government should be expended without discrimination in those states where segregated schools existed. He opposed such safeguards on the ground that they would alienate Southern votes for the bill, without which it would have no chance of passage. "Education is the answer to the race question, not legislation," he assured us. "When white Southerners are educated and given economic security there will be less prejudice against the Negro—fewer lynchings, more jobs, greater justice for the Negro."

Washington was dumfounded when Senator Black's name was sent to the Senate for the Supreme Court vacancy. At least three other candidates were known to be above Senator Black on the list which the President was considering.

I have always believed that President Roosevelt was at least partly moved to nominate Senator Black by his resentment against the selfishness of Southern senators. He knew that the Senate almost never turned down the nomination of a fellow senator for fear of establishing a precedent. Roosevelt knew that Black was more loathed by some of his fellow senators from the South than he was by Northern Republicans, because Black refused to follow the Southern pattern of conservatism and sectional greed.

Senator Black was confirmed with great speed by the Senate and before an investigation could be made of his allegedly having been a member of the Klan. Several of his closest friends in the Senate had scoffed at the rumor and assured me that Senator Black had never been a member of that infamous organization.

Revelation by a Pittsburgh newspaper that Senator Black had indeed been a member of the Klan at the beginning of his political career created a national sensation which is still remembered. Shortly afterward the Justice-elect granted an interview in London to Paul Ward of the *Baltimore Sun* in which Mr. Black gave as answer to a question as to whether he agreed with the Klan's principles the statement that his secretary was a Catholic, his law clerk a Jew, and one of his closest friends "Walter White of the NAACP."

Black's interview was featured on the front page and commented upon editorially in virtually every American newspaper. I was swamped by newspaper reporters for comment. It seemed wisest to answer briefly and simply that my firsthand acquaintance with the new Supreme Court Justice's views on racial, economic and political questions convinced me that Mr. Black would prove to be one of the most valued and able members of the Court.

My statement was used by enemies and critics of the Association and myself as basis for attack. But it was gratifying to read a number of editorials and letters from persons both white and Negro who were willing to reserve judgment on the new member of the Supreme Court. The first proof of Justice Black's freedom from race prejudice, now that the necessity of appealing for votes for reelection was ended, came in a decision which he read on Lincoln's Birthday, 1938. Three Negroes had been unmercifully tortured in Florida to extract a confession to a crime of which they were innocent. Justice Black's language was blunt and unequivocal in excoriating the Florida legal procedure in this case; a new trial was ordered, and the defendants were later acquitted. His record during his decade on the Supreme Court bench measured up to the high standard set in that first decision.

XXII

Marian Anderson and the DAR

On an early spring afternoon in Washington in March 1939 a vivacious, auburn-haired Washington newspaper correspondent, Mary Johnston, excitedly called me out of the Senate gallery, where I was listening to another filibuster. She had just come from an interview with the president of the Daughters of the American Revolution, Mrs. Henry M. Robert, Jr., who had bluntly told Miss Johnston that neither Marian Anderson nor any other Negro artist would be permitted to appear in Constitution Hall. Indignant at this lily-white policy, Miss Johnston wanted me to give her a statement which she could use in a story.

I had watched Miss Anderson's struggle against poverty and prejudice with more than ordinary interest. Following the success of Roland Hayes, she gave a recital in New York's Town Hall in 1925 which might better have been postponed a year or so. That evening Marian sang badly, though those who have listened to her in later years will find difficulty in believing that anyone with so great a voice could ever sing other than perfectly. Perhaps her performance that evening was due to stage fright. Some believe that the fault was due to the voice teacher with whom she was studying. He was a devotee of the bel canto school, and had attempted to raise Marian's voice a full octave. The New York critics that next day were harsh, even bitter. Most of them recognized the existence of a great voice, but some of them pontifically declared that it had been ruined.

Marian was so heartbroken that she vowed never to sing again. Some months later the NAACP was holding its annual conference in Philadelphia. Roland Hayes was to be presented with the Spingarn Medal and the presentation was to be made by the provost of the University of Pennsylvania, the scholarly and eloquent Josiah H. Penniman. Harry T. Burleigh, the famous composer and baritone of New York's St. George's and Temple Emanu-El, was scheduled to accept the medal for Roland in absentia, as Roland was then on a concert tour in Europe. We invited Marian to sing, but received a flat refusal. It took long persuasion to induce her to change her mind. But on Spingarn Medal night in crowded Witherspoon Hall she sang superbly and was forced to give encore after encore and then to take curtain call after curtain call. When at last the applause had subsided and the ordeal ended, Marian burst into tears and exclaimed, "Thank God! I've got my faith again!"

Now I welcomed Mary Johnston's suggestion, but pointed out that no one would be surprised to learn that I was indignant at the action of the DAR, and suggested that we get statements instead from some of Miss Anderson's famous fellow artists.

Mary agreed. Utilizing one of the high window sills of the Senate gallery as a desk, we drafted a telegram and compiled a list of distinguished musicians whom we would telegraph for comments. With gratifying speed the replies poured in from Lawrence Tibbett, Leopold Stokowski, Walter Damrosch, Kirsten Flagstad, Geraldine Farrar, and others, all praising Miss Anderson as a great artist and expressing indignation and almost disbelief that the DAR had taken the action we had reported.

On my return to New York, I found Sam Hurok, Miss Anderson's manager, as indignant as I have ever known him to be. He proposed that attention be focused on the bigotry of the Daughters of the American Revolution by asking Miss Anderson to sing an open-air, free concert in Washington.

The idea was exciting. The most logical place was the Lincoln Memorial. Mr. Hurok agreed, and asked Gerald Goode to go to Washington with me to see if arrangements could be made. Virginia-born Oscar Chapman, Assistant Secretary of the Interior, with characteristic intelligence was enormously enthusiastic. He made an immediate appointment with Harold Ickes, Secretary of the Interior, and throughout his life an unequivocal battler for justice to the

Negro. Mr. Ickes was equally excited over the prospect of such a demonstration of democracy. President Roosevelt was leaving that afternoon for Warm Springs. But Mr. Ickes would not let him leave until the President had permitted him to come to the White House to tell the story. Hearing it, the President gave his approval and told Mr. Ickes to provide whatever facilities were necessary to make the concert the greatest event of its kind ever held.

The engagement for which the Daughters of the American Revolution had refused the use of Constitution Hall had been arranged by Howard University. Since the University was dependent for support upon congressional appropriations, Mr. Hurok did not want to involve it in a protest which might have widespread repercussions. He, therefore, made a proposal which was more difficult to turn down than any other I have received in all the years of my connection with the Association. He suggested that the Lincoln Memorial concert be under the auspices of the NAACP. It would have meant publicity for the Association which could not have been bought for many tens of thousands of dollars.

But there was a broader issue involved than publicity. Because the NAACP is known as a fighting propaganda agency, its sponsorship of the concert might have created the impression that propaganda for the Negro was the objective instead of the emphasizing of a principle. I, therefore, proposed that the concert be given under the most distinguished and nonpartisan auspices possible—namely, a sponsoring committee on which would be asked to serve such persons as members of the Cabinet and the Supreme Court, senators, congressmen, editors, artists, and others who believed that art should know no color line.

It was natural that we should think instantly of Mrs. Eleanor Roosevelt as chairman of such a sponsoring committee. She had invited me to her apartment in New York a few days before to ask my advice on her resigning from the DAR in protest against the treatment accorded Miss Anderson. She had resigned, and this focused world-wide attention on the episode. However, I did not feel that Mrs. Roosevelt should put herself on the spot, particularly since reactionaries in the South were already pillorying her for her attitude on the Negro.

I therefore went to Mrs. Caroline O'Day, Congresswoman-at-large from New York state, whose Southern birth in Savannah, Georgia, and whose standing and integrity were such as to make her the next logical choice as chairman of the sponsoring committee. Mrs. O'Day enthusiastically accepted the chairmanship and turned over all the facilities of her office to us for use in sending telegraphic invitations to those selected to be asked to serve on the sponsoring committee.

A few politically minded individuals—chiefly in Congress—were cagey. Some had their secretaries wire that the invitations would be "brought to the attention" of their employers. A few sought refuge in excuses like "my position makes it unwise for me to participate in controversial issues of this character." But the overwhelming majority of those invited accepted membership with promptness and enthusiasm. Justices of the Supreme Court, top-flight artists of world reputation, writers, diplomats, Cabinet officers, congressmen and senators, men and women of lesser renown, agreed to serve and thereby express their admiration for Miss Anderson and their indignation at the cavalier treatment the DAR had given her. Seldom in history had a more distinguished group of Americans rallied to affirmation of democracy.

Among the sponsors were Mrs. Franklin D. Roosevelt and many other nationally and internationally known figures.

Gladys, Jane, and Pidge drove down to Washington with me on Easter Eve. The weather was crisp and cold but heavy with the promise of approaching spring. However, as we approached Washington sleet began to fall. With it fell our hopes. We went to bed low in spirits because of the snow piling up on the streets outside. Weeks of thought and all our hard work seemed about to be thwarted by nature. I was almost afraid to look out of the window when I awoke early the next morning. I shouted with happiness to see the sun.

The concert was scheduled to begin at five o'clock. We drove to the Lincoln Memorial, approaching it from the rear. We had to park the car blocks away because every available place near by had already been preempted. What a sight greeted us when we came around to the front of the Memorial! Every one of the several hundred chairs which had been placed on the lower platform was occupied. Seldom in the history even of Washington had a more distinguished group of sponsors been gathered. But much more important to us was the audience itself. Seventy-five thousand white and colored Americans not only from Washington but from cities, towns, and villages within a radius of hundreds of miles had gathered at the Memorial of the Great Emancipator to hear a singer of whom Toscanini had said: "A voice like yours comes but once in a century."

No member of that audience will ever forget the sight of Miss Anderson emerging from a small anteroom beside Gaudens's statue of Lincoln. She was apparently calm, but those of us who knew her were aware of the great perturbation beneath her serene exterior. On her right was gentle Georgia-born Caroline O'Day. On her left was Virginia-born Oscar Chapman. A tremendous wave of applause rose from the vast throng, which was silenced only when Miss Anderson gently raised her hand to ask that the concert be permitted to begin. Amplifiers poured out the thunderous chords of the opening bars of "America." Clasping her hands before her Miss Anderson poured out in her superb voice "sweet land of liberty" almost as though it was a prayer.

As the last notes of "Nobody Knows the Trouble I've Seen" faded away the spell was broken by the rush of the audience toward Miss Anderson, which almost threatened tragedy. Oscar Chapman plowed through the crowd and directed me to the microphone to plead with them not to create a panic. As I did so, but with indifferent success, a single figure caught my eye in the mass of people below which seemed one of the most important and touching symbols of the occasion. It was a slender black girl dressed in somewhat too garishly hued Easter finery. Hers was not the face of one who had been the beneficiary of much education or opportunity. Her hands were particularly noticeable as she thrust them forward and upward, trying desperately, though she was some distance away from Miss Anderson, to touch the singer. They were hands which despite their youth had known only the dreary work of manual labor. Tears streamed down the girl's dark face. Her hat was askew, but in her eyes flamed hope bordering on ecstacy. Life which had been none too easy for her now held out greater hope because one who was also colored and who, like herself, had known poverty, privation, and prejudice, had, by her genius, gone a long way toward conquering bigotry. If Marian Anderson could do it, the girl's eyes seemed to say, then I can, too.

XXIII

Fighters Wanted—No Negroes

Despite the well-organized and generously financed activities of isolationists, it became increasingly apparent toward the end of 1939 that the United States would inevitably be drawn into the European war. This issue was overshadowed in the 1940 presidential elections only by the third-term issue.

On September 14, 1940, America moved closer to the conflict when President Roosevelt signed the Selective Service Act. Two weeks later, on September 27th, the President complied with a request I had made that he receive a delegation consisting of A. Philip Randolph, of the Brotherhood of Sleeping Car Porters; T. Arnold Hill, who was at the time acting secretary of the National Urban League, and myself, to discuss discrimination against the Negro in the armed services and defense industries. The three of us met in the NAACP Washington Bureau office on the morning of the appointment to discuss the points we wished to make and to decide on which of us should act as spokesman. Mr. Hill made the wise suggestion that we should put these points in writing and leave a memorandum with the President so that there could be no misunderstanding of our position. In the light of subsequent events, this proved to be a precaution which saved us from grave embarrassment.

One of the steps most emphatically urged upon the President was the immediate and total abolition in the armed services of segregation based on race or color. The President listened attentively and apparently sympathetically, and assured us that he would look into possible methods of lessening, if not destroying, discrimination and segregation against Negroes. He promised to write or talk to us again after conferring with Cabinet officers and other government officials on the problem. But day after day passed without action by the White House.

On October 9th, Stephen Early, White House press secretary, handed to newspaper correspondents an official statement of a new government policy regarding Negroes in the Army and Navy. Far from diminishing jimcrowism, the new plan actually extended it! The statement declared that the traditional policy of segregation would be continued and that, except for the three already established Negro regiments, all present and future Negro units in the Army would be officered by whites. Early, apparently of his own initiative, added to the published statement the implication that this policy had been discussed with Randolph, Hill, and myself, and that we were in agreement with it.

The statement fell like a bomb on public opinion. Angry and puzzled telegrams, long-distance and local telephone calls, and letters poured in upon us from all parts of the country. It was heartening to note that the overwhelming majority of these messages assumed as a matter of course that the White House statement was either inadvertently or deliberately in error. Randolph, Hill, and I immediately issued a vigorous denial.

"We are inexpressibly shocked," one statement added, "that a President of the United States at a time of national peril should surrender so completely to enemies of democracy who would destroy national unity by advocating segregation. Official approval by the Commander-in-Chief of the Army and Navy of such discrimination and segregation is a stab in the back of democracy." We also quoted what we had fortunately declared in our written memorandum to the President to prove the utter falsehood of Early's statement.

Our charges proved to be a sensation. Wendell Willkie's vigorous campaign for the Republican nomination and his rugged honesty were attracting such crowds and favorable comment that the Democrats were becoming increasingly alarmed. Various polls had indicated that Willkie was gaining ground and that his popular vote would be large. The election appeared to depend on certain pivotal states in which the Negro vote would hold the balance of power.

Northern Democratic leaders were furious at Early for putting them on the spot and jeopardizing the Negro vote by this stupid blunder. Apprehension was changed to consternation when shortly afterward Early kicked in the groin a New York City Negro police-man who had been assigned to protect the President, when the officer refused to permit Early to cross a police line. Republicans gleefully seized upon the incident and saw to it that every town and hamlet in the United States where Negroes lived received full details of the assault. My telephone rang night and day with calls from friends of the President such as Governor Herbert H. Lehman of New York, Justice Felix Frankfurter, Anna Rosenberg of the War Manpower Commission, and others of lesser fame, who asked what could be done to repair the damage Early had done. I told all in-quirers that the White House would have to repudiate Early's statement and that he should be dismissed. The former was done—the latter was not. Early was forced to issue a retraction of his state-ment that Randolph, Hill, and I had approved the new Army policy and to make clear we had unequivocally urged abolishing segrega-tion. But he insisted the kicking was an "accident."

His statement was so unsatisfactory that I told alarmed friends of the President that the only way the damage could be repaired would be to take steps immediately to end discrimination in the armed services and industry. Judge William H. Hastie was ap-pointed Civilian Aide to the Secretary of War. Colonel Benjamin O. Davis, the only Negro officer of that rank in the Regular Army, was promoted to Brigadier General, the first Negro to achieve that rank. Colonel Campbell Johnson was appointed Special Aide to the Director of Selective Service. These three men worked valiantly in the face of heartbreaking opposition and achieved some results. But had they been twenty men each, the problems faced could be amel-iorated only to a slight degree as long as the basic evil of segregation was not ended.

Disturbed by the situation, Senator Wagner introduced a resolu-tion in the Senate to investigate the extent to which minorities were being denied employment in defense industries. As usual, this resolu-tion was subjected to delays although industrial plants throughout the country were begging for workers. Several Senate leaders expressed themselves vigorously as believing that the committee which had just been authorized to investigate defense contracts under the chairmanship of Senator Harry S. Truman was the logical agency to inquire into discrimination and that there was no necessity for setting up another investigatory committee.

This seemed reasonable, so I obtained an appointment with Senator Truman. He was quite frank in telling me that although his committee had only recently been established the number of hearings which had already been scheduled would keep it busy for a period of at least six months, and that even then he would be able to hear not more than three or four witnesses on the nature and extent of discrimination against minorities in defense plants.

We had already lined up approximately one hundred witnesses ranging from persons of national reputation to Negroes who had been refused employment despite possession of training. Senate Resolution 75, moreover, proposed an investigation of discrimination not only in employment but in vocational training, and of racial segregation in the Army, Navy, Air Forces, Medical Corps, and the operation of the draft law under local draft boards. Despite the fact that, in addition to Senator Wagner, two prominent Republican senators, Charles L. McNary of Oregon and Arthur Capper of Kansas, and a Democratic senator, Prentiss M. Brown of Michigan, joined in fighting for passage of the resolution, foes of the measure succeeded in keeping it buried in the Senate committee to which it had been referred.

Meanwhile Hitler's armies were marching across Europe spreading destruction and devastation. Nothing seemed able to stop the Japanese in Asia and the Pacific. But still the doors of war plants, with but few exceptions, remained closed to Negroes. Bitterness grew at alarming pace throughout the country. Philip Randolph and I talked almost daily regarding his proposal that a protest march on Washington be staged by Negroes. Because it afforded action, the proposal had fired the imagination of the disheartened Negroes throughout the nation. The NAACP board of directors voted to participate in the march. Official Washington was skeptical at first, but later began to show signs of alarm. Mayor Fiorello H. La Guardia invited Randolph and me to a conference at City Hall which was attended by Mrs. Roosevelt, Aubrey Williams, at that time Director of the National Youth Administration, and Anna Rosenberg. Randolph and I were asked not to stage the march.

"You know where I stand," said Mrs. Roosevelt. "But the attitude of the Washington police, most of them Southerners, and the general feeling of Washington itself are such that I fear that there may be trouble if the march occurs."

I told Mrs. Roosevelt of numerous requests we had made that the President receive a delegation to discuss again the steadily worsening conditions, which requests had not been granted. After she had heard the facts, Mrs. Roosevelt, with her usual honesty, agreed. "I will get in touch with my husband immediately because I think you are right," she declared.

On June 18, 1941, the President received Randolph and myself. Robert P. Patterson, at that time Assistant Secretary of War, was present in place of Henry L. Stimson, who was out of Washington. The late Frank Knox, Secretary of the Navy, was there. So were William S. Knudsen, president of the General Motors Corporation; Sidney Hillman of the Office of Production Management; Aubrey Williams, and Anna Rosenberg.

Randolph and I reiterated our adamant opposition to segregation. Judge Patterson agreed with us, but wanted to know how integration could be achieved. I pointed out the anachronism of an Army presumably trained to fight against Hitler's theories of race while it practiced a similar philosophy. We discussed practical means of abolishing segregation. Some years later, he told me that integration had seemed impossible to him at the time of the 1941 conference, but that he was convinced the methods we then discussed were workable when Negro and white soldiers fought together in the Battle of the Bulge.

I pointed out to the President that both the Army and Navy were handicapped with inefficient and prejudiced Southern officers in the higher ranks; that the backwardness of the South was responsible for fewer opportunities to make good in business and the professions for whites as well as for Negroes; that Northern graduates from West Point and Annapolis frequently did not remain in the Army or Navy but got better-paying jobs as engineers and in other vocations, while Southerners, because of lack of opportunity in the South, and because many of the Southerners were lacking in energy and ambition, stayed in the Army, where they found a ready-made career.

I further pointed out to him that these were some of the same men who had virtually lynched General "Billy" Mitchell for his advocacy of development of air power, and that they resisted any modernization of the armed services, which might conceivably prove disastrous. I concluded by telling the President that the seniority rule in the Army and Navy had thus placed Southerners in more than fifty per cent of the top-ranking positions of the armed services. Although, of course, some of the Southerners were able men and a few of them free of racial prejudice, the majority were neither able nor racially democratic in spirit or attitude.

When I finished, President Roosevelt turned to the Assistant Secretary of War and asked, "Bob, is that true of the Army?" to which Mr. Patterson sadly replied that it was.

The President then turned to the Secretary of the Navy to ask about that service. Mr. Knox replied that he thought the estimate far too low for the Navy, but added, "We can't do a thing about it because men live in such intimacy aboard ship that we simply can't enlist Negroes above the rank of messman."

"Hold on, Frank," the President interrupted. "We've got some good Negro bands in the Navy. Why don't we make a beginning by putting some of these bands aboard battleships? White and Negro men aboard ship will thereby learn to know and respect each other and then we can move on from there." Knox promised to look into the matter and to see what could be done. But we had the distinct conviction that he had no real interest in the matter and had agreed only because the President had suggested it. We found this opinion correct when more than a year later Knox, when asked by the President at another White House conference what he had done on the suggestion, admitted that he had done nothing.

We then turned to discussion of the only reason the conference had been called—the threat of a march on Washington. No success attended the President's skillful attempts to dissuade us. The NAACP was the only one of the organizations sponsoring the march which had a large mass membership. The President turned to me and asked "Walter, how many people will *really* march?"

I told him no less than one hundred thousand. The President looked me full in the eye for a long time in an obvious effort to find out if I were bluffing or exaggerating. Eventually he appeared to believe that I meant what I said.

"What do you want me to do?" he asked.

Philip Randolph told the President that we wanted him to issue an unequivocal executive order to effectuate the speediest possible abolition of discrimination in war industries and the armed services. William Knudsen had been silent up to this point, although he had scrutinized Randolph and me with ill-concealed hostility. He now spoke in blunt opposition to any such step by the President, declaring that industry itself would hire such Negroes as it saw fit to employ. We told him with equal frankness that one of the worst records of discrimination by any large industry had been that of General Motors, of which Knudsen was president. Knudsen angrily denied this and demanded proof. We told him that we had not brought the record of his company with us but that we would be very happy to supply him with the facts. I happened to look at the President during this interchange and saw that with his love of a fight he was enjoying the episode.

"And send me a copy too of General Motors' record when you send it to Bill, won't you?" he asked, his eyes twinkling.

Knudsen subsided and took no active part in the discussion thereafter. The President asked us to go into the Cabinet Room and there make a draft of the kind of order he thought he should issue. On one side of the table were Randolph and myself and two of Randolph's coworkers, Frank S. Crosswaithe of the Harlem Labor Committee and Layle Lane, a New York City schoolteacher, who had not been permitted to sit in on the conference with the President. With us were Mayor LaGuardia and Aubrey Williams. We completed the draft and I returned to New York, to leave a few days later for Houston, Texas, to attend the annual conference of the NAACP.

Randolph telephoned me there one blistering hot day just as I had finished speaking to the summer school session of the Prairie View State College for Negroes. Philip told me that there had been steady whittling down of the draft we had made in Washington. The emasculated version was so weak that I told him that in my opinion it was worthless and that we should repudiate it and stage the march. Randolph returned to the conference in agreement with this and fought doggedly for an order which had at least some power.

On June 25, 1941, the President issued Executive Order 8802 specifically banning discrimination on account of race, creed, color, or national origin in industries holding government contracts for war production and in the training for jobs in war industries. The Order set up a Committee on Fair Employment Practices responsible only to the President to investigate and take corrective action against discrimination.

Mark Ethridge of the *Louisville Courier-Journal* was named by President Roosevelt as chairman. Earl B. Dickerson, Negro lawyer and alderman of Chicago; David Sarnoff, president of the Radio Corporation of America; Presidents Philip Murray of the CIO and William Green of the AFL, and Milton P. Webster, vice-president of the Sleeping Car Porters, were chosen as members of the committee.

Immediately sniping at the Committee began from politicians, unfriendly newspapers, and hostile employers and labor unions who were determined to continue their practice of discrimination despite the desperate need for workers. An excellent and devoted staff, with former Governor of the Virgin Islands Lawrence Cramer as director, and George M. Johnson, formerly of the University of California and Howard University Law Schools, as associate director, began the seemingly impossible task of breaking down racial barriers. Their budget was at no time sufficient to the needs of the committee. Funds were supplied from the contingent fund of the President. However, more progress was made by the FEPC toward employment on the basis of ability in the face of racial and religious discrimination than at any other period in American history.

When, in 1944, enemies of the FEPC succeeded in placing the agency under the control of Congress, the death knell of the committee was sounded. A relentless filibuster from January 17 to

February 8, 1946, defeated efforts to secure appropriations to continue its work. Thus ended the career of the agency which, more than any other, established the right of minority Americans to work at their skills and thereby increased their faith in the democratic process.

XXIV

Mother Stops Climbing Stairs

George wrote Mother during the spring of 1940 that he had arranged a Southern speaking tour which would enable him to stop off in Atlanta to spend a day with her. A change in his schedule enabled him to reach there a day early. As his taxicab drew up in front of the house on Houston Street, the vision which greeted him made him wish he were elsewhere. For Mother, clad in a gingham dress and sunbonnet, was perched perilously at the top of a swaying and shaky ladder, touching up with a paintbrush some spots under the eaves of the second story of the house. George was afraid to call out to her, as he feared the excitement of seeing him would cause her to lose her balance and come toppling down the thirty or more feet to the ground. Instead, he left quietly and got a neighbor, who induced her to descend in safety and only then let her see that he had arrived.

When he returned to New York he told me how Mother had berated him for arriving ahead of schedule, before she had completed the preparations for his visit. Over our protests, Mother, with the strong determination which had carried her through life, had refused to leave the large old house in which she now carried on a lonely existence to come live with one of us.

"All you children were born here, and I am going to stay right here until they carry me out," she told us, and her words brooked no argument.

A few weeks later Mother mentioned in a letter an attack of indigestion she had suffered, but dismissed the illness as being of such slight and temporary importance that doses of baking soda and

Epsom salts, to which she was addicted, had "straightened her out."

Gladys and the children were spending the summer at Northampton, Massachusetts, and I stopped off there on my way back from a trip to Chicago. Just as I entered the house my brother-in-law, Eugene Martin, telephoned from Atlanta that "your mother has just left us." She died as she had lived—with courage. My sister Olive had sent Mother some soup that afternoon by her husband, Will. He and Eugene had stopped on the front porch to talk with her, and she casually mentioned a recurrence of the pain in her chest. Suddenly her lips became blue and she rose to her feet, somewhat unsteadily, and told Eugene and Will that she thought she ought to go upstairs and lie down. Alarmed, my two brothers-in-law offered to carry her up the stairs, but Mother dismissed such an intimation of weakness contemptuously.

"I've been climbing stairs for seventy years and I'm still able to do so under my own power," she said proudly and rejected their offer of help.

Feminine to the last, Mother conveniently forgot some nine years which should have been added to the seventy she confessed. She knew, although she would never admit it, that her illness was more serious than indigestion. When Olive and Helen got her comfortably into bed she mustered her fast-failing strength to give directions about routine household matters.

"The gas, electric light, and water bills with the money to pay them are in the upper right-hand drawer of my dresser there—be sure and pay them tomorrow when they are due," she told them. "And the new gray dress I bought for the Twelve Club is good enough to bury me in. Use it and don't waste money on a new one."

Just then Mother noticed Mae, the maid, standing at the foot of the bed silently weeping. Mother asked her anxiously if she had eaten, and when Mae, choking back her grief, replied that she did not want any food, Mother sharply insisted that she go downstairs immediately, heat up the soup Will had brought, and drink it.

"I'm afraid I won't be needing it," Mother said somewhat regretfully, because she loved Olive's excellent cooking. "You'll find fruit in the icebox, and some fresh rolls in the breadbox which I won't be needing either."

She looked at the grieved faces around the bed and asked all of them except Olive and Helen to leave. The pain in her heart by now was so intense that even the drug which Dr. Slater had given her to ease it was obviously having little effect. When the others had left the room Mother voiced for the last time her very great pride of spirit and person.

"Don't let any undertaker touch me—you two girls dress me for burial. And do take care of my baby and see that she gets well" —referring to Madeline, who was ill in New York.

She closed her eyes and never opened them again.

XXV

Wendell Willkie and the Good Fight

I knew Wendell Willkie only during the last few years of his extraordinary life. Our meeting, which grew into one of the three or four closest and richest friendships of my life, developed out of the increasing political strength and independence of the Negro vote.

An important figure in one of America's greatest industrial corporations telephoned me during the spring of 1940 to ask if he could come to see me. When he arrived he told me of his deep interest in the election of Mr. Willkie as president, though it was at times difficult to determine whether he was for Willkie or merely against Roosevelt. My visitor was courteous and almost ingratiating. Over cocktails he made the usual offers of jobs for myself and other Negroes if I would support Willkie and he were elected. My telling him that the NAACP was a nonpartisan and nonpolitical organization seemed to be without effect.

He proposed to me that I fly out to Chicago in a private plane and ride into New York with Willkie on his campaign trip, with, of course, newsreel shots and photographs of the two of us apparently in agreement. In this way, he assured me, I would not be violating the Association's rule against political activity by any of its personnel. He seemed quite startled when I refused to participate in any such attempt to evade the Association policy. He was even more startled when I informed him that although I did not like many of the elements in the Democratic Party, particularly the anti-Negro

198

Southern wing, I had far more faith in Franklin D. Roosevelt's devotion to the common man, and even more in Mrs. Roosevelt's sincerity, than in Mr. Willkie or any other candidate who could obtain the nomination of a party so committed to the interests of big business.

This was the first of a number of attempts to inveigle me into participation in the election campaign. The situation became so difficult that I was almost afraid to answer the telephone either at the office or at home lest it be another importuning politician whose pleas it would require much time and energy to shake off.

A few weeks after the election I received a very friendly note from Mr. Willkie inviting me to have luncheon with him. He stated that he was anxious to meet "the fellow" who had refused to meet him during the campaign. We tried unsuccessfully to arrange a mutually convenient date, finally abandoning the effort after several failures. And then one night I saw him at a private dinner at the Waldorf-Astoria given in honor of a Catholic bishop. I approached Mr. Willkie and introduced myself. Before the evening was over a friendship developed which grew steadily in warmth and meaning to me to the day of his untimely death.

As we were discussing, at luncheon not long afterward, the inside story of the fight Mr. Willkie had made as counsel to the motion picture industry in the Senate hearings, I pointed out that the most widely circulated medium yet devised to reach the minds and emotions of people all over America and the world was perpetuating and spreading dangerous and harmful stereotypes of the Negro.

Wendell's (he insisted on our using each other's first names the second time we met) response was immediate.

"I ought to have a tiny bit of influence right now—I don't know how long it will last—with the moving picture people. Let's go out to Hollywood and talk with the more intelligent people in the industry to see what can be done to change this situation," he said.

Naturally I was delighted to have the help of so powerful an ally, but knowing how busy he was I did not dare hope that he could find the time to go to California for this purpose. However, not long afterward he telephoned me to say that he had been asked to speak at the Annual Award dinner of the Motion Picture Academy of the Arts and Sciences.

"Let's kill two birds with one stone," he suggested. "Let me know what day will be convenient for you to go to Hollywood, and I will tell them that I can speak on that day, since they have left the date up to me." We both enjoyed the idea of a Negro, secretary of a "radical" organization like the NAACP, thus setting the date for movie stars to receive their "Oscars," which Wendell called their "Oakies."

Late in the afternoon of the day we arrived in Los Angeles, Walter Wanger and Darryl Zanuck of Twentieth Century-Fox called and the four of us discussed ways and means of presenting to motion picture producers, writers, directors, and actors the justice of picturing the Negro as a normal human being instead of as a monstrosity.

A few hours later we entered the Biltmore Bowl dining room, which was packed to the point of suffocation with movie stars and figures of the industry. When Willkie spoke he told his "moral degradation" story, which brought down the house.

It will be remembered that not long after the 1940 election Willkie had come out vigorously in support of Roosevelt's foreign policy program, which step brought to light the venom and reaction which had motivated some of his erstwhile supporters. Following his pronouncement he had received a lengthy letter, written on expensive stationery, from a wealthy woman in California. She indignantly related how she had contributed generously to the Willkie campaign fund and had worked assiduously in his behalf. Her epistolary rage mounted in denunciation of his post-election agreement with "that man in the White House." "As long as I live I will never contribute another penny to you or anything with which you are connected," she stormed. "I know not what others may think of you, but as for myself, it would take an act of Divine Providence to raise you to the level of moral degradation."

Wendell and I went back to Hollywood again in 1942, when he accepted our invitation to deliver the principal address at the closing mass meeting of the Thirty-first Annual Conference of the NAACP.

Walter Wanger and Darryl Zanuck were hosts at a magnificent

luncheon in the Café de Paris on the Twentieth Century-Fox lot. To it they invited what one of the motion picture trade journals called one of the most select groups of producers, writers, directors, and heads of the important motion picture guilds ever assembled in the moving picture capital.

Walter Wanger introduced me to make the opening statement. I knew that the boards of censorship in Southern states, through their objection to the appearance of any Negro in films except as a comic or menial figure, had frightened most motion picture producers into slavish following of these stereotypes. I was aware of the dependence of the moving picture industry on mass consumption and of its increasing fear, born of such attacks, of any reforms which might cut down box-office returns.

I attempted as best I could to allay these doubts, and at the same time to present without equivocation the resentment of colored peoples at home and abroad against racial caricatures. I pointed out that we did not ask that Negroes be pictured as superhuman heroes, because they, like all humans, are made of weaknesses as well as strengths. I urged Hollywood to have courage enough to shake off its fears and taboos and to depict the Negro in films as a normal human being and an integral part of the life of America and the world.

Willkie's speech was hard-hitting and uncompromising. He reminded the audience that on his recent world tour he had found growing resentment, not only against the motion picture industry but against America itself, because American films almost invariably caricatured people with dark skins. He reminded his audience that, whether they wished it or not, one world had come into existence, and that the fate of every human being was inextricably tied up with the outcome of the war which was swiftly enveloping the globe. And then he bluntly pointed out that many of the persons responsible for Hollywood films belonged to a racial and religious group which had been the target of Hitler, and that they should be the last to be guilty of doing to another minority the things which had been done to them. Few men could have made this latter statement without giving offense. Not only was no perceptible offense taken, but, instead, Willkie's frank admonition was cheered. His earnestness, his integrity, and his complete sincerity had won over his audience.

Many of the guests remained long after the luncheon was over to discuss ways of implementing the proposals we had made. I had been warned—not without reason, as I discovered—that Hollywood acquired a new enthusiasm whenever a protagonist for a cause came to the film capital, only to lose it and acquire another as soon as a new protagonist arrived. But we found a surprising number of writers, directors, actors, and actresses, and a smaller number of producers, who were genuinely disturbed by the situation and eager to find practical ways of solving it.

One or two producers and several writers and directors told us that many of the mistakes they had made were errors of the head rather than of the heart, and arose from the lack of unbiased and authoritative sources of information. Two producers suggested that the NAACP establish a Hollywood bureau for which the funds would be contributed by producers. Willkie and I doubted the wisdom of this, because we knew that he who pays the piper calls the tune. It is still the hope of the NAACP to establish an independent Hollywood bureau so competently and objectively conducted as to make it influential in changing the movie stereotypes of Negroes which influence scores of millions of human beings all over the earth.

As long as Wendell Willkie lived, the trend set by the 1942 luncheon continued. A noticeable diminution of objectional Negro roles could be observed. A few innovations were to be noted in the films made by Warner Brothers, Twentieth Century-Fox, and Metro-Goldwyn-Mayer. But with the tragedy of Willkie's death in 1944 most of those responsible in Hollywood for changing the pattern appeared to feel that the pressure upon them had been removed.

Willkie and I were confronted constantly with evidence of the terrifying power to intimidate Hollywood which a few people possessed. Repeatedly producers told us frankly that they dared not risk offending boards of censorship in Southern states. We learned how one man acting as a censorship board to pass on the suitability of pictures for five states belligerently objected to any Negroes in moving picture films unless they played roles in conformity with his own prejudices. Although the five states produced only 1.25 per cent of the estimated income from any picture made in Hollywood, the prejudices of this one octogenarian censor were kept constantly in mind by moving picture makers whenever a Negro character was involved. In this fashion, one man was determining what the entire world would be permitted to learn about the Negro through the medium of American movies.

But my friendship with Wendell Willkie did not exist only on the basis of what we sought to do about the presentation of the Negro in films. In 1943 he expressed a desire to talk frankly, and off the record, with a group of Negroes who had vision and character. Gladys and I invited such a group to meet him at our home in Harlem. Bill Hastie and George Johnson, then of Washington, Ira Lewis of the *Pittsburgh Courier*, and about thirty others were there.

Fortunately two of the five rooms of our apartment are so arranged as to make one fairly large room, but even its capacity was taxed. Wendell came early, arranged himself in a comfortable chair, and called for a Scotch and soda. With him as its focal point, the conversation sparkled and crackled like electricity. We discussed, of course, the war. Wendell told us intimate details of recent events in England, Europe, Russia, Africa, and Asia, where he had recently visited. It was fascinating to watch the eager faces of men who sat on every available chair and on the floor as they matched wits and information with the man who also was striving to find answers to questions which had to be solved to save the world from chaos.

As we learned to know each other, Willkie and I saw more and more of each other, and we often talked of his political points of view. One day, as we were discussing in his office a suggestion that he be a candidate for the governorship of New York, he expressed the conviction which ruled his thinking during the last months of his life. He was leaning back in his chair, with his feet on the desk. It was a little startling in that luxurious office to notice that his shoes were half-soled. He watched an outbound troop ship, dreary with the dull gray paint of war, its deck crowded with young Americans pathetically absorbing their last view of New York harbor.

"Look at those kids out there on that ship," he said. "I believe I can do more in fighting for what they believe and for what they deserve by staying out of public office, even including the presidency. I would gladly say to hell with the presidency and all political offices if I felt I could do more as an individual than as governor or president or anything else."

Such a statement made by any other man in public life would have sounded hypocritical. But Wendell Willkie believed implicitly what he had just said. If any proof were needed of his sincerity, that proof was supplied a few months later when he and I had breakfast together in a Western state on the day that he had had a conference with the governor. That evening Wendell returned to his hotel in more dejected spirit than I had ever seen him. Wearily he asked me whether I had ever heard a more brazen proposal than the one which had been made to him that day. This governor was a "favorite son" of a state with a sizable bloc of electoral votes. He had proposed that if Wendell would promise him a certain post in the Cabinet if elected, the governor would deliver his state's electoral votes to Wendell.

"What did you tell him?" I asked.

"I told him to go to hell," Wendell replied, his anger mounting again. "I have never made a deal yet and I'll be God-damned if I'll make one now, even to be president of the United States." I telephoned room service for two double Scotches to celebrate the decision and to alleviate his weariness and disgust.

Some sentimental persons attributed Willkie's death in 1944 to a broken heart over his repudiation by his party and his apparent failure to unite effectively the liberal elements among the Republicans. If he had a broken heart I saw no evidence of it. Instead he appeared to me to be happier, and more determined to fight for his ideals, now that he was free of any suspicion of doing and saying things solely for political reasons.

None of us believed that his last illness was as serious as it turned out to be. He had just written an article for *Collier's* dealing with the Negro question. He and I had been asked by a publisher to do a book together dealing with the race problem as a world issue of prime importance which had to be faced and met if lasting peace were to be attained. A day or two before he died I received a note from him written in the hospital. He said that he was being held there for no good reason but that he hoped to "escape" in a few days. "Then let's get together for a couple of cocktails to discuss the book, though God alone knows when either you or I will ever get the time to write a book." He added a postscript. "Whatever you are writing in seclusion, for my sake please give them hell." He was referring to *A Rising Wind*, the story of my experiences in the European, North African, and Italian theaters of war which I was then writing against a deadline before leaving for the Pacific.

I telephoned Ruth Lipper Saturday afternoon before leaving to speak in Charleston, West Virginia, on Sunday, October 8, 1944. Ruth told me that she had just been told at the hospital that Willkie's fever had subsided and that his doctors believed he would be able to leave the hospital within a few days.

The next morning I stepped off the train at Charleston to be told by President John W. Davis of the West Virginia State College that Wendell Willkie had died during the night.

XXVI

The Fifth Estate

One of the first objects of criticism and attack after Pearl Harbor was the Negro press. For a time it appeared possible that an hysterical use of charges of "sedition" and "interference with the war effort," as well as denial of newsprint to these papers, would be used to cripple or drive them out of existence. John Temple Graves of Birmingham, Alabama, wrote a blistering attack on the Negro press in the *Virginia Quarterly Review*. Mr. Graves' article was quoted widely and commented upon editorially, particularly in the Southern press. His allegation thereby gained a circulation far in excess of that usual to material in a university publication.

Warren Brown wrote another attack which appeared first in the *Saturday Review of Literature* and later in the *Reader's Digest*. Brown, a Negro, had been well educated through the generosity of certain philanthropic agencies which sought to soft-pedal attacks by Negroes on racial proscription. Great emphasis was placed on Brown's race in order to prove that both Negro and white Americans believed the Negro press to be irresponsible, inaccurate, and inflammatory.

More fuel was added to the mounting flames by an article in the *Atlantic Monthly* written by Virginius Dabney, editor of the *Richmond Times-Dispatch*. Mr. Dabney titled his article "Nearer and Nearer the Precipice." He passed over lightly and mildly legitimate Negro grievances and blamed virtually all friction between whites and Negroes in America on the Negro press.

It must be admitted in all truth that there was some justification for criticisms by these three writers and others. Either because of insufficient staff or carelessness, too many of these papers would publish insufficiently corroborated stories, and sometimes printed rumor for truth. Even when the facts had been carefully checked flamboyant headlines were placed over the stories, sometimes with incorrect emphasis. Lynchings, assaults on Negro soldiers, refusals of war plants to employ colored workers, and similar items were given preference over less sensational news.

But the fault was far from being that of the Negro press alone. These papers are relied upon by Negroes for the news they cannot find in white newspapers. If they specialized in seeking out and publishing stories about racial discrimination it was because their readers wanted and expected them to perform this service, generally ignored by the white press. And what was generally overlooked by critics was that they were only following, with comparative restraint, a pattern which had long been set for them by the white press. The worst distortions in the Negro press could not equal the inflammatory misrepresentations which had been given the public by anti-Negro white papers, especially in the South, for years. As is so often the case, a minority had followed, to a limited extent, the bad leadership of a part of a powerful majority.

I was brought into this situation almost by accident. As I was leaving his office one day in December of 1942 President Roosevelt called me back to say that pressure was being brought to bear on him and the Department of Justice to indict the editors of some of the more flamboyant Negro newspapers for "sedition" and "interference with the war effort." The idea to me was fantastic and absurd. I asked the President what evidence, if any, there was that any of the editors he mentioned were guilty of relations with any foreign power, or of any act which could be interpreted as treasonable, under the wise and tolerant provisions of the Constitution. The President told me he had seen no evidence which would stand up in court, but that the stories which had been published in a few of the papers were so clearly biased and inaccurate that some of the men high in government believed that convictions could be secured.

I urged upon the President a remedy quite different from that offered by the courts. I told him that decisive action to abolish segregation in the armed services and to end discrimination in government-financed war industries would transform these papers from critics of the war effort into enthusiastic supporters. I suggested that it would be most revealing to investigate the records of the government officials who were demanding the suppression of the Negro press, and if he would invite some Negro editors to the White House, along with the white newspaper and magazine editors whom he occasionally asked to come in for pep talks, he would accomplish a great deal.

The President agreed to do this, but suggested that a good deal more needed to be done in addition to such conferences. Apparently the President called in his advisers and ordered them to abandon the absurd and dangerous proposal to charge Negro editors with disloyalty. But those who wanted to silence these newspapers were not to be discouraged. A new device was concocted shortly afterward—sharp limitation or complete denial of newsprint to Negro newspapers which exposed or attacked discrimination. When I had gathered the facts I presented them to the President, who promptly squelched this attempt.

In the meantime we called a conference at our office in New York on January 23, 1943, to which were invited editors of the twenty-four largest Negro newspapers, whose combined circulation totaled close to three million copies weekly.

We talked frankly. We offered the services of our Washington Bureau to check without cost any story or statement originating in the capital. Cooperative use of the facilities of the papers were devised, which resulted in the formation not long afterward of the Negro Newspaper Publishers Association. A code of journalistic ethics was planned and more rigid methods of checking the details of stories prior to publication were perfected.

Almost immediate results were to be observed. Sensationalism was curbed in the treatment of news with little loss of militancy in attacking discrimination. Racial hypersensitiveness was lessened at least to the extent of playing up more fully and prominently constructive acts by whites against discrimination. Objectionable or questionable advertising of love powders, dream books, and luck stones, which a few of the papers continued to accept, almost totally disappeared.

Some amusing developments, however, so far as the NAACP is concerned, were to be observed among some of the editors after the suggestion had been put into effect that these editors be invited to conferences at the White House and in the offices of Cabinet officials in Washington. Armed with a sense of new importance, a few of the editors proposed to take over "leadership" by forming a new organization, which editors would head, to replace the NAACP. One of the editors asserted belligerently at a meeting of the Negro Newspaper Publishers Association that the Negro press had "made" the NAACP, and why therefore should editors pay any attention to what "Walter White says, because there are a dozen of us here who make many times as much money as he does." We noticed also that in many instances the Association's name was deleted from stories of important legal or other victories which had been won through its efforts.

In many ways the establishment and rise of the Negro press in America has been a miracle in journalism. Until quite recently no Negro could obtain employment as reporter, editor, or craftsman on any white daily newspaper or magazine. The Negro thereby had been denied the opportunity to learn the newspaper trade by working at it. A few Negroes have graduated from schools of journalism and more are taking such courses as opportunities on both Negro and white publications increase. But as a rule the Negro newspaperman has had to establish his own practices and standards, and the results have not always been uniformly good.

Even more disadvantageous has been the difficulty the Negro newspaper publisher has experienced in obtaining credit for the purchase of expensive printing and other machinery. Along with this handicap has been the fact that his revenue from advertising has been microscopic. The result has been the perpetuation in the Negro press of personal journalism, with its advantages and disadvantages, which has almost totally disappeared from the white press.

The Negro press has been and is today the only large segment of American journalism whose major support comes from its readers rather than its advertisers. It has therefore of necessity remained more responsive to its readers' wishes than has any other. It is probable that this situation will not last much longer, first, because advertisers are awakening to the fact which they have hitherto ignored, that Negroes spend in excess of ten billion dollars annually, and, second, because of the increasing costs of production.

With its obvious faults, the Negro press is a phenomenon of immense significance to the whole United States as well as to the Negro minority. It is one of the products of segregation. Its shortcomings are in considerable degree the result of the proscription which it and Negroes as a whole have suffered. Its function as a watchdog of Negro interests has given it power and influence which will continue and increase as long as prejudice and proscription plague the Negro.

XXVII

Turn to the Left at Detroit

I was involved in the famous Ford strike of 1941, and thereby hangs a tale of the increasing importance of the Negro worker in the American industrial scene. In 1919 Negro steel workers had been used successfully as strikebreakers. At that time most of the American Federation of Labor unions and the four railroad brotherhoods barred Negroes from membership. Only a few heavy-industry unions such as mine workers and longshoremen admitted colored workers. The inevitable result of exclusion had been a steadily growing antagonism which worked to the disadvantage of organized labor and the Negro until the Committee on Industrial Organization was formed in 1935. As head of the United Mine Workers John L. Lewis had recognized no color line, and the incorporation of that philosophy in the CIO offered the first reason for confidence of Negro workers in labor unions.

The first real test of the CIO came in the attempt to organize Ford workers. Henry Ford had provided for Negroes the first opportunity for employment in considerable numbers above the rank of porter or common laborer in any large-scale American industry.

The Ford public relations and employment departments had quite cleverly capitalized upon this departure from the traditional pattern of employment. Liaison was established between the Ford employment office and large Negro churches in Detroit. Whenever there was need for labor the pastors of these churches would be telephoned that there were openings and that applicants bearing letters from the clergymen of these churches would be given special consideration. It was natural that communicants who had received employment through intercession of their pastors would contribute more generously to support of their churches, and many Negro ministers cooperated fully. But it inevitably provided a serious conflict when a decision had to be made by Negroes, who constituted a sizable percentage of Ford employees, between Ford and the United Automobile Workers of the CIO.

The first serious manifestation of the cleavage in Negro thinking I encountered was the dilemma I faced when I arrived in Detroit in June 1937 for the annual conference of the NAACP. Tired and soiled by the long automobile drive from New York, we reached Detroit to be confronted by an angry and belligerent delegation of Negro ministers who informed me that unless Homer L. Martin, at that time president of the United Automobile Workers, was removed from the program, or a representative of the Ford Motor Company placed on the program with Martin to answer whatever statements he made, these ministers would order their parishioners to boycott the convention.

The public relations department of the Ford Motor Company was much more subtle—and intelligent. They offered to place at the disposal of the national officers of the NAACP a fleet of shiny new cars for our convenience during the convention.

We decided not to use the cars.

Perhaps if I had been less exhausted from the heat and the long trip I might have been more respectful to the Negro ministers. But I was tired and wanted nothing on earth so much as a bath. I resented the dictatorial belligerence of the ministers and curtly told them that "the law compelling anyone to attend an NAACP meeting had long since been repealed," and that they could do whatever they pleased about boycotting our meetings. Despite—or perhaps because of—their attacks, the auditorium in which Homer Martin spoke was not large enough to accommodate more than one-third of those who wished to attend the meeting.

It was not until four years later that the United Automobile Workers were strong enough to challenge Henry Ford's determination to permit neither Wall Street nor any labor union to have any say about the policies of the Ford Motor Company.

In the interim Mrs. Edsel Ford had become interested in the

NAACP through her friendship with Mary White Ovington. The Edsel Fords and Miss Ovington had been neighbors at Seal Harbor, Maine, Edsel Ford had shared his wife's interest and had made an annual contribution to the NAACP from a special bank account, so as not to disturb or give offense to his father, who would probably not have approved.

When the Ford strike broke in 1941 the Negro issue was brought decisively into the picture and there was general recognition of the profound effect it would have upon the eventual outcome. A considerable percentage of Negro Ford employees refused to go out on strike. Other Negroes were rushed into the plant as strikebreakers as Harry Bennett marshaled his forces, and they were told that they would be "paid around the clock" for no more arduous task than punching a time clock every eight hours. An ugly situation of dangerous proportions swiftly developed. Many of the Ford workers were Southern whites who had brought to Detroit the traditional racial prejudices of Mississippi and other Southern states.

The ominous atmosphere seemed almost a tangible thing when I arrived in Detroit. Eddie Levinson, formerly the labor editor of the *New York Evening Post* and then publicity director of the UAW-CIO, and Dr. James J. McClendon, president of our Detroit branch, met me at the airport. We drove to the Statler Hotel, where R. J. Thomas, president of the UAW-CIO, George Addes, and other union officials were waiting. They began promptly to tell me the dolorous story of how the strike was threatened with failure because of the Negro workers. The union officials, with the exception of Eddie Levinson, put almost the entire responsibility upon the Negro ministers.

I asked Thomas what steps had been taken by the union to convince Negro Ford workers that it was to their advantage to join the union. I asked him what proof had been offered that the union's seniority rule would not be utilized to victimize Negro workers as soon as employment peaks declined.

Thomas was embarrassed but honest in his reply.

"We've got so many Southern whites in the Ford plant, we've been afraid to conduct an open campaign to recruit Negro members in the union," he admitted. "We've sent organizers to the homes of Negroes to talk to them privately," he added.

I pointed out to the union leaders that whatever may have been the wisdom of a surreptitious campaign of this character in the past, they were now faced with the grim reality of losing the strike unless they could induce Negro workers to leave the Ford plant at River Rouge by demonstrations that these workers would not be double-crossed. I learned that the union leaders were less disturbed by the numbers of Negroes who distrusted the union than by the fear that rioting would force the governor to call out troops. It was believed not only by the union but also by the public generally that some of the Ford company officials were counting on the development of sufficient violence to necessitate the calling of troops and that the troops would break the strike.

We decided that the most immediately effective way for the union to make clear its position would be to place advertisments in the Detroit newspapers, setting forth in unequivocal terms the union's position toward Negro workers. The following day an advertisement in both white and colored newspapers stated that under a UAW-CIO contract Negro Ford workers would receive the same pay as whites, and that Negroes would lose no privileges by joining the union, but on the contrary would enjoy greater security and receive promotions on the basis of seniority.

Since as far as we knew no newspapers were getting into the River Rouge plant, our next problem was that of getting the union's pledges to the Negro workers who had been in the plant since the inception of the strike.

But even before that task was undertaken another hurdle had to be surmounted—the attitude of the executive committee of our Detroit branch. Most of its members at that time were businessmen, doctors, and other representatives of the upper middle class of Negro life. All of them were sincerely devoted to the cause of Negro freedom. Most of them had worked faithfully and for many years to make the Detroit branch large and successful. But they were symbols of the dilemma of members of the Negro middle class. The bulk of their incomes was derived from sales or professional services to Negroes employed in the Ford plant. It was inevitable therefore that they identify their own economic interest with that of anti-union Negro Ford employees.

We met at the colored YMCA to discuss the issue. I sensed the moment I entered the room that I was in an atmosphere as definitely anti-union as would have been that of a meeting of the board of directors of the Ford Motor Company. But fortunately for me the atmosphere was tempered with respect for the judgment of the national office. I pointed out that Ford's employment of Negroes had been unique in the Detroit scene and that it was perfectly understandable that they should be concerned about the perpetuation of jobs upon which their livelihood in large measure depended. But, I added, it was inevitable that the Ford workers would eventually be organized by some labor union. I told them of the pledges that had been made that afternoon by the union leaders. No good would come from labor-management warfare, and peace in the Ford plant could be obtained only by an impartial election under the National Labor Relations Board to determine in democratic fashion whether the Ford workers wanted to be organized, and, if so, by which unions.

Jimmy McClendon, who had been my fellow student at Atlanta University, broke the silence which followed my presentation of the facts.

"Okay, pal, if you say it's that way, I'm with you," he told me.

Not all the skepticism vanished. But they were willing at least to find out whether the union would keep its pledges.

The union offered us the use of its sound trucks to get the news of the pledges which had been made into the plant. But our judgment was against incurring obligations of any character to either side in the industrial quarrel. We hired our own sound trucks. The Reverend Horace White, Dr. McClendon, and several others of us circled the huge Ford plant. Over loud-speakers we read the union's statement and pointed out that the best interests of neither the union nor the Ford Company nor Negroes would be served by their remaining in the plant and causing almost certain rioting.

The effect at first was slight. The pall of distrust was too impenetrable. Newspapers in Detroit and throughout the country had featured photographs of strikers beating Negro "scabs" and of Negro "strikebreakers" fighting with white unionists on the picket lines. No Negro pickets had been assigned to the plant by the union because of fear of trouble. I suggested that nonsegregated groups of pickets be assigned, and that efforts be made to get photographers to picture unity of this character instead of the discord and racial antagonism which had monopolized the news.

I walked in the picket line around the plant and attempted to talk to a Negro inside who brandished a frightening weapon several feet in length made of tool steel which he had sharpened to razor-keenness. In answer to my plea that he come out of the plant he told me in exceedingly profane and biological language what he thought of unions in general and of me in particular. He said that Ford's was the only place in Detroit where he had been able to find a job to support himself and his family, and that the union had not done a blankety-blank thing to break down employment discrimination in other Detroit plants.

After a few hours, however, our loud-speaker appeals began to produce results. Across the main entrance of the River Rouge plant stood an apparently impregnable wall of human flesh made up of armed guards placed there to prevent not only entrance into the plant by unauthorized persons, but also to prevent departure of those inside from the plant. Across the road, which formed a kind of no man's land, was a solid mass of strikers. I remember one sturdy Negro from the plant standing poised on the other side of the guards like a halfback waiting for the ball to be snapped. As one of the guards momentarily turned away the Negro charged through the split-second opening and across the road. A great cheer arose and he was greeted warmly by the strikers, who provided him transportation to his home. We did not succeed in getting all of the Negroes out of the plant, but many of them did leave. An NLRB election shortly afterward demonstrated that a majority of the workers wished to be represented by the UAW-CIO in preference to the UAW-AFL or a Ford company union.

The position taken in the Ford strike bore fruit in a number of ways. As amicable labor relations as any American industry has consummated with a labor union have been established between the Ford Motor Company and the UAW-CIO. The union has assiduously attempted to live up to its pledges and has vigorously and continuously fought racial discrimination within the union and in American life generally.

During the terrible race riots in Detroit in 1943 white union members fought against white mobbists to protect Negroes, and Negro unionists fought Negroes in protection of white fellow workers. There were two areas in Detroit during the riot where peace was maintained—in the plants which had been organized by the UAW-CIO and in the nonsegregated residential areas.

Four years after the Ford strike, in 1945, I was again called to Detroit in connection with an industrial dispute. This was the General Motors strike. Walter Reuther, the redheaded, ebullient anti-Communist president of the automobile workers, conceived the idea of an impartial citizens' committee to listen to the evidence on both sides of the dispute and render an opinion if it saw fit to do so. The men and women who either served in person, or expressed their approval but were unable to serve, formed an interesting cross-section of America. They included the Reverend Henry Hitt Crane, pastor of one of Detroit's largest Protestant churches, who acted as chairman; Leon Henderson, former OPA director; Mrs. M. E. Tilly of Atlanta, Georgia, a powerful figure in Southern church and civic affairs; Josephus Daniels, former Secretary of the Navy; Walter Lippmann; James G. Patton of the National Farmers Union; F. R. Von Windegger, St. Louis banker; Ralph McGill, editor of the *Atlanta Constitution;* Mrs. William H. Hastings, president of the National Congress of Parents and Teachers; and ten other distinguished Americans.

Reuther had insisted that the thirty per cent increase in wages which the union demanded should be considered in relation to the profits which General Motors was making and the prices which it charged the public for its products. To this a corporation spokesman had belligerently retorted that the prices General Motors charged and the salaries, bonuses, or other benefits to corporation executives were not the business either of the union, the government, or the public. Reuther had shrewdly put General Motors on the spot by offering to reduce the wage demands from thirty per cent to one per cent if the corporation would agree to make no increase to the public in prices and to reveal fully and frankly whatever hidden profits to management had been made. The union leader pointed out that increased wages would be meaningless if prices skyrocketed and that such wage increases would do great harm to the American economy. General Motors promptly and indignantly refused this offer.

During the General Motors dispute I learned a lot about how shrewd corporation lawyers can enable management to concentrate control of American industry in the hands of a small oligarchy at the expense of stockholders and workers. Certain General Motors stockholders, dissatisfied with the manner in which the business of the company was being conducted, had appealed to the courts for redress. Such impudence was rebuked and safeguards against its repetition set up, by revision of the corporation's rules so that virtually dictatorial power was given to a handful of top executives. The result was a situation which made those whose money had been invested in the company through the purchase of stock even more impotent than the workers. At least the latter had the strength which comes from being organized.

Our committee had no official status, nor was there any compulsion upon any party to the dispute to pay any attention to us. General Motors was asked to produce such witnesses as it wished heard and to submit whatever documentary evidence it cared to prepare. We were amazed at the ineptitude of the corporation from the standpoint of public relations. It refused to send any witness, which of course it had a perfect right to do, while at the same time it submitted a substantial mass of data in the form of printed reports and mimeographed statements, most of which it would have been greatly to the advantage of the corporation to have withheld.

Although I had made it my business for many years to read as widely as time permitted available material on labor-management relations in the United States, the attitude of General Motors as presented by its spokesmen was a distinct shock to me. I knew that General Motors was not only one of the most powerful corporations in human history, but also one of the more enlightened units of our modern industrial society. If its attitude toward not only its employees but the public as well was so intransigent, the even more arrogant attitudes of less enlightened corporations pointed toward ever-increasing conflict. I wondered as I listened to the testimony how long a system of free enterprise could last under such conditions. What I heard and saw during those days at Detroit convinced me that there was little hope of industrial democracy if we continued the conflict of the immovable object of stubborn employers with the irresistible force of aroused organized labor.

I also learned much at first hand of the terrific stresses and strains within the labor movement. Reuther was then emerging as the most vocal and implacable enemy of communism in the trade-union movement generally and in the United Automobile Workers in particular. Pitted against him was a small but powerful coalition which sought control of the union either because of political beliefs, personal ambitions, or honest disagreement with Reuther's opinions and tactics. It was obvious that some of the members of this opposing faction would gladly have seen the negotiations fail rather than see Reuther with his anti-Communist views emerge victor and thereby become a more powerful figure in American affairs.

XXVIII

No Social Experiments, Please!

Crushing defeats suffered by the Allied armies in Europe and the Pacific and the dire possibilities of the entire world being conquered by Hitler and Hirohito had little discernible effect on race prejudice in the United States. During the dark days immediately following Pearl Harbor bitterness against the Japanese seemed to find expression in Southern communities through acts of violence against Negro soldiers. It became increasingly apparent that as long as white and Negro soldiers were kept in rigidly segregated units the chasm of racial bitterness and misunderstanding would be steadily widened. As long as Frank Knox was Secretary of the Navy, where colored Americans were permitted to serve only in the messmen's division, no change of the status of Negroes in that service was considered.

Some progress was made in the Army, due primarily to the attitudes and efforts of Robert P. Patterson, Under Secretary of War, and William H. Hastie, Civilian Aide to the Secretary of War. I made a proposal to General George C. Marshall, then Chief of Staff, in December 1941, which had the sympathetic support of Mr. Patterson and some others in the War Department and which, had it been adopted, I am convinced would have set a new and successful pattern of democracy. I urged the creation of a volunteer Army division open to all Americans irrespective of race, creed, color, or national origin. I was not naïve enough to believe that a Regular Army division free of segregation could be established without friction, during the tension of war. I knew that if men were forced against their will into Army units with those against whom they held strong prejudices, there would be clashes, some of them deliberately fomented, which would defeat the whole experiment.

This was not idle speculation on my part. There had been many instances to prove that there were young Americans gravely bestirred by the conflict inherent in their country's declaration that it was fighting a war against dangerous Nazi racial theories, while a similar racial philosophy dominated our Army and Navy. Roger Starr, a handsome young white New Yorker and Yale graduate, had written the War Department for permission to serve in a Negro regiment. He wanted thereby to contribute his bit to the elimination of racial segregation, since his presence as a white man would make the all-Negro regiment at least a token mixed unit. Mr. Starr's idealistic and gallant gesture was widely publicized in the press. Almost immediately he was inundated with letters from other young white men, including a number from the South, applauding the stand he had taken and pledging themselves to follow his example.

I had the opportunity to see another dramatic demonstration of the eagerness of young white Americans to do something tangible on this question. I was invited to deliver the mid-year convocation address at the University of California at Berkeley. Just before leaving for California I was told by friends in the War Department that if a sufficient number of prospective soldiers indicated their desire to serve in a mixed division the chances of the establishment of such a unit would be greatly increased.

At Berkeley, after an eloquent introduction by Dr. Robert Gordon Sproul, president of the University of California, I spoke to a vast audience of several thousand students, faculty members, and others. I mentioned with elaborate casualness the proposal I had just made to the War Department of a nonsegregated division. No sooner had the meeting ended than an avalanche of young men poured down upon me from the great amphitheater. The first student to speak was a blond, tousleheaded young giant of a Southerner, whose accent was so thick that even I as a native of Georgia had difficulty in understanding him. But there was no mistaking the gleam of idealism in his eye.

"Ah want to be the first as a native of Jawja to volunteah for

ah mixed division," he said, his words tumbling forth in his eagerness. "A lettah will be too slow—Ah'm goin' to telegraph the Wah
Depahtment."

All my associates and I encountered the same reaction wherever we
went. Not long after the speaking engagement at the University of
California I talked at a student conference at Campobello Island at
which were present representatives of a large number of universities
and colleges from all over the United States. Every student there
was delighted to find a concrete means of implementation of his faith
and belief in democracy and his opposition to the color line.

But the War Department was not moved. Despite the best efforts
of Robert Patterson and a few others, including a general from Arkansas, the tradition-bound and prejudice-indoctrinated majority felt
that "we must not indulge in social experimentation in time of war."
One of my letters was coldly dismissed by Major General E. S.
Adams, at that time Adjutant General of the Army, with the curt
statement that "your comments have been made a matter of official
record for such reference as circumstances may warrant." In answer
to a request that a conference be held on the subject, General Adams
wrote six days later that "the War Department does not contemplate
the organization of a division such as suggested, and consequently a
conference on the subject is not deemed necessary."

The cowardice of the War Department and of the government generally in this and other instances continued despite a steadily mounting
number of racial clashes. In Beaumont, Texas, policemen followed a
Negro soldier, Charles Reco, after he had debarked from a bus to
avoid an argument with the driver, and shot him in the back, killing
him instantly. Louisiana state troopers killed in cold blood Private
Raymond Carr and were not even reprimanded, despite a mass of evidence that the killing was wholly without provocation. Lieutenant
Nora Green, an Army nurse stationed at the Tuskegee Army Air
Forces training school, boarded a bus in Montgomery after a shopping tour in preparation for overseas duty. She was ordered by the
driver to get out of the bus because it was a "white" bus. When she
refused she was badly beaten and thrown into jail, where she was
confined until three the next morning, when she was released upon
payment of a fine. When we protested to the War Department and

the Department of Justice, Lieutenant Green was ordered not to talk about it, and the case was hushed up.

A selected group of Negro officers and soldiers from the famous 368th Infantry Regiment was returned to the United States from the Pacific and sent as cadres to a camp in South Georgia. When they arrived, a deliberate campaign was instituted to "teach them their place," in view of the fact that they were from the North, and show them that they must conform to the Southern pattern of Negro behavior and accept the treatment to which Southern Negroes are accustomed. One officer of the Coast Artillery went so far as to issue an order providing the death penalty for any Negro soldier a party to "relations between white and colored males and females whether voluntary or not." Even the War Department thought this went too far and issued an order, when we protested the action, declaring that "the order was found to be contrary to the purport of verbal orders of the regimental commander, who has caused the order to be withdrawn."

Courts-martial of Negro service men both within the continental United States and overseas increasingly became a weapon against men believed by prejudiced superiors to be too "militant."

We protested in season and out of season as we saw a storm approaching, but to little avail. The spinelessness of Army and Navy policy became even more inexplicable as hundreds of Northern white soldiers in Southern camps voiced their bitter opposition to treatment of their Negro comrades in arms and urged the abolition of segregation and discrimination. But their protests were as futile as ours.

The most severe jolt to Washington complacency came when William H. Hastie resigned as Civilian Aide to the Secretary of War in protest against the continued policy of discrimination in the Army Air Forces. Judge Hastie wrote a brilliant series of articles which we released to the press and published later in pamphlet form. The arguments he presented were so carefully documented and unanswerable that they served as an excellent focal point of the growing resentment among both Negro and white Americans against the system of segregation.

XXIX

Machine Guns and Tear Gas in Detroit

Meanwhile segregationist hysteria in civil life increased. Our fears of explosion as a result of unchecked violence against Negroes and the pent-up bitterness these attacks engendered began to be realized in 1942, and spread with dismaying frequency during the following year.

Detroit was the stage of two of these outbreaks. The first of them was a dispute over the question of whether whites or Negroes would occupy Sojourner Truth Homes, a federally financed housing project which had been named after the famous Negro abolitionist. When vacillating Washington eventually decided on Negro occupancy, mobs of whites attacked Negro tenants as they moved into the project, smashing furniture and brutally beating men, women, and children. Detroit policemen stood by idly and raised no hand to protect Negroes.

But the Sojourner Truth riot was but a mild prelude to the disorders which took place the following year.

Early in June 1943, some twenty-five thousand employees of the Packard plant, which was manufacturing Rolls-Royce engines for American bombers and marine engines for the famous P-T boats, struck in protest against the upgrading of three Negroes. It was a wildcat strike bitterly opposed by the UAW-CIO. R. J. Thomas, at the time president of the union, had charged that the fomenters of the strike were members of the Ku Klux Klan, which though few in number were exceedingly and bitterly active in fighting the employ-

ment and promotion of Negro workers despite a desperate labor shortage. I had seen evidence of the accuracy of Thomas's charges. One
night as the shifts of workers changed, I listened to a fiery orator
with a thick Southern accent haranguing a crowd in front of one of
the gates to the Packard plant.

"I'd rather see Hitler and Hirohito win the war than work beside
a nigger on the assembly line," he screamed.

Not only the Klan but a number of other organizations such as the
National Workers League, followers of Gerald L. K. Smith and Father
Coughlin, the Southern Voters League, certain Polish Catholic priests
and their followers, and remnants of the notorious Black Legion, had
industriously utilized anti-Negro and other prejudices in the same
manner as the Nazis had utilized anti-Semitism in Germany. None of
these organizations was numerically strong, but they made up in
venom and aggressiveness for their lack of size.

But not all of those responsible for the Detroit riot belonged to the
lunatic fringe. Preceding and during the Packard strike the personnel
manager and the general foreman of the Packard plant had openly
urged the strikers to hold out in their demand against the employment or promotion of Negroes. Although no attempt was made by
such individuals to conceal their activities or opinions, no disciplinary
action was taken against them by the Packard Motor Car Company.
Similar conditions existed in other Detroit plants.

Even more disheartening was the failure of most of the top-ranking
industrialists to manifest any concern with the spreading of hate, the
incredibly bad housing, recreation, and transportation facilities, or
any of the other evils to which their Negro workers were subjected.

Early on Monday morning, June 21st, I was wakened by a telephone call from the president of our branch in Detroit. The long-
expected riot had come. A few hours later I was on a plane. The
drive into the city from Detroit airport was marked by fleeting
glimpses of mobs roaming the streets in search of Negro victims.

The trouble had started on the previous night at Belle Isle, a mu-
nicipally owned recreation park. On a crowded bridge, two automobiles, one driven by a white Detroiter and the other by a Negro, had
collided. It was a steaming hot night and the tempers of the two
drivers were short. The quarrel which followed did not last long,

but it immediately set off a fantastic variety of dangerous rumors.

In the white sections of Detroit a story was industriously spread that a Negro had raped a white woman on Belle Isle and that Negroes were rioting at the resort. In Negro Detroit the rumor spread like a a prairie fire that white sailors had thrown a Negro woman and her baby into the lake at Belle Isle and that police were beating innocent Negroes.

A white mob invaded the Roxy Theater on Woodward Avenue to drag out Negro patrons and beat them. Other mobs stoned automobiles driven by Negroes, stopping them and also streetcars to pull out Negro passengers, who were beaten, stabbed, or shot. Meanwhile policemen stood by and made no effort to check the assaults. Within a few hours nearly all of Detroit was a battlefield, the exceptions being those areas in which Negroes and whites lived as neighbors. One Detroit policeman diverted automobiles driven by Negroes and ordered them to detour to Woodward Avenue, where mobs were waiting. Not even in the South had I ever seen so total a breakdown of law enforcement machinery. Not only the police officers but Mayor Jeffries and Police Commissioner Witherspoon were as inactive in checking the mob as were the peace officers under their command.

It was apparent to anyone that the rioting would not be stopped by the local officials. Judge Ira W. Jayne of the Wayne County Circuit Court, who has served for many years as a member of the NAACP board of directors, arranged an interview for me with Governor Harry S. Kelly. I asked Governor Kelly to request federal troops, because it was evident that the sporadic rioting in open daylight would be greatly increased with the coming of nightfall.

But neither Governor Kelly nor any of the city officials acted with vigor and promptness. I therefore telephoned the War Department at Washington who told me that an official would have to get in touch with the Commanding General of the area, stationed at Chicago. I passed this information on to the Governor, the phone call was finally made, and federal troops reached the city at nightfall, a curfew was established, and order was restored.

But the thirty hours of rioting had cost Detroit thirty-four lives, injuries to more than six hundred persons, the destruction of a million dollars' worth of property, and the almost complete stoppage of war production during the period of rioting. Of the thirty-four killed, twenty-five were Negroes, seventeen of them killed by policemen. More than three-fourths of the six hundred injured were colored. But eighty-five per cent of the 1,832 persons arrested were Negroes who had been the attacked instead of the attackers. The police charged most of the Negroes they killed with looting. It is true that there was a considerable amount of wanton lawlessness by some Negroes. Penned in ghettos from which their color barred them from escape, two hundred thousand Negroes occupied virtually the same areas in which one-quarter of that number had lived twenty years before. Maddened by the long series of unchecked and unrebuked assaults upon them, some of the Negroes during the rioting took the only vengeance simple minds could find under the circumstances—smashing the windows of white stores in the Negro districts and pillaging the establishments. But the looting was not confined to Negroes. At the height of the rioting a white policeman was seen carrying two large cans of lard from a store, which he placed in the police car he was driving, presumably to take to his home. There were many instances of similar thefts.

But there were instances, too, of heroism by both whites and Negroes.

Three white sailors recklessly plunged into a mob of more than a hundred whites to rescue the helpless Negro who was being beaten to death. Their faces bloody and their uniforms torn to shreds, the three sailors fought so ably that they succeeded in rescuing the victim.

The Detroit superintendent of schools told me another story of courage and cowardice on a Woodward Avenue streetcar. A police captain boarded the car with several patrolmen to announce that a mob was lying in wait near by and that he would take into custody the eight Negroes aboard the car and protect them. Four of the Negroes accepted the offer—and were promptly turned over to the mob to be beaten to death. The four colored men who chose to take their chances by remaining aboard the streetcar were saved when they crouched on the floor and were covered by the skirts of sympathetic white women.

In a town gone mad, Negroes were as gallant in protecting their white friends from infuriated Negroes. A white druggist operating a store in the heart of the Negro district was safely conducted by a Negro doctor to the edge of the Negro area. There were many instances of Negroes defending their white neighbors and white neighbors protecting Negro friends in the sections of the city where there was no racial segregation in housing. Equally remarkable was the attitude in the automobile and other plants where Negro and white trade unionists had learned to be friends. There were no instances of fighting or other friction within the plants even as rioting raged in the streets outside.

Thurgood Marshall joined me in Detroit the second day of the riot and, with the assistance of investigators we brought from New York, we set about the difficult task of getting the facts, attempting to stimulate city and state officials to action, and allaying the fears of the Negro community. Fortunately we had a large and active branch of the NAACP in Detroit, whose able executive secretary, Gloster Current, was an indefatigable worker. Two other members of our national office staff, Daisy Lampkin and Lucille Black, were also in Detroit at the time assisting in the annual membership campaign.

With the assistance of our local branch we set up headquarters in the basement of the colored YMCA in the heart of the Negro ghetto near the City Hall. The Wolverine Bar Association and the Detroit chapter of the National Lawyers Guild volunteered their aid in interviewing and counseling the seemingly unending number of bandaged, bewildered, and angered Negroes who passed through the office seeking help. Not long afterward I was destined to see bombed-out victims of Nazi terror in Europe. In Detroit I found the same bewilderment at senseless human cruelty on the faces of Negro victims of the same foul hate which Hitler had spewed upon Europe and the world. Men, women, and even children told us their stories of violence inflicted upon them not only by members of the mob but also by Michigan state troopers and the Detroit police.

There was the story, for example, of what happened on Monday night to Negroes living in the crowded Vernor Apartments. A Detroit policeman had been shot and slightly wounded by a Negro who was then killed by another police officer. We were never able to find out why the state and city police connected this shooting with the Vernor Apartments, other than that they were occupied by Negroes. Police searchlights lighted up the building as though it were a Hollywood stage setting. Then the police began riddling the building with machine guns, revolvers, rifles, and deerguns. Tear gas was shot into the building to force the terrified tenants to evacuate it. It was a terrible sight when men, women, and children who had escaped death only by throwing themselves flat on the floors of the building emerged, some of them wounded, with hands high in the air at the orders of the heavily armed policemen. The helpless victims were beaten by officers as every obscene gutter phrase was hurled at them.

The destruction which had not been total up to that point from bullets was then completed when police smashed locks and doors, ransacked the apartments, and took whatever money, jewelry, or other items of value they wanted. Thurgood Marshall remarked when we went to the Vernor Apartments after the police had completed their destruction that the building "resembles a battlefield." This was a masterpiece of understatement.

The following night, around ten o'clock, forty-six hours after the initial outbreak at Belle Isle, a squad car of state policemen drove up to the colored YMCA and searched every resident of the institution, as well as passers-by, for weapons. When none was found, the Negroes were permitted to go on their way. As the last of them entered the building, one called to a friend, "Hi, Ridley!" One of the state policemen, who afterward said that the Negro had called out, "Heil Hitler!" jumped out of the police car in which he had been sitting, put one foot on the bottom step of the building entrance to steady his aim, and began firing into the building, seriously wounding one of the Negroes in the lobby. Two policemen entered the building and forced all the men in the lobby, and the desk clerk, to stand along the wall with hands above their heads. They were struck repeatedly and otherwise mistreated as the officers again searched them. The YMCA employees were forced to open all locked drawers and were threatened with death if they did not comply immediately. When no weapons were found, the police departed, leaving it to the YMCA officials to get the wounded to hospitals.

Thurgood and I worked incessantly to get the state authorities to take some action against the state policeman and his fellow officers for their wanton brutality. We were never able even to have them queried or reprimanded, much less punished.

A committee of local citizens accompanied me to present to Mayor Jeffries the evidence which had been gathered. The Mayor's office was a large room with his desk near a row of windows through which one could see the grimy public square. We were seated at a long table in one corner of the office while the Mayor talked with a young sailor. But Mayor Jeffries kept looking at us with quick glances as he prolonged the conversation, in which it was not difficult to read his reluctance to hear from us the evidence we had come to present. When at last he could prolong the interview with the sailor no further, he walked hesitantly across the room to where we sat. He fingered gingerly the mass of material I handed him as he complained that it was too much for him to read at the time and discuss with the delegation. I told him that he was not expected to read it at once, but that I would summarize it if he wished. In a manner which seemed to indicate that he didn't want to listen to any of it, Mayor Jeffries asked me if I could not come back to see him "sometime next week."

On no occasion have I ever felt time so completely wasted as I did on leaving Detroit City Hall that afternoon.

No balm in Gilead was ever more soothing than the reaction to the Detroit massacre which I found on my return to New York. Mayor LaGuardia summoned me to Gracie Mansion with a group of others to hear the report of two New York City police officials, one Negro and one white, who had been sent to Detroit by the Mayor to observe the manner in which the police force there had handled the riot and to devise means of preventing repetition in New York City of the mistakes which had been made in Detroit. We did not know how soon those plans were to be needed in New York City itself.

No sooner had I returned to the office than a request was made for me to meet with a group of distinguished persons in the theater and radio world who were eager to find some means of making known their opposition to race riots.

A resourceful and energetic young woman by the name of June Blythe, a member of the publicity and promotion staff at RKO, was the moving spirit and indefatigable worker in this push for a program through which well-known figures in the entertainment world could utilize their influence to create a countersentiment to mobbism. So shocked had many of these stars been by the brutality of the Detroit riot that they were willing to do everything possible to prevent its repetition.

We formed the Emergency Committee of the Entertainment Industry. Our first task was that of attempting to arrange a coast-to-coast broadcast, utilizing services which would have cost many tens of thousands of dollars had it been on any other than a voluntary basis. This was almost our undoing. So many top-flight artists offered to appear that there would have been time only to list their names, which would not have made a very entertaining show. We finally decided to do a reenactment of some episodes of the riot, with a brief speech by an outstanding American. William N. Robson of CBS agreed to write the script. We supplied him with the facts and in the meantime arranged an interview with Wendell Willkie to ask his support and participation. Aline McMahon came into New York from the country for this purpose on an oppressively sultry day.

Willkie agreed almost instantly to appear on the program. He and Bill Robson and I worked on revisions of the script until it was as good as we could make it. We then faced the question of free time at a good hour on the air, since the committee had no money. The Columbia Broadcasting System gave us a half hour on the evening of July 10th. When William S. Paley read the script he became so enthusiastic that CBS broke precedent by officially sponsoring the broadcast. This was, so far as I know, the first instance of a radio network's taking an editorial position on a controversial issue of this sort. There was understandable apprehension by CBS and by ourselves as to the reception the broadcast would receive in Detroit and in Southern cities. To our delight the overwhelming majority of comments were favorable, and the program was given the Peabody Award by the University of Georgia as the best program of its type for the year.

During its unfortunately short life the Emergency Committee of the Entertainment Industry drafted a code with respect to the treatment of minorities on the stage, radio, and screen which has materially affected these entertainment media. I have always regretted that this committee, which was strictly nonpolitical but at the same time deeply concerned with implementing American protestations of democracy, was forced to disband because of lack of staff and money. Some of those who were active included: Herman Shumlin, Jane Cowl, Aline McMahon, Billy Rose, Maxwell Anderson, Jean Arthur, Tallulah Bankhead, Ralph Bellamy, Erskine Caldwell, Ilka Chase, Duke Ellington, William Feinberg, John Garfield, Benny Goodman, Max Gordon, George Heller, Lillian Hellman, Jean Hersholt, James Hilton, Miriam Hopkins, Lena Horne, Thomas Mann, Groucho Marx, Ralph Morgan, Jean Muir, Paul Muni, Arch Oboler, Elmer Rice, Paul Robeson, Edward G. Robinson, Jonas Rosenthal, Robert Rossen, Lawrence Tibbett, Walter Wanger, and Orson Welles.

XXX

Harlem Boils Over

On Sunday night, August 1, 1943, I went to bed early, exhausted in mind and body by three speaking engagements that day. I told Gladys that I did not want to be disturbed under any circumstances, even if President Roosevelt or Cleopatra called. I had been asleep only a few minutes when one of the members of our staff, Lucille Black, telephoned. Gladys told her of my request not to be disturbed and asked her to call back the next morning.

"But does Mr. White know there is a riot going on in Harlem?" Lucille asked.

Five minutes later I was dressed and ready to leave the house when Mayor LaGuardia phoned asking me to meet him as quickly as possible at the West 123rd Street police station. Roy Wilkins joined me in the lobby and we took a cab to 125th Street and Seventh Avenue, where the worst of the rioting was then centered. Neither of us thought of it at the time we left the house, but it was fortunate for me that Roy was in the same taxicab. As we rode down Seventh Avenue we could hear the smashing of plate glass windows and the roar of the crowd, as far north as 135th Street. We saw Negroes attempting to get at white people in automobiles who, unaware of the riot, had driven into the heart of it. Our cab got through safely because Roy's brown skin saved us from attack.

Mayor LaGuardia and Police Commissioner Louis Valentine were already at the police station when we reached it. With the energy and resourcefulness which made him so great a mayor of New York, LaGuardia had ordered all available police officers into the Harlem area and had telephoned Governor's Island for military police to get all soldiers and sailors out of Harlem. But unfortunately Governor's Island was sending only white MP's, and the temper of the crowds had already reached such a peak of frenzy that I feared mobs would attack them. I suggested to the Mayor that he telephone Governor's Island again to send an equal number of colored MP's and to issue instructions that they be assigned to work in racially mixed pairs. This was done and there was no instance of any trouble. Negroes could not object as violently, even to the use of force, if one of the two MP's handling a recalcitrant Negro soldier happened also to be a Negro.

Like many riots, this one had been caused by a wholly false rumor: that a Negro soldier had been shot in the back and killed without cause by a white policeman. There is in Harlem a hotel whose reputation has been questionable back to the days when that section of New York City was inhabited by whites. Unaware of its reputation, the mother of a Negro soldier stationed in New Jersey had gone there on Saturday night to await the arrival of her son from camp early the next morning. The soldier had brought his fiancée to the hotel for breakfast with his mother, after which the three had gone to church, visited friends, spent several pleasant hours at a moving picture theater, and then returned to the hotel to pick up the mother's luggage for her return home.

That afternoon a group of men and women had rented a room in the hotel for a drinking party. One of the women became intoxicated and boisterous. As the soldier with his mother and fiancée entered the lobby, the drunken woman was arguing vociferously with a policeman who was stationed on the premises because the hotel had been raided previously. The policeman in line with his duty was attempting to quiet the obstreperous female who was becoming increasingly abusive, as she appealed to other guests to "protect me from this white man!"

Not thoroughly informed nor understanding what was going on, the soldier remonstrated with the policeman who curtly advised him to mind his own business. Both men became angry and the policeman brandished his blackjack. The soldier seized the blackjack and started to run, whereupon the policeman, an inexperienced rookie, drew his revolver and shot the service man in the shoulder.

Under normal conditions the episode would have caused no more commotion than the average altercation that occurs in a huge city like New York scores of times daily. But conditions were far from normal in Harlem that sweltering summer night. A steady stream of letters had poured into the mailboxes of relatives and friends from Camp Stewart, Georgia, written by men of the 369th Infantry and telling of gratuitous insults and beatings and humiliations suffered by men who had fought in the Pacific and had been returned home to train other fighters. Not only Harlem's newspapers but the daily press had been filled with countless stories of lynchings and mistreatment of Negro soldiers. Long Island airplane factories and other war industries were begging for men and women workers, but those with black skins were daily told contemptuously that they were not wanted. These conditions existed while Harlem radios pleaded around the clock for Americans to do their utmost to win the war.

This was the caldron of brooding misery and frustration into which the rumor of another black soldier "murdered without provocation" was dropped. Down from the fire escapes where men and women sought futilely for a breath of fresh air, and out of the old-law tenements where color prejudice and poverty had packed human beings like sardines, poured an angry stream of Negroes. Fresh in their memories were the riots of Detroit and Beaumont, Texas, and the gory tales of black men hunted like wild beasts and killed. Symbols of a cruel and oppressive white world were the shiny plate-glass windows of the stores along 125th Street whose patronage was almost entirely Negro but many of which had refused bluntly to give employment to Negroes however qualified. Whatever missile could be found went hurtling through the windows, and the sound of crashing glass was like strong drink to the mob.

A strange and to me highly significant phenomenon was the fact that at the beginning of the riot, that is, from around ten P.M. on Sunday night until the early hours of the next morning, there was little looting. It was only after the first rage had spent itself that the looters became active. Throughout that first night food and clothing lay in tempting profusion behind smashed windows accessible to hordes of men and women who all their lives had been forced

to work long hours at miserable pay to earn enough for bare sub-
sistence. But the crowds, inflamed by injustice, real and fancied,
were beyond greed, and their berserk rage found expression only in
lashing out at the symbols of the hostile world which hemmed
them in.

When the MP's had arrived and were sent out in pairs to round
up service men, and assignments had been given to the steady stream
of police officers who poured into the 28th Precinct Police Station,
LaGuardia suggested that he and I go on a tour of the area. Police
Commissioner Valentine wanted to assign a squad car to precede
and one to follow the Mayor's car for protection. The impetuous
Mayor refused to wait the two or three minutes it would have taken
to arrange this. I attempted to induce LaGuardia to sit between me
and the driver of the one-seat police car to avoid possible injury to
the Mayor in the more exposed position. I was concerned not only
for his sake, but also because I knew and feared the terrible publicity
all Negroes would receive if any harm befell a man so well-known
and beloved. But the Mayor would have none of this arrangement.

"They know my face better than yours," he ordered me, "so you
sit in the middle."

Along Fifth, Lenox, and Madison Avenues north of 125th Street
wild-eyed men and women, whose poverty was pathetically obvious
in their shabbiness, roamed the streets, screaming imprecations. I
thought of the stories I had read of the French Revolution when
the starved hordes had poured from the sewers and slums of Paris,
shouting their hatred of oppression and oppressors. As we drove up
Lenox Avenue we heard the crash of a brick against a store front
and LaGuardia ordered the policeman to drive us to the spot. Although it took us but a minute or two to reach the scene, a fire
broke out inside the store before the car came to a stop. Heedless
of his own safety, LaGuardia jumped from the car and screamed at
the crowd before the building. I doubt that in the excitement the
Mayor was recognized, but such was the fury with which he lashed
out at the marauders that his moral indignation shamed and quieted
the crowd, which rapidly dispersed.

It was apparent to me that the situation was becoming increasingly
dangerous and that one-man campaigns to restore sanity, even when

conducted by as popular a figure as Mayor LaGuardia, could not stop the madness which had seized the community. I suggested to the Mayor that he order to Harlem city-owned sound trucks and that we get well-known Negro citizens to ride the streets of the area to appeal to the people to stop rioting and go home, explaining that the rumor which touched off the disorder was false. LaGuardia thought this a good idea and asked us to round up as many well-known citizens of Harlem as possible. Roy and I got on the telephone, to learn to our disappointment that many of those we wanted, such as Duke Ellington, Adam Powell, Joe Louis, and Cab Calloway, were out of the city. But we got the Reverend John H. Johnson, rector of St. Martin's Protestant Episcopal Church; Parole Commissioner Samuel Battle; and Ferdinand Smith, secretary of the National Maritime Union.

Smith and I rode one sound truck together. Up Eighth Avenue from 123rd to 155th Street we cruised where the crowds were densest and angriest. Over and over again, as the huge vehicle nosed its way through crowded streets, we repeated our plea: "The rumor is false that a Negro soldier was killed at the Braddock Hotel tonight. He is only slightly wounded and is in no danger. Go to your homes! Don't form mobs or break the law! Don't destroy in one night the reputation as good citizens you have taken a lifetime to build! Go home—now!"

During our first trip up Eighth Avenue our pleas were greeted with raucous shouts of disbelief, frequently couched in language as violent as the action of the window-smashers. I remember particularly one giant of a man who stood on the sidewalk, his clenched fists raised in frenzied anger, and from whose face all semblance of patience had been stripped, leaving bare the fears and bitternesses which his dark skin had brought upon him. His voice was as loud as his body was big and strong, and the imprecations he hurled at us almost drowned the lesser voices of the others. He was still there when we came back down Eighth Avenue half an hour later, his upthrust arms still betokened his rage, but I fancied his face was slightly calmer and his language had diminished from obscenity to colorful profanity. The third time I saw him he was silent and his arms hung limply at his sides as he listened again to our statement that no Negro soldier had been killed that afternoon in Harlem.

Sheer repetition seemed to have its effect; on the second half of the second round trip, the giant was shouting to the thinning crowds to go home.

I began to notice also the cessation or at least the diminishing of another sound which had puzzled me—a rat-tat-tat on the roof of the sound truck as we moved into dense groups on the streets. It was the sound of missiles thrown at us from rooftops and windows of the tenements which lined Eighth Avenue and made it a canyon of poverty and sordid misery.

Toward morning the looters who always take advantage of disorder began to appear, especially from the more poverty-stricken areas east of Lenox Avenue. I remember especially a toothless old woman in front of a grocery store who moved about the edge of a crowd which had just smashed a store window. In one hand she clutched two grimy pillow cases which apparently she had snatched from the bed in which she had been sleeping. With the other hand she held the arm of a fourteen- or fifteen-year-old boy, possibly a grandson. The minute an opening appeared in the crowd the old woman, with an agility surprising in one of her age and emaciated appearance, climbed through the broken glass into the store window to fill the pillow cases with canned goods and cereals which lay in scattered disorder. When the bags were filled she turned toward the street and looked toward the police car in which LaGuardia and I were sitting. Exultation, vengeance, the supreme satisfaction of having secured food for a few days, lighted her face, and then I looked at the sleepy-eyed child by her side. I felt nausea that an abundant society like America's could so degrade and starve a human being, and I was equally sickened to contemplate the kind of man the boy would become under such conditions.

By daylight the fury of the mob had spent itself. Mayor La-Guardia and I went on the air in a broadcast to tell a startled New York what had happened. Over and over again the Mayor emphasized that the disorder had not been a race riot and to point out that no white person had been attacked nor had any white mob attempted to form. Both of us stated that resentment at the mistreatment of Negro soldiers, overcrowding, exorbitant rents, insufficient recreational facilities for both children and adults, poverty, and job proscription had caused the outbreak and that nothing could prevent its repetition except correction of these evils. Both press and radio handled the riot in the same sober and realistic fashion. I was amazed and delighted at the frequency of comment, ranging from husky taxi drivers to city officials, who said that they wondered why such an explosion had not occurred sooner considering the conditions under which the Negroes of Harlem lived.

Toward morning scores of prisoners were brought into the 28th Precinct station. Doctor Johnson, Mayor LaGuardia, Commissioner Valentine, and I stood behind the desk watching the faces of the prisoners as they were booked. I have lived in Harlem since 1918, but I had never seen such concentrated despair as I witnessed that morning. Their anger spent, the men, women, and children were pathetic specimens of humanity as the consequences of their acts loomed before them. The loot which had been captured with them steadily mounted in the large lobby of the police station—clothing and household furnishings and food—particularly food. The majority of the citizens of Harlem awoke that morning stupefied at what had happened the night before because most of them had been at home in bed before the outbreak, totally unaware of the rioting.

The streets of Harlem where the rioting had been fiercest were a distressing sight in the glare of daylight. Ministers, social workers, newspapermen, housewives, and others, sickened with the disgrace which had been brought upon New York City and Negro citizens, begged to be assigned tasks to repair as far as possible the damage that had been done. We were faced with the immediate problem of getting food and particularly milk for children into the area where only a few of the stores were undamaged or unlooted. Some merchants whose property had escaped damage were fearful of opening their stores. It was significant that in the majority of cases those who had not been molested were the establishments which had not attempted to sell inferior goods at exorbitant prices and whose employment policies had been more liberal.

Under Mayor LaGuardia's chairmanship a hastily arranged committee, through the New York City Department of Markets, made provisions for stocking the stores in Harlem with immediate necessities. It was not until late afternoon that we dared leave the scene to go to our homes to get baths and hot food and rest. Again on Monday night we patroled the streets which were then as quiet and empty as the financial district of lower Broadway on a Sunday morning.

As is usually the case, there were many meetings and conferences after the riot was over to discuss its causes and cures. The City-Wide Citizens Committee on Harlem was formed; it functioned for several years and did achieve some results in obtaining jobs for Negroes and in keeping before the consciousness of the people of New York the issues involved.

Algernon Black, leader of the Ethical Culture Society, and I were cochairmen for a while until the pressure of other work made it necessary for me to relinquish the responsibility. When I had to resign Dr. Black expressed his regret, saying, "The Black-White Committee is an ideal combination, especially since the man named 'Black' is white and the man named 'White' is black—or calls himself black."

But despite the efforts of individuals and organizations there has been little change in the basic causes of the 1943 riot in the thousands of Harlems—North and South—in the United States. Thrift of Negroes has been penalized by the attitude of banks, insurance companies, and investment corporations with respect to mortgages and other loans for improvement of housing in Harlem or other segregated areas in New York City. Restrictive covenants in deeds to property and the pressures of landlords and real estate agents continue to make it difficult if not impossible for Negroes, whatever their financial or cultural status, to purchase or rent property outside the ghetto. Amazingly and dishearteningly true is the fact that such covenants against Negroes have been used by members of other minorities who are themselves often the target of restrictive covenants.

More progress of a permanent nature has been made in the field of employment, but it is still a far higher hurdle for trained Negroes to utilize their training than for other Americans to do so. Yet I can see considerable progress when I look back at the situation in 1918 when I first arrived in New York. Today there are many more Americans who are aware that they too have a stake in the finding of a solution to the problem of the treatment of minorities in the United States and the world at large.

XXIX

"I Seen Them Work"

I found myself during this period increasingly eager to go overseas to learn at first hand the facts about the clashes between white and Negro American soldiers which seeped through to us despite war-time censorship. Occasionally a brief and cryptic item would be published in American newspapers concerning the more serious of these disorders; and between the lines of letters which we received from both Negro and white service men it was evident that the number of such conflicts was far greater than any of us knew with certainty. I made application to the War Department for permission to go overseas in any capacity which would permit me to travel freely and talk with whomever I chose. There were many delays, discussions, inoculations, papers to be filled out, and repetitious farewells, as day after day I expected orders to report to the air-field, but finally, on January 2, 1944, I left America for England as a war correspondent.

No sooner had I been billeted in a small hotel in the outskirts of London than newspaper correspondents swooped down upon me to ask if it were true that I had come overseas as a special investigator for the White House. The more vehemently I denied the rumor, the more skeptical some of them became. I was never able to learn who in the War Department had sent word of my coming and, apparently, warned that I be "handled carefully." It was obvious from the beginning that wherever I went and with whomever I talked, my every movement was closely watched. It was equally apparent that quite elaborate efforts were being made to steer me away from areas where there had been racial clashes and to keep me from talking with those, both white and Negro, who wanted to tell me what they knew.

But there were notable exceptions. Soon after I arrived in London, Major General John C. H. Lee invited me to dinner. On arriving at his flat I found that General Lee had also invited top-ranking officers of the Service of Supply to talk frankly about the problems which some prejudiced white American officers and enlisted men had created in the European Theater of Operations. Among them was Colonel Roy Lord, who later became Major General Lord because of his quiet genius in handling vast numbers of men and quantities of war materials. There were present those in charge of Special Service (which later became Information and Education), and those dealing with legal, security, and other phases of the vast operation necessary to a global war. There was my old friend, Jock Lawrence, whom I had known in Hollywood, who had just been made Chief of Army Public Relations.

General Lee talked with refreshing frankness about the dangerous situation between white and Negro American soldiers which was slowing up preparations for the invasion of Normandy and making us as a nation exceedingly unpopular with the British. General Lee told the officers that I should be given access to whatever areas, individuals, or documents I wished to see to permit me to get at the truth and to recommend corrective action. General Lee assigned Captain Max Gilstrap of his staff to act as my guide and put at my disposal a staff car and chauffeur. The next morning he sent an order to the commanding officers of areas and base sections to permit me to see whatever I wanted to see under circumstances of my own choosing.

The effect was all one could imagine it to be. I was the recipient of jittery respect in camps throughout the European Theater which I visited. Almost invariably commanding officers would offer either to guide me themselves or to assign several subordinates to do so. It was quite apparent in most cases that these commanding officers were more concerned with keeping soldiers, Negroes in particular, from talking freely with me, than in extending courtesies to me. Such was the effect of General Lee's order, however, that I soon learned to take full advantage of it by pleasantly but firmly refus-

ing escorts so that I could talk in barracks, mess halls, or wherever
I chose with soldiers so that they need not fear reprisals.

Although it had its bright spots, the picture I saw was no credit
to America. I found an appalling number of men who put their
prejudices above their patriotism. This was especially true of officers. Many of them used every device, official or personal, which
could be developed to make the lot of the Negro soldier as unpleasant as possible. The same tactics were used against white officers and enlisted men who dared oppose such mistreatment and
humiliation.

I came across innumerable instances where Negro soldiers were
court-martialed, found guilty, and sentenced to long terms for minor
offenses while white soldiers who were clearly guilty of much
graver crimes were either acquitted or meted out light punishment.
When some of these cases were reported to General Eisenhower and
other top-ranking Army officers, the corrective action which followed was characterized by some of the prejudiced whites as
"babying" and protecting Negroes.

I spent some time at an Army prison commanded by Colonel
James E. Killian, who was later court-martialed for the brutal treatment of American soldiers. Some of his subordinates, at a time when
there was no danger of our being interrupted by the Colonel,
showed me the records of some of the prisoners. I remember particularly a young Southerner whose eyes at one point filled with
tears of anger and frustration as he told me the facts about some of
the cases.

A Negro private in an engineering company had been court-
martialed for missing bed-check, and given six months, although he
was on the post and returned to his bunk a few minutes after inspection by an officer had found him absent. Outraged by what he
considered unfairness during his trial, he had told the Court, when
asked if he wished to say anything before sentence was passed, that
he considered the Court a prejudiced one. For this "crime" he had
been given two additional sentences of six months each to run con-
secutively.

The young Southern officer showed me the record of a white
soldier in comparison. The latter had struck and kicked his lieu-

tenant, cursed and struck his captain, and committed other of
for which he had been given a total of six months—one third
length of the term given the Negro soldier.

I do not mean to charge or imply that the administration of military justice was uniformly as one-sided as these two cases indicate.
But they were sufficiently typical of every theater of war I visited
to establish a sound basis for grievance. When I placed the facts as
I had discovered them before General Eisenhower, he ordered the
Judge Advocate General of the European Theater to investigate
each case and take corrective action both on individual cases and on
court-martial procedure. Some of the more flagrant injustices were
corrected. But I gained the distinct impression from checking (as
far as military practice and wartime regulations would permit) that
most of the investigators assigned to the task were more interested
in exculpation of the officers responsible for these miscarriages of
justice and of the court-martial system than in anything else.

Especially were courts-martial used against Negro soldiers who
had the fortitude to protest against discrimination. These were considered "bad Negroes" who were to be assigned the most unpleasant
and humiliating tasks to break their spirit and to be court-martialed
if other methods failed. An example of this kind of treatment is the
following incident which took place in North Africa.

A captain of military police swaggered through a Negro camp
cursing the men and calling them "niggers." Some of the Negro
soldiers drafted and circulated a petition to their commanding officer
protesting against such treatment. The signers of the petition were
immediately called on the carpet, denounced for their "impudence,"
and assigned to malaria-control work in the desert. One of their
comrades, who is a university graduate, but who had not been
allowed to sign the petition because he was already labeled an
"agitator," wrote a letter through military channels to General
Eisenhower protesting the treatment which had been given his
fellow soldiers. When several weeks had passed without any action
or reply to his letter, he wrote direct to General Eisenhower. Action
was immediate. He was court-martialed for violating Army regulations against sending any communication to superior officers except

through "channels." The young Negro was sentenced to six months, forfeiture of pay, and other penalties.

Wherever I went in the British Isles, North Africa, and the Middle East, and later in the Pacific, I found the same situation. The majority of American service men, particularly enlisted men, were either decent in their racial attitudes or indifferent on the subject. But everywhere there was a minority of bigots who were more determined to force their bigotry on others than they were to win the war. This was true almost as much of Northerners as of Southerners, especially among officers. I have never heard as much concentrated prejudice voiced against Negroes, Jews, Roosevelt, Catholics, and "foreigners"—particularly the "foreigners" in whose country these officers were stationed—as I have heard in officers' clubs around the globe. Frequently I would become so angry or nauseated that I would leave the club to find greater human decency among enlisted men.

I soon learned to judge the caliber of the commanding officers of Negro units within a few minutes after arriving in camp. In the majority of cases Negro soldiers would eye me almost furtively as they saw me moving about the camp with the commanding officer or one of his white subordinates. But as soon as I was able to shake off my guides and the news spread that the secretary of the NAACP was in camp, the atmosphere of caution disappeared. A torrent of complaints, many of them well-founded, as I learned upon investigation, would descend upon me. But with the complaints of mistreatment invariably came little acts of gratitude and kindness which touched me deeply.

There was the time, for example, when a Negro chaplain, Captain William Perkins, arranged for a special concert for me of the Army Negro chorus which Captain Perkins had organized and trained. Captain Gilstrap, our driver, and I drove for hours through an impenetrable blackout to reach the place in East Anglia where the chorus was to sing for us. Incessant rains had made a quagmire of the area where airfields for B-17's were being constructed with lightning speed and efficiency. We arrived dinnerless, half an hour late. The huge Quonset hut seemed icier because of the tiny British stove than it would have been had there been no visible attempt to warm the building. During the concert we munched sandwiches and drank coffee which Captain Perkins thoughtfully supplied. I wondered as I listened to some of the most beautiful singing I had ever heard how such melody could come through teeth which must have chattered with the cold.

We stumbled through the pitch-darkness and the ankle-deep mud to Captain Perkins' hut, where we were to spend the night. A fat-bellied American stove had been stoked so full that it glowed ruby red. There were mounds of chocolates and cigarettes which the soldiers had contributed from their rations. In some fashion snowy white sheets and pillow cases had been obtained for our beds. After months of sleeping in the rough texture of Army blankets, I slept that night with a sense of luxury greater than I have ever known, before or since.

Despite a bombing, we sat up late talking. As I was about to go to sleep one of the soldiers asked me what I wanted for breakfast the next morning. Knowing full well that it would be the inevitable and omnipresent powdered eggs and Spam, I told him sleepily that I wanted steak and hot biscuits. To my amazement and delight, that miracle was achieved. Small slices were carved by the mess sergeant from stewing beef and thus we had our steaks!

On my return to London, Ambassador Winant and Generals Eisenhower and Lee seemed gravely disturbed by the reports I gave them. Mr. Winant wanted material which could be used by the Joint Anglo-American Board of which he was a member, which largely determined both civilian and military life in England. Various civil and military British agencies had vigorously and sometimes belligerently resisted, at the outset of the war, the demands made by some Americans that a rigid color line, which had not existed before the war, be established. But various and steady pressures had changed this initial attitude considerably, especially with respect to contacts between British civilians and American Negro soldiers. General Eisenhower also asked me to prepare a detailed report of my observations and to include in it recommendations for whatever action could be undertaken to correct or ease the situation. These include: The establishment of an impartial and biracial board to re-view court-martial records of Negro troops and to re-examine the entire procedure with recommendations of methods to reduce the incidence of prejudice. I urged the abolition of the custom of declaring "off limits" to Negro soldiers virtually all the areas contiguous to Negro camps. I recommended the assignment of white and Negro military police to work in mixed pairs in all areas where white and Negro troops were billeted near each other. I pointed out that I had found that in practically every instance where there had been friction, the commanding officers had been either prejudiced or weak or both, and, contrariwise, the commanding officers where little or no trouble had occurred were men who enforced the orders against discrimination which had been issued by General Eisenhower and others in the higher echelons.

Army G-2 was urged to take action on the spreading of fantastic falsehoods by some white Americans that Negroes had tails, were addicted to barking instead of talking as a means of communication, that they were savages brought from Africa, and so on. I recommended that more high-ranking Negro officers and more combat troops be brought to the European Theater.

I urged that Negro air units be utilized on a nonsegregated basis; that qualified Negro medical officers be assigned to the Medical Corps; that more indoctrination of both white and Negro troops on the facts about the nature and quality of Negro troops be added; that United Nations canteens be established by the United States Army and the American Red Cross in cooperation with the British and other allies to enable soldiers of all nations and colors to associate under decent circumstances instead of in pubs and places of questionable character.

I had discovered several instances where Negro combat troops had been transformed after arrival overseas into service units. This had been one of the most damaging of all practices to the morale of Negro troops.

One of the most dramatic examples of the abandonment of interracial antagonisms in combat on the part of combat troops themselves, and the tragic perpetuation of it by the Army High Command, occurred during and after the Battle of the Bulge.

Von Rundstedt's sudden and dismayingly effective break-through

threatened disaster. The tide of war might have been chan,
at that point. At the very least, the war would have been prolong
had this daring maneuver succeeded, even though superior numbers
of men and infinitely greater war materials would probably have
brought Allied victory. Many Americans now alive would have
died in the interim.

Every available man was thrown into the breach to stop the German advance, but even then there were not enough. Desperate appeals were sent to the United States to rush more combat troops as
quickly as possible. Many were sent by plane, but even these proved
insufficient. It was at this point during some of the fiercest fighting
that Lieutenant General John C. H. Lee issued an appeal to colored
Service of Supply troops to volunteer as combat troops.

"It is planned to assign you without regard to color or race to
units where assistance is most needed," General Lee promised. He
made no effort to minimize the desperate character of the fighting
nor the great number of casualties caused by the German break-
through. He pointed out that all noncommissioned officers would
have to surrender their ratings to qualify for service as combat
troops.

An avalanche of volunteers answered General Lee's appeal. In
some units as high as eighty per cent of the soldiers offered their
services. In one engineer unit, 171 out of the 186 men volunteered.
One pfc. in an ordnance company declared, "We've been giving
a lot of sweat. Now I think we'll mix some blood with it!"

Delighted at this first opportunity to function as "real" soldiers,
the response was so great that the entire structure of required service units was threatened. The Army had to set up a quota to prevent
complete disorganization of its service units.

Generals George Patton, Omar Bradley, and Courtney Hodges
gave their approval to the use of Negro soldiers in completely unsegregated combat units. General Eisenhower was enthusiastic. But
Eisenhower's Chief of Staff, Lieutenant General W. Bedell Smith,
now United States Ambassador to Russia, insisted that the plan be
submitted to General George C. Marshall, Army Chief of Staff.

Washington was aghast at the unprecedented idea of an unsegregated, genuinely democratic army. It ordered the plan abandoned.

But the need for combat troops was so critical that the high command in Washington was forced by persuasion and the circumstance to agree to a compromise—the inclusion of all-Negro platoons in white regiments, instead of the admixture of whites and Negroes throughout regiments. Although the Negro soldiers felt that they had been let down, their ardor was not too greatly diminished. The Negro platoons were distributed among eleven combat divisions of the First and Seventh Armies. They fought through the latter and crucial stages of the Battle of the Bulge and through the subsequent Allied drive across Germany.

Of all the Negroes who were thus permitted to fight, only two went AWOL. Their platoon had not at the time seen action because it was stationed in the rear as reserve troops. The whereabouts of the two deserters was discovered a few days after their disappearance when a front-line division commander reported that the two Negroes had "reported to him to fight!"

Several of the Negro volunteers won the Distinguished Service Cross, Silver Star, and were otherwise cited for bravery over and beyond the call of duty.

The Army took a poll among the white officers and soldiers who had fought with Negro troops. The results are to me a striking example of the fact that race prejudice is not as immovable as timorous people imagine. The Army poll showed that after having served in the same unit with colored combat soldiers, seventy-seven per cent of the officers favored integration as contrasted with thirty-three per cent prior to the experience. The figures among enlisted men were seventy-seven per cent and thirty-five per cent, after and before the experience of serving with Negroes,

A white South Carolina sergeant was quoted by the Army as saying, "When I heard about it, I said I'd be damned if I'd wear the same shoulder patch they did. After that first day, when we saw how they fought, I changed my mind. They are just like any of the other boys to us."

Another sergeant from Alabama, after telling how bitterly he had opposed serving with Negroes at first, emphatically confessed a total change of attitude. "I used to think they would be yellow in combat, but I seen them work."

Eighty-four per cent of white company officers and eighty-one per cent of white platoon sergeants declared on inquiry that Negro troops had fought superbly, and seventeen per cent of officers and nine per cent of enlisted men even went so far as to say that Negroes fought better than white troops. Seventy-three per cent of the officers and sixty per cent of the enlisted men expressed the opinion that white and colored soldiers had got along together very well even in the close contact which comes from serving together.

General Patton highly praised the colored volunteers. General Eisenhower declared: "All my commanders reported that these volunteers did excellent work." General Charles Lanham of the 104th Division, presenting combat decorations to eleven Negroes, went even further to declare: "I have never seen any soldiers who have performed better in combat than you have."

But General Eisenhower, to the dismay of many of us who had faith in him, testified before the Senate Armed Services Committee in 1948 that he believed racial segregation in the Army should continue at the platoon level. And on April 26, 1948, Kenneth C. Royall, Secretary of War, who comes from North Carolina, bluntly told a distinguished group of fifteen Negro leaders that the Army would continue segregation.

Even after V-E Day, the amity between white and Negro comrades in the Battle of the Bulge continued and many warm friendships developed. One of the Negro veterans of the Battle of the Bulge recently shared with me correspondence with a Louisianian who had been his buddy in Patton's Third Army. The young white veteran voiced his dismay at conditions he had found on returning home.

"What can I do with people who haven't the slightest understanding of what the war was fought for?" he asked.

Negro and white soldiers alike believed that the policy of integration would be continued at least for those Negroes who had fought in this emergency. But after V-E Day, most of the Negro platoons were ordered out of the combat divisions and assigned once more to the menial tasks of service units. The emergency ended, it was apparent that powerful forces in the Army were determined that, however well Negroes had fought and behaved, they should not have the glory and publicity of returning to America as part of victorious combat divisions or be permitted to wear the insignia of those combat divisions. The flaming high morale of the Negro volunteers plummeted to an all-time low. Four Negro sergeants determined on direct action—appeal to General Eisenhower. Their efforts to get permission failed, so they went AWOL to Allied Headquarters at Frankfurt. General Eisenhower, they learned to their dismay, had left for Potsdam for the conference President Truman was holding there with the heads of Allied nations. But a military aide, Colonel Lee, who, either through his own liberality or through contact with Generals Eisenhower and Lee, had attained a deep understanding of and sympathy with the Negro volunteer, invited them in and talked frankly with them, saw to it that they were fed in the cafeteria of Supreme Allied Headquarters, and invited them to return four days later for a decision on rectification of the situation.

The following Monday the men returned to Allied Headquarters —to learn that Colonel Lee had been suddenly transferred to the United States. All their efforts and those of others, white as well as Negro, to preserve their combat status which had been won under fire, were in vain. All the Negro volunteers were restored to their previous status as Army menials.

But a dent in the pattern of segregation has been made. Lieutenant General Robert L. Eichelberger, Commanding General of the Eighth Army, on January 20, 1947, at Gifu, Japan, announced the formation of a modified nonsegregated division, consisting of two white regiments and one Negro regiment. This action was taken following War Department approval of the recommendations of a Board headed by Lieutenant General Alvan C. Gillem, himself a Southerner, which had outlined steps to eliminate segregation. Perhaps the United States Army and Navy will eventually have courage enough to make our armed services genuinely democratic.

XXXII

Good Enough to Unload Ships

To jump ahead in my story: I found the most bitterly resented incident of racial discrimination in the Army in North Africa. Major General George Barr, Chief of Staff of the Mediterranean Theater, had arranged for me to fly in his personal plane from Algiers to Oran. He had declined to tell me the reason for the trip. But shortly after arriving I was conducted to a sort of natural amphitheater where the Negro Second Cavalry Division was gathered. The sight of thousands of men sitting morosely on the ground and looking unhappily at me from beneath battle helmets as I stood at the hastily erected microphone was one not easily forgotten. The white and colored officers headed by General Harry Johnson of Texas formed a thin line of officialdom at the bottom of the amphitheater. Behind them rose great masses of dark faces to the top of the curved hillside.

I was told in answer to my query as to the reason for the assemblage that both officers and men were exceedingly embittered because the Division had been trained for combat duty but on arrival in North Africa had been ordered transformed into port battalions to unload ships. They had been called together so that I could talk to them and tell them to be "good boys."

The story infuriated me because there was no rhyme or reason for the transformation which had depressed and enraged the men of the Second Cavalry Division and all other Negro troops. There was at Oran at the time a huge casual camp in which there were between forty thousand and fifty thousand misfits who had been relieved from combat duty. These men had nothing to do except to keep their tents clean. Idleness was causing considerable trouble. The most intelligent step which could have been taken would have been to use these men in unloading ships and handling supplies for transshipment into the Italian Theater of War where the desperate battles of the Anzio beachhead and Cassino were then being fought. But these soldiers were white—and the high command for that reason apparently thought their energies should not be used in unloading ships, even though most of the men had failed in combat.

But the Second Cavalry Division, a colored unit, was deemed by the high command, because it was made up of Negroes, the instrument for unloading ships, despite the fact that many hours and dollars had been devoted in the States to training them for combat duty.

When I discovered that I had been selected to assuage the wounded pride of the Negro troops and to tell them to be "good soldiers," I bluntly refused to be a party to pulling out of the fire chestnuts which had been thrown in by stupidity and racial ignorance. As we stood arguing the point a few yards from the microphone I could feel thousands of eyes in dark faces glaring hostilely down upon us. I did not need to be told that the question was pounding through the minds of each one of the Negro troops as to whether or not I would let them down. Few if any of the white officers who were pleading with me to urge the cavalrymen to accept the situation were intelligent enough to know that my advising them, as secretary of the NAACP, to submit to indignity would have added fuel to their resentment instead of quenching it.

I walked to the microphone and told the men that I knew what was passing through their minds and that I shared their anger. I promised to do whatever I could to enable them to serve in the capacity for which they had been trained. I could not tell them that I had exacted a promise from a representative of the War Department who was present to permit me to send a cable to Washington urging that the order be rescinded and the Second Cavalry Division permitted to fight instead of perform menial duties. The faces of the men became somewhat less morose because of my pledge. But although the theater commander and his subordinates expressed to me their agreement with my contention that the order had been both unnecessary and unwise, it was never recalled.

In Italy I found the situation only a little better. The overwhelming majority of Negro troops there were unloading ships, repairing airfields, and driving trucks. But there was a new pride among them because of the 99th Pursuit Squadron, which as a part of the 79th Pursuit Group, was making a distinguished record in combat. Negroes were being given an opportunity to do something more than menial army chores. Although the 79th Pursuit Group was still flying fairly slow, low-altitude planes, such was the determination of the 99th to prove the mettle of Negroes as fighters that the flyers were almost pathetically reckless in strafing and bombing enemy targets. German airmen had become so terrified by the "black flying devils" that they fled whenever they found their opponents to be members of the 99th. As a matter of record, the three white squadrons of the 79th Pursuit Group fought as skillfully and bravely as the Negro 99th Squadron, but pigmentation made the Negro airmen more discernible and more to be feared.

But to me the most remarkable development was the total obliteration of consciousness of difference in skin color among both white and Negro flyers of the 79th Group. An indication of this was given me by an episode which occurred while I was with the 99th. A dinner party had been arranged to celebrate the first anniversary of entrance into combat of the 79th Pursuit Group. The event was scheduled to be held in the flamboyantly luxurious officers' club at Naples. But the committee in making arrangements was confronted with an order which had been issued by Lieutenant General Jacob L. Devers as Commander of the Mediterranean Theater of Operations forbidding association of Negro and white Army personnel in any place there was dancing. The reaction of the white flyers was that of instantaneous anger and rebellion.

"We have fought together for a year, some of our members have died together, and when we celebrate we are going to do it together no matter what the top brass says," was their declaration of war on prejudice. The dinner was held as they had planned it.

Back in Algiers some weeks later I asked General Devers about the order and the reason for its issuance.

"It was brought in to me one afternoon as I was hurrying to an appointment," he told me. "They said it was necessary to prevent friction, so I signed it," he ended apologetically.

I asked him what he would now do if he was convinced that issuance of the order had been a mistake, and if he planned punitive action against the 79th Group for violating it.

"The Army never revokes orders of this sort," he answered lamely. He gave no answer to my question about punishment of the 79th Group, but left the impression that he preferred to ignore the incident.

At the Anzio beachhead Negro soldiers established a record for courage under fire which was never adequately reported or photographed. The lifting of Army censorship about that operation of exceedingly doubtful military value permits the telling now of this story. Military experts may be able to prove some tactical advantage of the beachhead landing at Anzio, but it would take an enormous amount of persuasion to convince the officers and men who served there. Several divisions were packed so tightly in the area shaped like a slice of pie, fourteen miles deep and eight miles from Anzio to Nettuno, that the American troops were easy targets for incessant German bombing and the three heavy German guns which the Americans nicknamed "The Anzio Express" and "Whistling Willies."

So great was the accuracy of the Nazi gunners that they could lay a 340-millimeter shell with deadly skill on almost any square yard of the beachhead. The heavy guns were mounted on railroad carriages so that the weapons could be hastily run back into tuntels when American planes strafed them. So continuous and destructive was the German barrage that food, ammunition, and medical supplies could be transported from Naples to Anzio only on LST's. These were operated by crews of which an average of seventy per cent were Negroes. A very high percentage of these Quartermaster and port battalion troops were killed or injured in the perilous running in of supplies, without which the Anzio operation would have taken an even greater toll of American lives. I found that within one week fifty-two members of a single Negro Quartermaster battalion had been killed and ninety-three injured. But such was the determination to prove their ability and courage under fire that the commanding officers of these Negro units had difficulty in dissuading Negro soldiers from returning to Anzio from Naples on afternoons when they had made the trip the night before.

But despite the record being made at Anzio and by the 99th Pursuit Squadron, the American spreaders of prejudice were found to be active even as close to the battle front as Naples. Many of the American white soldiers, especially officers, resented the association between Italian women and Negro soldiers.

While I was in Naples excellently printed placards twenty-four by thirty-six inches in size appeared on billboards throughout the city. On translation the words had an ominously familiar tone. They demanded that Italian women cease associating with American Negro soldiers because, according to the placard, "the Negro is an inferior human being" and "must live in America only among his own." Physical violence against any woman who was caught even talking to a Negro was threatened, in such phrases as "the machine gun will cut down the prostitute who sells the honor of her race, and the people will seek revenge upon her and her black son when this crime has been brought to light."

The placards were purportedly the work of the "Italian-American Committee for the Preservation of the Italian Race" and were allegedly authorized by "R. A. Jacono, President." The Italian officials and people with whom I talked were incredulous and indignant at the appearance of the cards. Major General Barr, Chief of Staff of the Mediterranean Theater, ordered an investigation. It was discovered that the signs had been printed in a small Naples shop at the order of an American Army colonel who paid cash in advance for the job. The same colonel, accompanied by two American soldiers, carried the placards away in an American Army truck. The following morning they mysteriously appeared on billboards. General Barr informed me later that three of the culprits had been court-martialed and sentenced for violation of the 96th Article of War, the catch-all provision which is often invoked when it is impossible to make specific charges under other Articles.

This was but one of several well-organized and financed attempts to spread racial hatred against fellow American soldiers which I found. Some of them were effective, but most of the Italians, having

learned by personal experience or that of friends of the warmheart-
edness and friendliness of Negro soldiers, refused to believe the
canard. A few of the top-ranking American Army officials, particularly Colonel Charles C. Poletti, former Lieutenant Governor of New
York, who at the time was Military Governor of Naples, attempted
in every way possible to stop the activities of prejudiced Americans. But the job was not an easy one, since most of the anti-Negro
propaganda was either conducted by word of mouth or in surreptitious methods such as by the posting of notices, presumably
issued by the United States Army, in hotels, stating that no American Negroes were to be permitted to patronize these establishments.

I became convinced in Italy of the soundness of the formula
which has almost mathematical exactitude—that race prejudice flour-
ishes in inverse ratio to proximity to actual fighting. The pettiness
of race and creedal differences are sloughed off when men face
sudden death. Sometimes the cleansing is permanent, but too frequently for the good of society the fears and prejudices are taken
on again once the danger is past.

In Cairo I had one of the most moving experiences of my entire
trip when I interviewed Felix Eboué, the black Governor General
of French Equatorial Africa. His story is one of the classics of the
war.

When France fell in June 1940, like a Japanese paper house in a
hurricane, the menace of her collapse to the Allied cause was greater
in French Equatorial Africa than in France itself. Hitler dominated
North Africa. His plan was to sweep south along the west coast of
Africa until he captured Dakar, with its magnificent harbor, but
a short plane jump across the South Atlantic to Natal, Brazil. From
there he was determined to move northward until the Nazis con-
trolled all of the northern half of South America. Attack upon the
United States was to be launched through the Caribbean from that
perilously close vantage point, simultaneously with an attack by the
Japanese on the West Coast.

Had these plans succeeded—and in 1940 who would have dared
assert they were impossible of achievement?—Hitler would have
become the ruler of the world. Every leader of France except De-

Gaulle conceded that Hitler could win the war. So did the governors of four of the five provinces of French Equatorial Africa. The four were white Frenchmen sent from France to rule over subdivisions of that vast and rich African colony. The sole exception was dark Felix Eboué, at that time governor of the province of Chad, whose strategic location dates back to the days when Ovid wrote: "Who holds Chad controls Africa." Eboué refused to yield to Hitler even when his wife (later a member of the French Chamber of Deputies) and his children were threatened with death by Vichy and the Nazis. He rallied the people of his own province and persuaded three of his four white fellow governors to stand fast despite the utter hopelessness of the situation. The fifth provincial governor he imprisoned. DeGaulle and his homeless government-in-exile were invited to use Equatorial Africa as a base. The powerful Brazzaville radio station, without which the war in Africa, the Middle East, and Europe could not have been prosecuted so successfully, was made possible by Eboué's keeping Equatorial Africa out of Hitler's hands. Airfields and roads were constructed to get arms, ammunition, food, and medical supplies to the beleaguered Allied forces in the Middle East. Troops were trained and later made history in the incredible march across desert and mountain under General LeClerc to play a crucial role in the battle against Rommel.

I spent two fascinating days with M. Eboué. He had been made Governor General of all French Equatorial Africa, but his health had deteriorated under the long years of physical and mental strain. He was scheduled to go a few days later to Lebanon to rest, and it was there he died. But if he had any premonition of his death while we were together in Egypt, he gave no sign whatever. He sloughed off fatigue and illness whenever we talked of the future of Africa and France. Schools, hospitals, irrigation projects, and facilities for marketing the minerals and agricultural products of Equatorial Africa and raising the living standards of his people were meat and drink to him. Once I interrupted his flow of words, meanwhile wishing fervently that my own country treated its minorities in such fashion as to create such loyalty and faith.

"Do you really believe France is going to keep her promises of full citizenship and equality of economic opportunity to her colonials, if keeping those pledges cuts down her income from the colonies?" I asked him.

He looked at me almost in anger, as though I had reflected on the virtue of his mother, and exclaimed in a voice which brooked no pursuance of the subject, "*Certainement!*"

Somewhat later I inquired if the natives of Equatorial Africa, and he in particular, as Governor-General, wished or planned to become independent of France. Again there was incredulity at such a question.

"Indeed, no! We are citizens of France and our loyalty to her and her principles of '*égalité, fraternité, liberté*' can never be shaken!"

I was deeply moved by the faith of a man who had altered the course of the war by the implicitness of his faith, despite the fact that already the white world was forgetting the contribution he had made with such selflessness and cost to himself. That morning in a Cairo newspaper I had read with sickened heart of a lynching in my own country even as it fought a war against the racist theory of Nazism. And a few days before I had seen in a sandswept airfield in the middle of the Libyan Desert a German propaganda leaflet dropped by plane. On it appeared a photograph of an elderly Negro being struck full in the face by a brutish member of a mob during the Detroit race riots while the Negro's arms were pinioned by two police officers. In Arabic was a hypocritical but effective appeal to Arabs to fight the Allies since the picture showed how dark-skinned people are treated in "white" nations like the United States and England.

I could not help but remember and be ashamed for my country as I saw on M. Eboué's face and heard in his voice the reward France was reaping for treating this great black man and others like him as human beings.

Even the terrible closeups I had experienced of lynching had not been able to shake my love for and loyalty to America. All the failures of the democratic ideal when it encountered the color line had not destroyed my belief in government of, by, and for the people, or caused me to wish in exchange any form of totalitarianism, however benevolent its nature or roseate its promises. But Eboué made me wish that the United States were less hypocritical and dishonest on the question of minorities so that I could love and trust it as much as this man of France loved and trusted his country.

XXXIII

Eyes on the Negro Vote

It was a great shock to me on returning home to learn how remote the war and its larger implications were to most of the people of the United States. This was especially true among the Republican conservatives, who were confident that any candidate they chose, the more conservative the better, could beat Roosevelt on the fourth-term issue. This strange and unjustified complacency was particularly noticeable in the attitude of most of the Republican leaders toward the Negro vote now that Wendell Willkie had been eliminated.

On June 17, 1944, delegates from twenty-five leading Negro American organizations met in New York to discuss the situation and to thresh out whatever differences might exist in order to enable us to present the legitimate demands of the Negro minority to the two major political parties.

It was a remarkable gathering in many ways. Whatever schisms had existed in the past between Northern and Southern Negroes, white-collar and laboring colored Americans, and between those of differing political beliefs, had been miraculously reduced to a minimum by the growing seriousness of the Negro fight and by the greatly developed political independence of the Negro.

We knew that we possessed a potent weapon in the fact that, in at least seventeen states with 281 votes in the electoral college, the Negro vote held the potential balance of power in any normally close election. We decided to draft an open letter to the Democratic and Republican parties which would let them know what Negroes were thinking and also serve as a yardstick to Negroes themselves by which the sincerity of political parties and politicians could be measured.

This statement was agreed to by representatives of twenty-five of the largest mass organizations of Negroes in the country with a total membership of six and a half million. It said in part:

In the coming November election, the Negro voter will judge political parties, as well as candidates, by their words and deeds as to whether they show a determination to work for full citizenship status for thirteen million American Negroes and to better the lot of all disadvantaged peoples. Political parties and candidates that seek the votes of Negroes must be committed to the wholehearted prosecution of the war to total victory, must agree to the elimination of the poll tax by Act of Congress, the passage of anti-lynching legislation, the unsegregated integration of Negroes into the armed forces, the establishment of a permanent federal committee on fair employment practices, and a foreign policy of international cooperation that promotes economic and political security for all peoples. . . .

Negroes no longer belong to any one political party. They will vote for men and measures. Negro voters played an important part in the election of a Negro Communist to the New York City Council, a Negro Republican as Judge in the same community, a Democratic Mayor in Cleveland, a Republican Governor in Kentucky, and in cooperation with organized labor and other progressive forces, in the withdrawal and defeat of hostile congressmen in Alabama, Texas and California. . . .

The Negro people, like all other Americans, recognize the war as the chief issue confronting our country. We demand of any political party desiring the support of Negroes a vigorous prosecution of the war. We are opposed to any negotiated peace as advocated by the Hitler-like forces within our country. Victory must crush Hitlerism at home as well as abroad.

In evaluating the merits of parties and candidates we must include all issues—those touching the life of Negroes as a group as well as those affecting the entire country. The party or candidate who refuses to help control prices, or fails to support the extension of social security, or refuses to support a progressive public program for full post war employment, or opposes an enlarged and unsegregated program of government-financed housing, or seeks to destroy organized labor, is as much the enemy of Negroes as is he who would prevent Negroes from voting.

We insist upon the right to vote in every state, unrestricted by poll taxes, white primaries, or lily-white party conventions, the gerrymandering of districts, or any other device designed to disfranchise Negroes and other voters. Any political party in power, or aspiring to power, must demonstrate its determination through legislation and through vigorous criminal prosecution by the Department of Justice to protect and secure voting as a fundamental right of citizenship.

The ever-serious evil of lynching and mob violence has become more critical as a result of unrestrained violence against Negroes in the armed services. No national administration can merit the support of Negroes unless it is committed to a legislative and administrative program for the elimination of this national disgrace.

The Senate rule requiring a two-thirds majority to limit debate, combined with the refusal of senators to vote for cloture, has recently prevented a vote on the Anti-Poll Tax bill. Negroes will not any longer accept the subterfuge of those who claim to favor anti-lynching, anti-poll tax and other progressive legislation yet refuse to invoke cloture so that their votes can be registered. . . .

The program now being carried on through the Fair Employment Practice Committee to secure and protect the right to work without racial or religious discrimination must be continued and expanded during and after the war. . . .

No injustice embitters Negroes more than continued segregation and discrimination in the armed forces. The national policy of segregating Negroes in the armed forces violates every principle of democracy. Any party or candidate that hopes to win the support and respect of Negroes and all progressive groups must prove their belief in democracy by adopting a democratic program for the integration of all Americans into unsegregated military forces. . . .

We are concerned that this war bring to an end imperialism and colonial exploitation. We believe that political and economic democracy must displace the present system of exploitation in Africa, the West Indies, India, and all other colonial areas. We insist that all parties and candidates formulate a foreign policy which will recognize China as an equal partner with America, England and Soviet Russia, and which will resolutely and unequivocally oppose either perpetuation or extension of exploitations based upon "white superiority" or economic or political advantage to "white" nations at the expense of the two-thirds of the people of the earth who are brown, yellow, or black of skin. The United States must point the way by including Negroes among its representatives at the peace conference or peace conferences and among its diplomatic, technical, and professional experts engaged in international post war reconstruction.

The full text of this statement was published in paid advertisements in a number of newspapers, white and Negro, and many thousands of reprints were distributed by the participating organizations.

I was also instructed by the NAACP board of directors to appear before the platform committees of both political parties to state the position of the Association and the church, labor, educational, and civic organizations which had joined in drafting the document.

Senator Robert A. Taft of Ohio, it will be remembered, served as chairman of the Republican platform committee. He was coolly courteous, but some other members of the committee seemed annoyed that Negroes who could neither be cajoled, intimidated, or bought should presume to state bluntly the shortcomings of democracy from which they suffered and to insist upon corrective action. We had no illusions that the pledges in party platforms would be long remembered once the election was over. We were well aware of the certainty that the South would block as far as it could even mild planks dealing with issues like lynching, the poll tax, segregation, or job discrimination. We also knew that the working agreement between the conservative wings of both parties in Congress would cause the Republicans to go no further in their platform than the pressure of the Negro vote forced it to go. But we also knew that, however coy and indirect the approach to the Negro vote of the two parties, each knew that it had to have that vote to win.

So far as the Republican platform of 1944 is concerned, our efforts obtained one unequivocal pledge of a federal Fair Employment Practice Committee and evasive references to disfranchisement and lynching. Senator Taft, although he was chairman of the drafting committee, subsequently announced that he would not vote for the FEPC bill. However, more liberal Republicans and Democrats have since made efforts to enact into law prohibition of discrimination in employment.

I was somewhat disturbed on arrival in the United States to learn that the annual conference of the NAACP had been scheduled to meet in Chicago between the Republican and Democratic national conventions. I felt that our conference should have been held prior to both conventions, but it was proved subsequently that the choice of dates was fortunate.

It will be remembered that the bitterest fight among the Democrats in 1944 was between those who feared and hated the liberal views of Henry Wallace and those who favored his renomination as a candidate for the vice-presidency. I have never seen such cold-blooded speculation as there was among the Democrats, particularly those from the Deep South, as to how many years of a fourth term President Roosevelt could last. Intoxicated with power, many Southern politicians believed that the vice-presidential nomination could be secured for a conservative Southerner if only Wallace could be eliminated. These politicians knew that no conservative Southerner could be the presidential nominee or be elected over the opposition of Negro and labor votes. They were unwilling to institute the reforms which would gain them the support of these two powerful blocs. Through naming a vice-president of whom they approved, they were confident that they were providing for a cooperative president before the term was over. Among the Southerners mentioned were Senator John Bankhead of Alabama, Representative Sam Rayburn of Texas, and, as the most likely prospect, former Senator James F. Byrnes, who was then director of the Office of War Mobilization.

Thirty thousand persons attended the closing meeting of the NAACP Conference in Washington Park in Chicago on Sunday afternoon, July 16th. The Democratic national convention was scheduled to open the following Wednesday. That morning Mr. Byrnes arrived in Chicago by plane from Washington, summoned newspaper reporters, and dramatically announced that he was a candidate for the vice-presidential nomination on the Democratic ticket. The Rebel yell figuratively and in some instances literally was loosed in Chicago hotel corridors by Southern delegates. Byrnes had been so exceedingly useful to President Roosevelt in steering legislation through the Senate and keeping the Southern opposition in hand, and had received so much publicity as a member of the United States Supreme Court, he and his supporters were certain that they could force the President to support him for the post. Most of all, they were certain that Byrnes was the one man who could insure the displacement of Henry Wallace from the Democratic ticket.

The news of Byrnes' candidacy, however, was calamitous to Negroes. His record in Congress had been consistent in only one respect—that of unrelenting, skilled, and uniformly successful opposition to every measure sought by Negroes. He had participated in numerous filibusters against anti-lynching legislation. Throughout his public career he had made no attempt to conceal his contempt for Negroes or his conviction that they should be content to submit meekly to whatever status they were assigned by white men.

The only favorable item, as far as Negroes were concerned, in Byrnes' long public career was a unanimous decision of the Supreme Court which he had read while a member of the Court, in the case of *Ward* v. *Texas*, in which a Negro had been subjected to the third degree to extort a confession of rape. The white woman who had made the charge had told an incredible story, which included the detail that she had pulled a blanket over her during the raping because the flies were annoying her.

The Supreme Court's reversal of the conviction by the Texas court, read by Mr. Byrnes, followed numerous precedents in reversing convictions based on confessions obtained through the third degree.

The vast audience at the Washington Park meeting listened attentively to Marshall Field's analysis of domestic and world problems. It applauded enthusiastically when Dr. Ernest A. Hooton of Harvard presented the Spingarn Medal to Dr. Charles R. Drew for his scientific work on blood plasma. The sun beat down relentlessly as the huge crowd, far greater than that for which we had provided seats, waited for a statement of the Association's position on the party platforms and candidates.

All my colleagues and as many members of the board of directors as could be reached had helped in drafting my speech. After reviewing briefly the manifestations of revolt against the racism and exploitation which had plunged the world into a global war, I analyzed the platform of the Republican Party which had just been adopted, which pledged a Permanent Fair Employment Practice Committee through congressional action on the one hand, and on the other advocated the return of the United States Employment Service to the control of the states, throwing minorities like the Negro to the mercy of state officials. GOP evasion or indefiniteness on housing, lynching, and segregation were discussed.

I then turned to the approaching Democratic convention, and the audience laughed and applauded appreciatively when I declared that "if you think the GOP platform as dishonest and stupid as I do, we 'ain't seen nothing yet!' Wait until the Democrats get going Wednesday." I quoted from the Open Letter of the twenty-five organizations of Negroes mentioned earlier in this chapter, and warned the Democratic convention that if it nominated a Southerner as vice-president it could kiss the Negro vote good-by.

The tumultuous applause and thundering cheers which greeted this statement could leave no possible doubt of American Negroes' feelings in the mind of the observers, both white and colored, from both Democratic and Republican parties, whom we had spotted in the audience.

We learned that evening and the next day some of the details of the reports which some of these agents carried back to the Democratic leaders. There was, of course, no means of measuring exactly the effect of the Negro opposition to Byrnes' ambition, nor that of organized labor, especially of the CIO, which was voiced later in the week. But it is certain that the pivotal Negro vote in key states which would determine whether Roosevelt or Dewey would be elected played a not inconsiderable part in Byrnes' withdrawal of his candidacy the following day.

Neither the war nor the increased strength through organization of Negroes and whites against bigotry lessened the determination of some members of Congress to "keep the Negro in his place." On the contrary, some demagogues like United States Senator Theodore G. Bilbo of Mississippi, Governor Eugene Talmadge of Georgia, and Congressman John E. Rankin of Mississippi intensified their attacks on minorities. Senator James O. Eastland of Mississippi loosed a blistering attack upon Negro soldiers, declaring that they had been a total failure. This was hard for me to bear because of the recent death in action of my nephew, a fighter pilot, who had been shot down in Hungary as he returned from his fifty-seventh mission over enemy territory.

If a casual observer had watched the Senate when the Fair Employment Practice Committee came before it, he would have concluded that the war had not changed American attitudes on minorities—unless to make them even worse. Pressure from the South and even from unenlightened businessmen in the North had forced the introduction of a bill to establish the FEPC as a governmental agency authorized by congressional enactment in lieu of one created by presidential executive order, in a move to render it ineffective. When President Roosevelt attempted to continue the agency through appropriations from his contingent fund, congressional enemies of governmental prohibition of discrimination in employment attached a rider to the appropriations bill for the President's contingent fund, forbidding expenditure of any moneys from that fund for the agency.

This was done in the face of extraordinary support for a permanent FEPC by labor, church, minority, and other organizations operating through the national committee. Significant fissure in the opposition of organized business groups was the support given the fight for the FEPC by a number of employers. Among these were the Sperry Gyroscope Company, which frankly admitted that prior to the establishment of the FEPC they had never even considered employment of Negroes, but had found colored workers eminently satisfactory after being persuaded by the FEPC to employ them.

But even such testimony had no effect upon such members of the Senate as Bilbo, who became more implacable in their opposition because of the rising tide of support for the FEPC and for laws to abolish lynching and the poll tax. The entire nation was shocked when Bilbo wrote "Dear Dago" and "Dear Kike" letters to correspondents whose names indicated Italian or Jewish ancestry. But there was one manifestation which indicated that attitudes were changing. The torrent of shocked protests from white soldiers and sailors overseas as well as from citizens in the United States caused me to be almost grateful to the Mississippi demagogue for extending the targets of his abuse.

Even this did not give courage to many members of the Senate to answer Bilbo's tirades. Aided by fellow Southerners like Senator Allen Ellender of Louisiana, and the aging Kenneth McKellar of

Tennessee and Tom Connally of Texas, Bilbo launched a filibuster against the FEPC bill which tied up completely the "greatest deliberative body in the world" for weeks.

There was, however, one bright spot during the filibuster which marked the growing public sentiment against such legislative farces. A sailor, recently returned from the Pacific, attempted to voice from his seat in the public gallery of the Senate his objection to the spectacle being enacted on the floor below. Instantaneously he was hustled out of the gallery by plain-clothes guards. The bewildered sailor protested his arrest and heatedly defended his right as a citizen and member of the armed services to protest against the smearing of his Negro comrades in arms with whom he had fought overseas. It seemed to me a distressing indication of the Washington mentality that the sailor was then examined for possible mental aberration. There seemed even to be amazement when he was found to be perfectly normal and was released from custody.

Although the protest received headlines in newspapers across the country, it had little effect upon the Senate itself. An attempt to invoke cloture to shut off the filibuster mustered enough support to come closer than had ever been the case before to stop the torrent of meaningless words. But the two-thirds vote required was not achieved. Despite the unequivocal pledge of the 1944 party platform to enact federal FEPC legislation, enough Republicans voted against cloture or absented themselves from the Senate floor to defeat the motion, which of course was solidly opposed by every Southern Democratic Senator except Pepper of Florida and Barkley of Kentucky.

Funds were voted to liquidate the FEPC, and the movement gained momentum to transfer control from the federal government to the states of the United States Employment Service. Thus nearly two years before the end of the war the stage was set to place disfranchised Southern Negroes and enfranchised ones in the North at the mercy of those who thought them entitled only to the most menial and least remunerative jobs. I left for the Pacific wondering how I would answer the questions which would inevitably be asked about the prospects of greater opportunity after the war.

XXXIV

Purity in the Pacific

The flight from San Francisco to Pearl Harbor in a converted Navy bomber was uneventful except for the surfacing of a Japanese submarine whose antiaircraft guns were too feeble and limited to do us damage. When I reported to Navy Public Relations, the lieutenant commander who greeted me demanded, "Where in the hell have you been? We've been expecting you for weeks to do something about the trouble Southerners have been causing out here."

I burst into laughter as I told my interrogator that I was amazed to hear such a statement from one whose accent was so obviously Southern.

He joined me in laughter but there was little merriment in his voice.

"I'm from Texas and I went home last Christmas for a visit before coming out here," he told me. "A Negro had been lynched there just before I arrived and I was shocked and infuriated to hear my friends and even members of my own family approve the lynching. They did this even though it had been found out after the Negro was lynched that he was innocent. It woke me up and I've been awakened even more by what I've seen out here in the Pacific," he added bitterly.

Joe Magee, the Texas lieutenant commander, proceeded to take me under his protective wing although it cost him the friendship of some of his fellow officers when it was discovered that I was a Negro war correspondent and secretary of the NAACP. If he regretted the loss of such acquaintanceships, Joe never showed it. We had been instructed before leaving San Francisco that Fleet

Admiral Chester W. Nimitz received the press only when occasion warranted and that under no circumstances was any correspondent to request individual interviews with him. Through Joe's intercession with his fellow Texan I sat down to the first of numerous and wholly delightful personal interviews with Admiral Nimitz within four hours after I had reported to Navy PRO.

"You and I have had many a quarrel," Admiral Nimitz reminded me, "about segregation and limiting Negroes to service as messmen in the Navy. I was certain—and I am still certain that I was right—that in peace time it wasn't practicable to put Negroes aboard ships where they would outrank whites. They would have been entitled to promotion on the basis of ability. I knew segregation would be both wrong and expensive. But now we are at war—and that's a different story."

A KA (cargo-attack) ship was due to arrive in Honolulu within a few days, manned by a mixed crew in which Negroes for the first time occupied ratings above that of messman. The Admiral suggested that I accompany him aboard ship to see how the experiment worked. The ship arrived on a day when I was on the other side of the island of Oahu experiencing my first ride in an amphibious truck known as a DUKW. A telephone call came from Admiral Nimitz asking me to report to his headquarters without delay.

Arriving there I found the captain and the first officer of the newly arrived cargo-attack boat waiting nervously in the anteroom of Admiral Nimitz' office.

"I decided not to go aboard because you were not here," Admiral Nimitz informed me, "so I asked the ship's officers to come up here to see us."

The interview went well until the ship's captain, apparently still quite conscious of Nimitz' Texas background, told the Admiral, in answer to his questions about the nonsegregation experiment, that although men of different races slept in the same quarters, he as captain had deemed it wisest, for the time being at least, to assign all the Negro crew members to hammocks at one end of the room.

"That's bad, Captain," the Admiral said. "If you put all the Negroes together they'll have a chance to share grievances and to plot among themselves, and this will damage discipline and morale. If they are distributed among other members of the crew, there will be less chance of trouble. And when we say we want integration, we mean *integration*."

The captain hastily promised that the "suggestion" of the Admiral would be complied with. When I went aboard the next morning, I found through inquiry of the crew that there were no longer any segregated sections aboard ship.

There was little, however, that Admiral Nimitz could do, because the United States Navy had not trained any Negro officers. In this respect it was woefully behind the United States Army, which had at least trained Negroes in segregated training schools up to the time of establishment of integrated Officer Candidate Schools during World War Two. There were therefore very few Negroes in the Navy who were qualified to become either commissioned or noncommissioned officers. At the time of my conversation with Admiral Nimitz at Pearl Harbor there were only six Negro officers in the Navy, three of them ensigns and the highest ranking being Lieutenant (j.g.) Edward S. Hope, who had formerly been superintendent of Plant and Grounds at Howard University in Washington, D. C., and who was the eldest son of the late Dr. John Hope, President of Atlanta University. But at least a start, however belated, had been made because Admiral Nimitz, in spite of the fact that he was a Southerner, had faced the issue without evasion.

The picture I found in the Army in the Hawaiian Islands was considerably less pleasant than that in the Navy, even though the latter was far from satisfactory. In contrast with Admiral Nimitz' forthrightness, the policy of Lieutenant General Robert C. Richardson, Jr., was to keep Negroes in service units and to use strong-arm methods when necessary to prevent clashes between white and Negro personnel—his basic assumption seeming to be that, whenever trouble occurred between Negroes and whites, the Negroes were invariably to blame.

I had read many books, articles, and news stories extolling Hawaii as having wiped out color distinctions to a greater extent than any other area under the American flag, but I found many disappointing evidences that the reports had been too optimistic. Prejudiced American whites, although a minority, had demanded that American Negroes, even though wearing Army and Navy uniforms, be excluded from restaurants, hotels, dance halls, and other such places. When some proprietors objected to drawing the color line which had not hitherto existed, threats were made to wreck their places of business. Even more effective was a persistent campaign of anti-Negro propaganda among the residents of Hawaii.

One day while I was in Honolulu a well-dressed and well-behaved soldier of the famous 369th Regiment sought to have his picture made in a photographic gallery with leis. The dark-skinned Hawaiian girl who was employed to be photographed with customers indignantly refused to pose with a "nigger." Restraining his anger, the soldier asked the girl, who was manifestly of Japanese and Hawaiian blood mixture, who had taught her to take such an attitude. Although her skin was darker than that of the Negro soldier, she replied that "the American whites tell us that you are inferior and that you have tails."

This kind of mind-poisoning was successful because the precarious economic future of the Islands and the desire for statehood convinced the majority of Hawaiians that subservience to whatever they construed as the dominant opinion of the United States was desirable and necessary. The editorial policy and treatment of news concerning Negroes by the *Honolulu Star-Bulletin* was so biased that the anti-Negro stories spread by some Americans were given printed confirmation and sanction.

I was received with elaborate friendliness and courtesy by General Richardson and his staff, but I never was able to obtain adequate answers to questions I asked about the courts-martial then in progress of seventy-six Negro soldiers of the 1320th Engineer General Service Regiment.

The trial was called to my attention by an anonymous note sent to my hotel. The writer identified himself as a white enlisted man who was so outraged by what he termed "racial injustice" that he wanted to see something done to protect the Negro prisoners but feared to sign his name lest he be penalized. The courts-martial had been kept so closely guarded a secret that even Lieutenant Commander Daniel Armstrong, son of the General Armstrong who founded Hampton Institute, and who had been assigned to act as my guide, had not mentioned the case to me.

Company E had been commanded by a Captain Roache, one of three Negro officers of the 1320th Engineer Regiment, who had been immensely popular despite the fact that he was a stern disciplinarian. The Negro soldiers had worked faithfully, but discontent had grown as Captain Roache and the other two Negro officers remained stationary while less qualified white officer replacements were promoted regularly and rapidly. The three Negro officers had eventually submitted a respectfully worded request through channels that they be given consideration for promotion on the basis of merit equal to that which was being given to other regimental officers. Within due time formal written assurance was received that the matter would be handled satisfactorily. A few days later the three Negro officers were transferred out of the regiment and replaced by white officers, one of whom began immediately to voice profanely his passionate dislike of Negroes, and to demonstrate it in his acts.

On the evening of the transfer of the Negro officers Company E was ordered out of barracks by eight-thirty P.M. to commence work. Angered by the treatment which had been accorded Captain Roache, and further infuriated by the language and tone of voice of the new commanding officer, some of the men refused to fall in. Later, however, a colonel, whom the men did not know but whose manner was less hostile, ordered the men to go to work and to make up for the two hours which had been lost. He assured them that if they did do so and caused no further trouble, their earlier refusal to work would be overlooked. The men complied and believed the matter forgotten until several days later, when sixty-seven were arrested, charged with mutiny. Nine more were arrested shortly afterward. Sixty-nine of the defendants were found guilty and their conviction approved by the Judge Advocate General of the Pacific Ocean Area.

Under strict military regulations during war time, refusal to obey an order from a superior officer is considered a grave offense. But whatever offense had been committed by the men of Company E was mitigated by the whole racial picture in Hawaii, I pointed out to such officers of the Pacific Ocean Area as I thought it important to discuss the case with. When these facts fell on deaf ears, I cabled a request to the Secretary of War that the conviction of the sixty-nine be reviewed, and that we be permitted to represent them. A rehearing was granted, but before it could be held the convicted men were released from prison and assigned to a rehabilitation company, Lieutenant General Richardson advised me, for "special training with a view to their restoration to duty at the earliest possible moment and their eventual separation from the services under honorable conditions." This swift corrective action was interpreted by most of those who heard of the trial as conclusive evidence of the nature of the facts and the racial attitudes which animated the trial.

XXXV

Jimcrow in the South Pacific

The red-headed Army orderly with a luxuriant Southern accent leaned over the bucket seat of the C-54 to point out the tiny green and brown speck in the Pacific blue which was Guam. We had left Kwajalein sixteen hundred miles behind us the night before. A brigadier general and pfc. were asleep on the floor at our feet. Considerate of their slumber, the orderly spoke softly about the number of times he had made the round trip shuttling back and forth between Guam and Kwajalein on an army transport.

"They almost had a race riot in Guam a few days ago," the orderly said as casually as he would have mentioned a slight thunder shower as being in the natural order of things.

"Race riot?" I echoed. "What happened?"

"Oh, some Navy niggers got uppity, but the MP's cooled them off in a hurry," was the nonchalant reply.

We landed a short while afterward, dragging our gear out of the plane and into a truck under a sun so hot, despite the fact that it was two days after Christmas, that it made the earth seem like a hamburger grill. We bumped over roads still in the making by Seabees and Army engineers until we arrived and reported to Island Command. An Army public relations officer escorted me to a tent filled with "jungle bunks"—Army cots with mosquito nets—so close together that one had to step carefully from his own cot in the morning lest his feet collide with the man in the next bunk. I put down my barracks bag and mopped the sweat from my face. Without preliminaries of any sort the Army officer, who was, incidentally, not from the South but from Pennsylvania, began telling me of the way "niggers" had been "raising hell" on Guam.

"The black sons-of-bitches are getting out of hand and we are going to teach 'em a lesson," he angrily declared. According to the story he told me, all of the white people on Guam of the Army, Navy, and Marine Corps had been perfect gentlemen, but the Negroes had stolen weapons and had gone on a rampage against the nice, kind white folks. It was manifest that the officer knew of me only as a war correspondent and had not the faintest idea either of my race or of my connection with the NAACP, if he knew there was such an organization. I decided, therefore, to let him talk as freely as he wished so that I might learn the worst.

Because what I heard and saw during the next few weeks in Guam is so tragically typical of the racial practices our country transported overseas during World War Two, the story of the trouble at Guam in December 1944 deserves recital here.

At that time the war in the Pacific had moved northward and westward to the Philippine Islands. Leyte had finally been taken and the mopping-up process of killing or driving into the jungle the Japanese yet on Leyte was being completed. Guam was, therefore, the chief base of supply, and frantic efforts were being made to speed the building of roads, supply stations, and fortifications. The Third Marines were undergoing there at that time final training for the assault on Iwo Jima. With the almost superhuman efficiency of American engineering genius, jungle land had been cleared and three magnificent B-29 airfields were being rushed to completion. Long, orderly rows of Quonset huts were packed tight with ammunition, food, clothing, and medical supplies. Apparently endless rows of refrigerators held enormous supplies of meats and other perishables.

But as was the almost invariable rule of the Army and Navy, the bulk of the hard, dirty work of construction and handling supplies had been given to Negroes. There were white construction units of the Army and white Seabees in Guam. But there were no Negro combat troops of the Navy or Army but only engineering, base company, sanitation, and other service units. Combat troops, as is their custom, looked with either indifference or contempt on noncombat troops, particularly if they were Negroes. But even more provocative than this was the fact that the traditional American attitudes of race had been brought from the United States to Guam, especially among the Marines, many of whom came from the South.

The very efficiency and progress of the transformation of Guam into a highly organized military and naval base increased the opportunity of some of the Negrophobes to translate their prejudices into action. Thanks to American mechanical equipment, a superb six-lane highway was built almost literally overnight from Island Command at one end of Guam to the Navy Supply Depot twenty-two miles away at the other end of the Island. Near the latter on one side of the new road were stationed the camps of four Negro Navy base companies. Everybody in Guam worked for long hours at top speed during that period, but the Negro base companies worked twelve hours a day, seven days a week at hard, sweaty work, handling supplies, cleaning up the area, and doing other necessary but menial chores. None of the excitement or glamour of war was theirs. One of the four Negro base companies had been made up of so-called "trouble makers" from Esperita Santos, their last base before moving to Guam. It was a case in human society of "giving a dog a bad name." The literacy rate was low, although there were a number of men with fair education and some with better than fair training and family background. But many a Negro was officially and privately classified as a "bad actor" by prejudiced superiors when he objected to discrimination or injustice. Thus this particular base company was made up of men who felt they had been given a raw deal, and who were understandably resentful.

But their resentment would probably never have been translated into action had not a long series of unchecked and unpunished insults and attacks been made upon these Negro sailors. Trucks rolled night and day along the Agat-Sumay Road from the part of the Island where the Third Marines were in training to the supply depots at the other end of the Island. Stones, empty beer bottles, and other missiles were thrown from the trucks into the Negro camp accompanied by such epithets as "niggers," "night-fighters," and "black sons-of-bitches." Twice hand grenades were hurled into the Negro camp. On one occasion, one of the Negroes had enough presence of mind and courage to pick up the hand grenade and throw it into a ravine back of the camp where it exploded a few seconds later. On the other occasion, injury or loss of life was prevented only by the fact that the grenade was a dud.

Near the Third Marines encampment was located a fuel dump where vast quantities of hundred-octane high-explosive gas was stored. One day a live grenade was thrown into the camp from a truck by four Marines. A tragedy was averted by one of the Negro soldiers who picked it up and threw it into a ravine outside the camp before it exploded. On another day a smoke bomb was thrown into the fuel dump. One of the Negroes working there smothered the bomb before it could explode.

And as in the United States, sexual jealousy and rivalry played a major role in fostering racial conflict.

Many of the Americans, particularly Southern-born Marines, bitterly resented the sight of a Negro talking to a female Guamanian. Small gangs of Marines began to run Negroes out of Agana—or what remained of that town, which was the largest on Guam before it was leveled by the sixteen inch guns of the American Navy. Negroes at first reported the attacks on them by whites to their commanding officers. Instead of acting to protect their men, these officers sought to cover up the attacks or to justify them. Negroes learned that it was a waste of time even to report the insults and assaults.

Events rapidly approached a climax on the afternoon of Christmas Eve, 1944. A group of Negroes had obtained liberty passes and had gone into Agana, where they were fired upon and driven out of town. Eight of them got safely back to camp. A ninth had disappeared. It was assumed that he had been injured or killed. Some forty men piled into two Navy trucks and set out for Agana to find their comrade. But a Negro assistant master-of-arms telephoned Military Police in Agana to inform the authorities that Negroes were headed into town. A road block was thrown up and the trucks stopped. When the men learned that their missing companion had not been killed or injured but instead had hidden in a ditch until nightfall and then had made his way back to camp, the Negroes climbed aboard the trucks and returned to their area.

Shortly after midnight a truck filled with white Marines drove into the Negro camp. The Marines angrily alleged that one of their number had been hit by a piece of coral thrown from a truck by a Negro. The spineless and scared white commanding officer of the Negro company, instead of arresting the men who were shouting threats that "if you don't do something about this, we are going to take the matter into our own hands," pleaded with the Marines to go away, which they finally did.

The invasion of the Negro camp shortly after midnight occurred just as the night crew came off duty and was going into the mess hall from which emerged the crew going on duty. Thus it was only a matter of a few minutes before all the Negroes in the four base companies knew about the invasion of the camp and the weakness on the part of their commanding officers. Apprehension mounted steadily throughout Christmas Day. Shortly before noon two intoxicated Marines shot and killed a Negro sailor. He and two companions were walking down the road past a native house. The Marine emerged, saw the three Negroes, whom he had never seen before, and went back into the native house to emerge with a carbine, which he raised to his shoulder and fired. On the afternoon of Christmas Day a white sailor shot and seriously wounded another Negro sailor. Neither of them had even been arrested when I reached Guam two days later.

Around nightfall, a jeep with a machine gun mounted on it drove past firing into the Negro camp and returned again firing. Guards who had been posted somewhat belatedly around the Negro camp returned the fire as did some of the Negro sailors. By this time the camp was in a state of almost hysterical apprehension. Negroes fired on a jeep containing two military police, which many of the Negroes believed was the same jeep which had fired into the camp shortly before. One of the MP's was injured. Again Negroes climbed aboard two trucks and set out for Agana. Again a road block was thrown up and this time all of them—forty-four in number—were arrested. The next morning a shakedown was given to the Negro camp. A considerable number of weapons, some of them handmade in the form of knives, and others stolen from the Navy

Supply Depot, were found. A number of the Negroes later testified that, despairing of any protection from the responsible authorities, they had been driven to the conclusion that they could hope for no protection save that which they gave themselves.

The book was thrown at the forty-four men arrested at Agana. Among the crimes charged against them were unlawful assemblage, rioting, theft of government property, and attempted murder.

Either because they were too busy or had not taken the trouble to find out what had been going on even on so small an island as Guam, the Island authorities had done virtually nothing up to that time. Then suddenly they awoke to the explosive character of the situation and a Navy Board of Inquiry was ordered before which I was invited to appear as an "expert witness" on race relations. The presiding officer of the three-man Board was a Marine colonel from South Carolina. His associates were a lieutenant colonel from New York and a Navy lieutenant from Philadelphia. The Judge Advocate or prosecutor for the Navy was a lieutenant commander who had practiced law for nineteen years in Dallas, Texas, whose attitude toward Negroes was traditionally Southern despite the fact that not infrequently he invited me to the Navy Officers' Club for a drink after adjournment of Court.

Toward the end of my testimony, the Judge Advocate, Lieutenant Commander James Swift, asked me if it were not true that I held the degree of Doctor of Laws. I admitted this to be true.

"Then you are competent, aren't you, to represent the defendants in this case, as defense counsel?"

I hastened to explain to him that the degree of Doctor of Laws (given to me by both Howard and Atlanta Universities) was an honorary one and did not mean that its possessor had any knowledge of the law. To this he replied that procedure in the Navy Board of Inquiry was more informal than legalistic and that I did not have to be a lawyer to serve as defense counsel. My first impulse was to decline, for I did not want to jeopardize the legal rights of any defendant because of my ignorance of the law and of Navy court-martial procedure. I suspected, as well, that the request for me to serve was at least in part based upon a determination to excuse whatever convictions or sentences might be imposed by saying that there could have been no injustice because the secretary of the NAACP had represented the accused. But as the words were forming on my lips, I looked at the forlorn and pleading faces of the defendants. They appeared to say, and later some of them did put their inner emotions into words, that they were without friends on Guam deep in the Pacific and if I failed them by refusing to do what I could, they were without hope, since there was no one else they trusted to do so.

I stated to the Court that I would serve as defense counsel if the Court and the Judge Advocate would agree officially for the record that no legal right of any of the defendants would be abridged or jeopardized by my ignorance of the law and that I be given complete latitude and not held strictly to legal procedure in the introduction of testimony or the examination and cross-examination of witnesses. The Court inquired as to the extent of the latitude desired. To this I replied that what had occurred on December 24th to 26th could not be isolated but was a direct outcome of the attacks which had been made on Negro service men over a period of many weeks and of the racial attitudes of Negroes and whites which had developed out of racial proscription in the United States. Somewhat reluctantly the Court agreed to the stipulations.

And then began one of the most trying and revealing experiences of my life. The Judge Advocate was an able lawyer and was assisted by a younger man who was also well versed and experienced in legal procedure. I had no assistants or investigators. The Judge Advocate also had at his disposal all of the confidential records of the Navy from which I was barred by Navy regulations and customs.

The Court sat during the day, so that the only time left for me to do my own work of locating witnesses and evidence was after nightfall, which required going through areas where American soldiers had quite recently been ambushed and either killed or wounded by Japanese lurking in the vicinity. (There were still 40,000 of them on the Island, hiding in the jungle, getting what food they could by foraging.)

But, despite the difficulties, the job had to be done as best it could be done. For three weeks, witness after witness told the story either from the white or the Negro angle with varying degrees of veracity. As I look back on it, the abysmal failure of both civilian and military America to face the race question honestly was epitomized by the testimony of a handsome, sensitive young Negro whose deep ivory skin and wavy dark brown hair reminded me of my own son. He had come to me and requested an opportunity to tell the Board of Inquiry what he had seen and experienced in Guam. The lad had been born and lived all of his nineteen years in an Eastern seaboard city. His parents were fairly prosperous and highly respected citizens. Earnestly and simply the young man told a straightforward story.

He said he had voluntarily enlisted in the Navy on his seventeenth birthday "to help my race and my country." Almost savagely, the Judge Advocate jumped on the young man's sequence of desire for service, challenging him, "So you place race above country, do you?"

And then the Judge Advocate demanded, "Isn't it true that you have been convicted before Captain's Mast [informal Navy hearing before the Captain] and served sentences for violation of Navy regulations?"

This was a bolt from a clear blue sky. I whispered to the Judge Advocate a request that I be permitted to examine the records of the Captain's Mast to learn the circumstances. This request was curtly refused by the prosecutor who suggested, "Ask him yourself to find out."

It was a tough decision to make. The young man's honest and open countenance might be deceptive. My querying him as defense counsel might put damaging evidence into the record of some crime or at least of moral turpitude. But I decided to take a chance anyway because the Judge Advocate's question and the young man's affirmative answer would look bad in the record and weaken the story he had told up to that point which had been most moving in its recital of the slurs and discriminations to which Negroes in the Navy, eager to serve their country, had been subjected. So I asked the questions which brought forth answers which explained in part the Judge Advocate's refusal to permit me to see the record.

Here are the "crimes" for which the young volunteer had been convicted and sentenced on each occasion to five days in solitary confinement on bread and water. One of them had been committed when he, after completion of boot training at the Great Lakes Naval Training Station in Illinois, had been ordered to service in the Navy Mine Depot at Yorktown, Virginia. One day he had boarded a bus within the Naval reservation in which, in accordance with Virginia law, a sign hung from the roof of the bus separating white from Negro passengers. As eleven of the seats to the rear of the sign were filled, the young man sat under the sign, part of his body being in the "Negro" section and part in the "white" section. The bus driver had driven the vehicle to the nearest shore patrol and caused the boy to be arrested, as a result of which he was convicted and sentenced. The other "crime" had been his entering a "white" restaurant in Virginia to purchase food.

Jubilant at the results of my fishing expedition, I asked the young man if in his native city he had been accustomed to patronizing restaurants and other places of public accommodation and if he had ever had to conform to jimcrow laws in public conveyances. The answer had been that until ordered to Virginia, he had never been in the South before in his life.

After I left Guam, the recommendations of the Board of Inquiry, despite the evidence, resulted in courts-martial and the sentencing of all forty-four men to prison terms, which, happily, were later reversed when we appealed the convictions. But we had to take the cases all the way to the Secretary of the Navy and the White House to achieve this.

A story I wrote in Guam on January 20, 1945, was passed by the censor before I left the Island and a promise was made to me that it would be cabled to the *New York Post* at once.

Fully aware that no dispatch telling the full story would ever be passed, I wrote my story as carefully as possible and leaned over backward in understatement. But it was never published. When I returned to the States some months later, I learned that the *New York Post* had never received it.

I found out what had happened to it only after I had told the story of the trouble on Guam on a nation-wide broadcast, my speech having been passed without alteration by both Army and Navy censors in the United States. Several days later I received a photostatic copy of the story which is for me one of the most amusing examples of the stupidity of military censorship I have ever encountered.

"For Release July 11, 1945" is written in large letters above my typed "Guam 20 January 1945" and the release date of July 11 is written in again four additional times in a three-page story. Throughout the story were interpolated phrases such as "I was told," "reportedly" and "allegedly."

I had written that the officer who had so spinelessly submitted to threats and abuse from enlisted men of the Marines had been relieved from duty following the Naval Board of Inquiry hearings. The censor had inserted "steps having been taken before the holiday incident," which I know was false. A general closely identified with the affair had told me that nothing had been done against the officer until the facts were uncovered in the hearings because the officer's unfitness was not known until that time.

There were other alterations and insertions of the censor's personal opinions—and prejudices—which would be ludicrous were not the episode and circumstances so filled with tragedy and oppression.

Later, in Leyte, I first ran into the oft-repeated and completely unjustified canard about the cowardice shown by Negroes of the 93rd Division. A public relations officer who believed that I was just another white newspaper correspondent went out of his way to tell me that Negroes were no good in combat. I asked him on what evidence he based his statement, and he told me that in the invasion of Bougainville the 93rd had been given an easy beachhead to take, but that the division had broken and run under fire, "causing death to many officers and men in the white divisions on either side of them."

I traced the story carefully, looked into the records, and talked with the commanding general of the 93rd (who was a Texan), to a brigadier general who had been with the division at Bougainville, and with officers of the white units who had been with the Negro division. The truth was that the 93rd had not been in the original invasion, which had taken place in October 1943, but had been sent in in March of the following year, after the island had been declared "secure." The 93rd had been given the task of pushing back the perimeter of the Japanese line, driving it deeper into the interior. The infantry had done a routine, but competent, job. The 93rd artillery, however, had been officially cited by General Dunckel of the 37th Division for the excellence and accuracy of its firing.

The story had apparently come from an actual instance in which the cowardice of a white officer had disorganized the men under him. A white captain had disobeyed orders to attack a Japanese position on either or both sides of what was roughly a horseshoe area. He had ordered his men to attack down the center. Doing so, they had found a much larger number of Japanese than scouts had reported. A Negro lieutenant and thirteen of his men had been killed. The captain had thereupon become hysterical, given conflicting orders, and eventually had fled in terror back to the safety of the command post far in the rear. He was quietly transferred to another division instead of being court-martialed.

My investigation also revealed that the 93rd, like other divisions in the Army, had been used as a promotion mill and a dumping ground for white officers who had failed in other divisions. Many of them were prejudiced against the men under their command, which the men were not long in sensing. After Bougainville, the 93rd had been broken up and relegated to unloading ships and other menial chores.

When I got to Luzon, and saw General MacArthur, I told him of the maligning of the 93rd Division and other Negro troops and the conditions which I had found. He told me of having served with the 24th Infantry in this youth and of his high regard for the fighting ability of Negroes. He questioned me closely about the morale and the possible effect on the fighting ability of the 93rd as a result of the Division's performing Quartermaster and port battalion duties for so long a time as to make them rusty in combat.

He assured me that the Division would be almost immediately reassembled as a unit and given refresher courses in combat so as to be used in action as soon as practicable. I think that at the time he meant it, but except for mopping up duties on the Island of Morotai, the 93rd Division was never used in any major engagement.

MacArthur promised to stop the practice of dumping on the 93rd officers who had been failures with other divisions. Some other officers had remained in the 93rd Division only long enough to achieve far more rapid promotions there than were possible in other divisions. Not all of these men were inefficient but unfortunately most of them were. Their rapid advancement had an effect on the morale of qualified Negro officers which needs no description here.

In Pacific Islands such as Dutch New Guinea I saw, as I had seen in North Africa, how swiftly the brave, beautiful promises born of fear of defeat in war were forgotten as soon as fighting ceased. But I also was stirred by the devoted and brilliant work of scientists in conquering the tropical diseases which have kept millions of human beings from achieving their fullest development.

I worked and lived for some weeks with the 93rd Division, but there was time, fortunately, to learn about other things which were happening in Dutch New Guinea. By this time I had grown weary of battle operations and of the equally difficult struggle with Army and Navy censors to get passed by them any but the most innocuous stories. I found myself becoming increasingly interested in the kind of life which would be established in these far-off places by the colonial powers. I had read the sweeping promises made by Queen Wilhelmina in London, promising on behalf of the Netherlands Government in Exile citizenship and better educational, health, and economic opportunities to the Dutch colonials after the war.

One day John Dos Passos and I went to see a new tropical hospital for the natives which had recently been erected not far from Hollandia. Set in a clearing surrounded by towering trees, it was a pleasant place although quite different from any hospital we had ever seen in the States or Europe. There were four large buildings of bamboo with thatched roofs and open sides. The beds were of bamboo with wooden pillows and no mattresses or linen. There were about a hundred patients and a daily average of two hundred out-patients were treated by a staff consisting of one Javanese doctor, two white Dutch nurses, and about a dozen native nurses. Two blond rosy-cheeked young Dutch civil servants guided Dos Passos, several medical officers of the 93rd Division, and me proudly through the buildings.

I told the civil servants how delighted I was to see Queen Wilhelmina's promises being put into practice and congratulated them on the fact that the Dutch government was spending money on improvement of health conditions and facilities in New Guinea even before the Netherlands were rebuilt. To my surprise he smiled deprecatingly and told me, "It isn't our money we are spending—we got this from your government through Lend-Lease."

I asked him, somewhat taken aback, how many additional hospitals were contemplated and was told that no more were being planned.

"We've got a small hospital in Hollandia [which I learned later was used almost entirely by Dutch officials] and these are sufficient for the Island."

I could see no brave new world for the many thousands of disease-burdened natives with only a hundred or so beds available.

Dos Passos then asked him what would be done about education and received the airy reply, "We'll continue to let the missionaries supply schools." Our questions as to the number of schools and the type of education supplied in them received the vaguest of answers and subsequently I saw no schools outside of Hollandia.

Our questions about plans to raise the living standards and economic status of the natives were treated with equal casualness.

"America is too far away to be a profitable market for the fruits, grains, and vegetables we could raise here in abundance. There are great possibilities in the mineral and natural gas resources which we will exploit after the war because our government will need every guilder it can obtain to restore our homeland."

As to native self-government which Queen Wilhelmina had promised, we were told, "We don't intend to do anything about that because we can rule the natives much better than they could rule themselves."

The civil servants were neither evil nor unkindly men, but it was not reassuring so far as solution of the rapidly rising demands of colonials for freedom was concerned.

Later with the aid of interpreters I talked with some of the native leaders. Isolated from the world, they were far less educated and in touch with the trends of world politics than the natives of other Dutch colonies like Java, Sumatra, and other units of Indonesia. But the war for human freedom had penetrated even into the most remote areas where neither newspapers, radio, or the omnipresent movies had reached before the war. These native leaders revealed only a meager knowledge of the details of the war, but they knew as clearly as any European or American the significance of the war to their own welfare. I found it both futile and unnecessary to spend much time attempting to convince them that I too belonged to a "colored" race. But they seemed in some uncanny way to sense that my questions were motivated by sympathy and honesty and they talked freely of the kind of world they were determined to achieve. They dreamed of freedom not only because the Japanese had done an excellent job of propaganda about the racial arrogance and imperialism of the white man, but because they were tired of being exploited.

It is not difficult for me to imagine from these conversations what these native leaders thought when later American airplanes, tanks, and guns bearing the familiar insignia of the United States Army were used by the Dutch and British in a futile effort to crush the independence movement in Indonesia. The white world had used the creative genius of mankind to make a word called "freedom" a dream and a goal wherever men live. All the war weapons now in existence or which may be devised will never be able to stifle the demands of non-white as well as white men for a more decent and just way of life. We seem so pathetically and abysmally unable to comprehend this simple fact.

Shortly after I reached Hollandia I met Major Hildrus Poindexter, a gifted Negro scientist, who reminded me of the late Dr. Robert Russa Moton of Tuskegee Institute. He had recently been awarded the Bronze Star for reducing the malaria rate in the Solomon Islands by 86.4 per cent in three months. He had done important work in the diagnosis and treatment of schistosomiasis, a disease which had taken heavy toll of American soldiers, caused by a tiny worm entering the bloodstream; was a holder of three degrees from the medical schools of Harvard and Columbia universities; and, having done extensive research in tropical diseases at the Institute of Tropical Medicine in San Juan, Puerto Rico, had taught for fourteen years in the medical school of Howard University in Washington. But his major passion was doing all that he could and learning as much as possible about tropical disease, which he believed to be the principal cause of the backwardness of dark-skinned people living in tropical countries.

Major Poindexter and I talked often of his specialty and plans.

"Because of my conviction that tropical disease is the largest handicap of the darker races of the world who live in the tropics," he told me one day as we sat in my tent, "I plan to devote my life to fighting it. Men with too much brain damage from sleeping sickness cannot think. Men suffering from malaria are too anemic to work. The muscles of men with hookworm are too flabby. Men who cannot think or work cannot contribute to civilization or compete with other men.

I found that even Major Poindexter's ability and devotion did not exempt him from the evil effects of prejudice. He expressed an almost heartbreaking eagerness to work in the Army Medical Laboratory which had been set up there because he believed that in the laboratory he could obtain the most practical experience with tropical maladies to be gained anywhere in the world.

The commanding officer was a kindly man, but he was from Kentucky. Both his education in medicine and his scientific contributions were considerably less than those of Major Poindexter. He freely expressed his admiration for the Negro doctor's ability when I talked to him a few days later, adding "and Major Poindexter works three times as hard as any of us and all of us work hard!"

The commanding officer, however, feared that some of the white officers would object to Major Poindexter's eating in the general mess hall and occupying a tent in Officers' Row.

The device to save the sensibilities of the white officers turned out to be one of those contradictory and ludicrous color-line stratagems, particularly as it had bearing on the hysterical fears of some white people regarding sexual relations between white women and Negro men. A special tent was erected for Major Poindexter at some distance from those of the white officers, but the isolated tent was placed near the quarters where the white nurses lived and was so remote, I reminded the commanding officer, that "you won't be able to keep as close an eye on Major Poindexter as you would if he were billeted with the other officers." This seemed to disturb the commanding officer, and shortly afterward Major Poindexter was assigned a tent close to that of the CO himself.

The eating arrangements in the officers' mess were solved in an amusing way by the arrival of Surgeon General Normal Kirk on a tour of inspection of the Pacific Islands. In General Kirk's party was an officer who demanded immediately upon arrival that he be permitted to see Major Poindexter to get him to check certain statements in an article for a scientific journal which he had written. The conference in the office of the commanding officer lasted all morning until time for luncheon. Impatient at the interruption, the officer who had accompanied General Kirk told Major Poindexter that they would continue their discussion over the luncheon table. There was no alternative to inviting Major Poindexter to join the official party at the commanding officer's table.

Thereafter Major Poindexter ate at that table because, as the commanding officer explained to me, "I felt I did not have the right to force any of my subordinates to eat at the same table with Major Poindexter, but I do have the right to invite whom I please to eat at my table."

In Australia, from Prime Minister Curtin and other officials of the Australian government I met at Canberra to barmaids and taxi drivers in Sydney, I encountered the familiar stories of bewilderment at the incessant conflict between white and colored American soldiers. I was forced to spend almost an entire afternoon answering questions from members of the Australian Sociological Society about the race question in the United States when I was much more eager to ask them questions about Australia and especially the "white Australia" policy. The American Red Cross had pursued its policy of setting up segregated clubs even though by that time the war had moved so far from Australia that relatively few American troops were left there. Again I encountered traces of the stories by some

American whites that all Negroes had tails and belonged to a lower order of human kind indistinguishable from the Australian bushmen. But many of the Australians had met and learned to know and to like the American Negro soldier. Learning that many of them were graduates of high schools, colleges, and universities had offset the falsehoods about Negro ability and behavior. Prime Minister Curtin told me he personally opposed any change in the "white Australia" policy so far as orientals were concerned, but that the impression which many of the American Negroes had made in Australia had caused him and others to favor a change in the regulations to permit American Negroes to settle there if they desired.

If these incidents—and many like them could be added—give a gloomy picture of the treatment accorded Negro troops in the Pacific, I have precisely accomplished my purpose.

The rigid pattern of segregation, the virtually unbroken custom of assignment of Negroes to service units, the heritage and pattern of prejudice brought from the United States was altered only in isolated instances where in athletics, music, or other diversions, Americans—white and black—were permitted to escape segregation and learn to associate as normal human beings joined in a common cause.

It was this pattern which was responsible for the cynical remark I heard so often from Negro troops—"We know that our battle for democracy will begin when we reach San Francisco on our way home!"

XXXVI

Cloudy Tomorrow

The special train arranged by the State Department for diplomats and correspondents from all over the world en route to the founding meeting of the United Nations at San Francisco was a delightful contrast to the privations I had so recently known in the Pacific. Dr. W. E. B. DuBois and I were attending the conference as consultants to the American delegation. Unlimited quantities of tender beef replaced the tough and tasteless hot cakes which were invariably icy cold and which I was sure were served no less than eight days a week. On the train one would never have suspected any shortage of cigarettes or Scotch from the quantities available. I'm afraid that Dr. DuBois and I received far more than was justly due us when our identity became known to the Negro waiters and porters.

But even more satisfying were the eager questions of the journalists and other writers from foreign countries which manifested how world-wide had become the recognition of the supreme importance of finding a way for the different races of men to live together in peace. All the way across the country we talked morning, noon, and night in an effort to explain how a country with such vast human and material resources, famed for its generosity in times of disaster and unquestionably believing the statements it was so addicted to making concerning democratic and Christian principles, could at the same time permit the continuance of bestialities based on hate and prejudice.

Our attempt to explain the contradictions of American action seemed increasingly futile at the first meeting of consultants with the American delegation at the Fairmount Hotel atop San

Francisco's Nob Hill. Handsome Edward Stettinius, Secretary of State and chairman of the United States delegation, told the group the position the United States planned to take on the crucial issues which were expected to arise. The very presence of the consultants represented a new and, most of us thought, a decidedly refreshing note in American diplomacy. The variety of organizations represented there ranged in political and economic orientation from quite conservative groups like the National Association of Manufacturers, the United States Chamber of Commerce, the American Bar Association and the American Medical Association, to women's, labor, and racial organizations. These included the CIO, the AFL, the General Federation of Women's Clubs, the American Jewish Committee, and the National Association for the Advancement of Colored People.

Never before on so important an occasion involving fundamental issues had there been such close affiliation between government—especially the State Department—and large mass organizations representing nearly ninety million Americans. It was excellent public relations, but it soon became apparent that as far as the "career boys" of the State Department were concerned, the consultants were intended to be merely window-dressing. But there were two men there who felt otherwise. Although the conservative press sneered at Mr. Stettinius's Long Island society, and Archibald MacLeish's poetry and "New Deal" backgrounds, these two State Department officials won the respect and affection of most of us because it soon became manifest that they genuinely desired the ideas and criticisms of the consultants and did not regard them as necessary nuisances.

Fireworks erupted at the first meeting of delegations and consultants when Mr. Stettinius, apparently nervous and embarrassed at being required to make such a report, announced that the American delegation had decided neither to introduce nor support a human rights declaration as an integral part of the charter which the nations had gathered to draft. All of us sat in stunned silence. I sat next to the representative of the National Association of Manufacturers, who seemed as much shocked as any of us. I thought of Vernon Bartlett's statement in *Tomorrow Always Comes* of the disastrous effect upon the entire world if the United States demanded and then did not use the moral leadership which its resources and geographic position gave to it as to no other nation.

I thought of the pathetic hordes of Jewish, Catholic, and Protestant victims of Hitlerism as they wandered homeless and starved and hopeless through the war-devastated countries of Europe. I remembered demolished Manila and the faith of the guerilla fighters of the Philippines who, having endured incredible hardship in fighting the Japanese invaders, believed implicitly when I had talked with them only a few days previously that the United States would do all it could to build a better and more just world. I remembered the Jews in Palestine, the impoverished Arabs in the Middle East and North Africa, and particularly the black natives of Africa who had told me of their dreams of a world after the war which would live up to at least some of the beautiful phrases of freedom in the Atlantic Charter.

Dreading the answer I knew I would receive, I asked what position the American spokesmen would take on the issue of colonies. I learned afterward from him that I was not in error when I thought I saw on Stettinius's face acute embarrassment at having to answer that question. His face reddened as the Secretary of State admitted that the delegation thought this basic cause of war—the fight for raw materials and markets, as well as the "right" to exploit colonial peoples—ought not to be taken up at San Francisco, but postponed to some vague date in the future.

The consultants were so dismayed by the weakness of the American representatives that the considerable differences in ideological viewpoints among us were wiped out almost completely in our common determination to muster the not inconsiderable strength of our respective organizations. Each of us had special axes to grind in our individual and organizational interests. But a remarkable phenomenon developed as each of us in his own way realized that inevitable failure of an international organization would result if the nations of the earth, particularly the United States, played politics of the prewar variety and permitted the old national rivalries to operate again despite the most devastating war in human history.

The consultants were driven into closer unity by rumors of the position which Senator Connally took on the proposal to establish an international office of education. His elevation by longevity of service in the Senate to the immeasurable power of Chairman of the Senate Foreign Relations Committee had in no wise, obviously, altered the views which the Texas senator had belligerently and interminably voiced during Senate filibusters against anti-lynching, anti-poll tax, and fair employment practice legislation. We were informed that in executive committee meetings of the American delegation, Connally had bitterly fought American support of an international office of education because, first, he did not propose to permit "Sovietizing" American education, as though that were possible, and second, because he feared this might mean interference with racial segregation in the schools of Texas, and that, he declared, would not be tolerated. That day I felt almost ill that American participation in the building of a warless world could thus be limited by race prejudice.

The consultants had been informed that one of the chief reasons for their appointment was the desire of the State Department that they act as spokesmen to keep the members of their organizations informed on progress at San Francisco so that public opinion in support of the international organization could thereby be created. We agreed among ourselves, therefore, to keep not only the members of our organizations informed, but the public as well. There was immediate reaction to this plan and the press and radio reports. An alarmed and highly vocal public opinion began to make itself felt. The American delegation began to edge warily toward a stronger and more definitive position on human rights, proposals for trusteeships to replace the mandates and protectorates of the Versailles Treaty and the League of Nations, and other procedures needed to make the flowery phrases in praise of freedom more nearly a reality.

It was quite evident throughout the Conference that those who thought to outmaneuver the United States, and frequently succeeded in doing so, counted on use of the circumstance that the hands of the United States were far from clean. This was especially true with respect to the treatment of minorities. Little effort was made to conceal faintly cynical smiles when American spokesmen talked of justice for all men. As we learned to recognize each other during the weeks which the Conference lasted, representatives of various nations asked me questions at meetings, receptions, and in the lobbies of the official hotels. Many of these queries were startling in their revelation of how detailed was the knowledge about internal affairs in the United States, even of events which had occurred during the war when censorship had been in effect. On several occasions I was embarrassed when I discovered that some of my questioners possessed more exact knowledge on the activities and objectives of anti-foreign-born, anti-Semitic, isolationist, and other subversive groups in the United States than I did.

But most of the questions were motivated by genuine bewilderment that the United States would permit so complacently the spreading of division and hate among its own people. Some said frankly that Americans were so friendly and generous that they found it impossible to believe the reports they had heard even when they had read them in American newspapers. There was almost a pathetic eagerness to hear me deny the reports because they did not want their faith in the one nation which could supply leadership to be destroyed or diminished. Frequently I found my voice filled with a somewhat hollow ring as I mustered all possible evidence of American opposition to bigotry, even as I was forced to admit the existence of sizable fissures in democracy as practiced in the United States.

I left San Francisco to fill speaking engagements about the Conference and what I had seen in the Pacific with very mixed emotions. Clark Eichelberger, who has devoted nearly all of his adult life to the cause of international organization for peace, and I talked nearly all the way to New York as our plane sped eastward.

The United Nations Charter, which was then about completed, was, we felt, like most other documents based on compromise, an imperfect instrument but the only hope of peace then visible on the horizon. The pressures of the colonial powers and the cloakroom appeals to the preservation of white overlordship had been disastrously effective in preventing adoption of any really effective machinery to wipe out colonialism. Clark was more optimistic by far than I was of any material change in the colonial system or improvement of the status of natives under the trusteeship plan which had been reluctantly incorporated in the Charter. The objectives of the trusteeship system were beautifully and admirably phrased—to promote the political, social, and educational advancement of dependent peoples and render assistance in development of the ability for self-government of natives. The Trusteeship Council set up in the Charter, made up of an equal number of member nations with so-called trust territories and of nations not holding such territories, was authorized to receive reports from administering nations, hear petitions from the trust territories, and to inspect them. The bitter fight over the latter provision had been revelatory in exposing the reluctance of not only colonial powers, but of other nations to permit even inspection, much less correction of evils. This did not portend any more improvement in the lot of natives than the system of mandates and protectorates. I was even more pessimistic because of the explicit provision that no nation was obligated to place a colony or dependency under United Nations trusteeship, such action being wholly permissive. It was certain in my mind that no nation would voluntarily surrender the economic or military benefits from a land until such benefits had either been exhausted or revolt by the native population forced the colonial power to relinquish the territory. I could see only trouble ahead but I did not know how soon and in what widely separated parts of the world, such as Southwest Africa and Palestine, trouble would erupt.

President Truman asked me to come to the White House shortly after I reached New York. In a way I dreaded going there to find no longer the skillfully genial Roosevelt. Something of the same thinking appeared to affect Mr. Truman, as he referred constantly to "the President" when speaking of his predecessor. He asked me innumerable questions about the San Francisco Conference and did not seem happy over the somewhat pessimistic report I gave him. He promised to consider the recommendation I made that when he flew to the Conference a few days later for the signing of the Charter, he boldly propose the immediate calling of another international conference to deal specifically with the problem of colonialism and human rights. I was strongly of the opinion that a bold stroke of that sort would give the United States the moral leadership on these two basic issues which it had not taken at San Francisco in the drafting of the Charter. Whatever might have come of such a proposal is admittedly problematical. But the United States would have thereby placed upon each nation which voted against immediate and decisive facing of these issues the moral responsibility and blame for postponement of action.

XXXVII

Freedom House-Warming

There were some compensations, however, which raised my spirits when I returned to New York. Thirty-six years of quiet but steady building of a genuinely mass organization, supported in the main by its membership, had begun to show phenomenal results. The NAACP had grown past the half million mark, adding, in 1945 alone, 170 new branches to bring our total of branches, youth councils, and college chapters to more than twelve hundred.

Our staff at the national office had so increased that we had long since outgrown our quarters in the rather down-at-heel loft building at 69 Fifth Avenue. But despite its shabbiness the years of struggle during which we had occupied space in the antiquated structure had created such affection for the building and the neighborhood that it was hard to think of leaving it. We tried to purchase the International Ladies Garment Workers' six-story building on Sixteenth Street, which that remarkable union had outgrown, but another organization beat us to it. It had been our plan to name the building as a memorial to Wendell Willkie. While we were considering this move, George Field of Freedom House, of whose board I was a member, came to see me. He proposed that we—Freedom House, the NAACP, and the outstanding organizations representative of Willkie's major interests—join in purchasing a building which would be a living memorial to him. We liked the idea. I have always shuddered at the usual method of perpetuating the memory of an individual by marble or metal statues or by other useless and usually hideous memorials. Most of the available places we found were either inadequate of space, obsolescent, or located too far from the centers of activity to make the building the meeting place we wanted it to be.

Eventually George Field learned that an ideally located building opposite the New York Public Library on Fortieth Street, which had formerly been a club but which was now owned by the Schenley Company, might be purchased. When the owners were told the purpose for which the building was to be used, an extraordinarily generous price was made and we set about raising the funds to purchase and remodel the property. Spyros Skouras of the Twentieth Century-Fox Company, of whose board of directors Wendell Willkie had been chairman, and others with means, contributed generously. Willkie would have appreciated this evidence that the principles for which he stood and fought so vigorously, particularly during the later years of his life, had so impressed themselves upon men like Skouras that they wanted to continue the fight. But I am sure that he would have felt even happier because of the contributions of small sums made by a large number of the so-called little people of America who sent what they could to the fund. I was especially pleased that more than thirty thousand dollars was raised with little effort through branches of the NAACP as an expression of the gratitude Negro and white members of the Association felt toward Willkie.

There were a few moments when I personally was almost tempted to abandon moving to more adequate and centrally located quarters. One of these times was the day Jim, the self-effacing and friendly superintendent of the shabby building at Fourteenth Street, was taking me to the fourth floor in the creaky elevator which happened that day, miraculously, to be running. Jim asked me in a voice filled with need of denial of the story he had heard, if we were really going to leave. When I told him that we were planning to make a change, his eyes grew misty as he urged me to reconsider the decision since "the building won't be the same without you," adding, "Everybody in the neighborhood will miss you when you're gone."

Across the street from our old office was a typical New York combination of restaurant and bar where magnificent hot pastrami sandwiches and kosher dill pickles and marvelous salami delicately flavored with garlic were menu stand-bys. Dave, the proprietor, was an ebullient naturalized Russian who had begged me, when I planned to go overseas, to take him to Russia with me as my interpreter, despite my telling him that because he had become such a capitalist since coming to America as a boy, I doubted he would be admitted to his homeland. Although I knew the not inconsiderable amount of money which our staff—now grown to more than seventy —spent in the establishment, was a part of the regret at our departure, it was very evident that more than monetary loss motivated his sorrow. The party he gave for us turned out to be more a wake than a celebration.

Our new quarters in the Wendell Willkie Memorial Building, luxurious in comparison with our old Fourteenth Street offices, almost immediately became as overcrowded as the old ones had been. The phenomenal growth of the Association and the shifting nature of the problems we sought to solve made it necessary for us to add new departments and new personnel. I often thought of race prejudice in terms of a bit of mercury—when one attempts to pin it down by pressing upon it, it scurries off to appear in another place. We were being deluged with appeals from Negro soldiers and sailors who had been convicted in courts-martial and who begged us to aid them in obtaining reconsideration of their convictions. Much of the working time of our recently established veterans' bureau in Washington, under the direction of Jesse O. Dedmon, ex-Army captain, and almost the full time of another veteran, Franklin Williams, in the legal department of our New York headquarters, were devoted to the examination of the voluminous records of these cases and the appealing of those which were found meritorious.

Appalling defects in the administration of military justice were discovered in many of these cases. The same discovery was made in other cases handled by the veterans' committees which were organized by many of the NAACP branches. The helplessness and hopelessness which many of the Negroes who fought in World War Two experienced in far places of the world was pathetically reflected in many of these cases. The considerable success of the appeals we made in behalf of these men reflected only relative credit on us; in most of these cases the injustices were so patent and flagrant, a scandal would have been created by refusal to reverse conviction. But the work required great care and the expenditure of considerable time and money to obtain justice.

Two other problems—jobs and housing—snowballed in importance after V-E Day and after it was apparent that the war in the Pacific could not last much longer.

For a time after Hiroshima, Americans could talk or think of little except the new power which science had given them. But the implications of that power on national and racial issues seemed apparent to only a few of the most intelligent individuals. The conservative coalition in Congress began to labor industriously, now that the danger of military defeat of the Allies was ended, to indulge in anti-labor tirades and machinations and to return to the states control of employment and other matters upon which the existence of minorities depended. The greatest advances in employment which the Negro had made during the war had been in shipyards, airplane factories, and other plants making war materials. When these plants ceased operation Negroes were the chief sufferers. Downgrading in jobs in other plants became the rule so far as Negroes were concerned, with but few exceptions. The predicted slump in overall employment in America did not materialize and even Negroes continued to have jobs, but usually at lower wages and requiring inferior skills. We therefore added a labor department to the Association's activities and placed in charge of it Clarence Mitchell, who had had excellent training and considerable experience in the War Manpower Commission and the Fair Employment Practice Committee when those agencies were in existence.

We were forced also to devote increasing attention to the question of housing. After we had won in the United States Supreme Court in a case arising in Louisville, Kentucky, a sweeping decision outlawing racial segregation by means of city ordinances or state laws, a new device to confine Negroes to ghettos had been concocted. Property owners in increasing numbers began to write into deeds clauses prohibiting the sale or rental to or occupancy by Negroes on pain of forfeiture or other monetary penalties. Soon such covenants against other minorities began to appear. At first the restrictions were set at a period usually of ninety-nine years, but when the United States Supreme Court on two occasions evaded the handing down of definitive decisions on such covenants, the use of such restrictions spread throughout the country in the absence of court prohibition of their use.

It was obvious to us that the Negro would soon be as ghettoized as the Jews of Poland if the practice were not stopped. No valid argument except the moral one could be effectively presented against an individual's refusal to sell a plot of land to, for example, anyone he did not want to sell the property to as a Jew or Negro or Episcopalian. But we felt that no person had a right to covenant against the purchasing of land after the covenanter had sold the property or died. Most reprehensible of all was the demand that the machinery of government, and particularly the courts which exist through the taxation of citizens of every race and creed, should be called upon and required to enforce private agreements of this character.

At the outset of our campaign against covenants we had to go it alone. We found many instances of such restrictions against Negroes by judges, educational institutions such as the University of Chicago, and so-called "property owners' protective associations," and others. It was not until such covenants began to spread to other groups that recognition of their danger to democratic society and the necessity of fighting them became more widespread.

More and more, during the war, as the migration of Negroes from rural to urban communities and from south to north continued, and as the demand for labor increased, these covenants and the virtual cessation of home-building imposed unbearable hardships on Negroes. Because they could not buy or rent dwelling places in the open market, they found increasingly difficult and expensive the purchase or rental of any but obsolescent dwellings. Ill health, juvenile and adult delinquency, frayed nerves, and increasing discontent inevitably followed. Only rent controls of the Office of Price Administration and the gradual breaking down of segregation by means of public pressure in housing projects financed by the federal and some of the state governments presented any hopeful aspects.

I remembered a conversation which I had had some years before with Langdon Post when he had headed the New York City Housing Authority, and wondered why more public officials did not possess the inquiring mind and courage which he had exhibited. He telephoned me one day during the period of selection of tenants for one of the first and largest public housing projects in New York City. He wanted advice regarding nine Negro families which had met all the requirements for admission.

"What do you think will happen to these nine Negro families," he asked, "and do you think the Housing Authority should submit them to possible and probable acts of hostility from some of the white people in the project?"

I told him that the decision should be made not by the Housing Authority or by me, but by the nine Negro families. I expressed doubt that there would be much, if any, hostility in a metropolitan city like New York and suggested that if any white tenants did object their apartments be given to others on the long waiting list. The Negro families were admitted and were soon accepted by their neighbors without friction of any sort.

I recalled this experience not long ago when the mayor of Chicago became alarmed by the threats of a mob made up of individuals from another part of Chicago against the admittance of Negro veterans to a public housing project for veterans in that city. He sought to persuade the Chicago Housing Authority to abandon its no-discrimination policy, but fortunately without success. Thus faced with the necessity for action, the mayor supplied police protection and the threatened rioting subsided.

Our legal department and the board of directors decided to attempt a third time to present the restrictive covenant issue to the United States Supreme Court in the hope that a definitive ruling could be obtained from that tribunal. Not only was the national office flooded with appeals from Negro prospective home buyers but so were our branches from Los Angeles to Long Island. We ventured to hope that the considerable changes in the composition and the philosophy of the Supreme Court, particularly in its greater concern with human as contrasted with property rights, would result in a clear ruling on the issue. The brilliant work in presentation to the Court of a considerable number of cases by young Negro lawyers like William H. Hastie, Leon A. Ransom, Charles H. Houston, George M. Johnson, W. Robert Ming, Jr., Loren Miller, and others, as well as Thurgood Marshall, had created a profound respect for NAACP attorneys. We have made almost a fetish of careful preparation so that none of the issues we present to the Court can be dismissed because of defects in the record or argument.

We were loath to confine our approach to the purely legal one because the social and economic consequences of covenants seemed to us to be an essential part of the question. We therefore spent considerable time and thought in preparation of a sizable portion of the brief devoted to the socio-economic factors in housing, particularly insofar as housing was worsened by racial restrictive covenants. We were fortunate in having the assistance, in addition to our own staff, of outstanding sociologists and economists such as Dr. Robert C. Weaver and Dr. Louis Wirth of Chicago.

The results of our combined legal and other research produced, in 1938, a brief in one of the covenant cases arising in Detroit which competent lawyers characterize as one of the ablest presentations ever made in a court of law.

XXXVIII

"Read and Run"

The increasingly shorter interval between wars had enabled the world to see all too vividly that once men have been taught that mass killing is both necessary and noble, it is almost impossible to unteach them in the art of murder. Blood lust and hatred cannot be shut off as simply as one turns off a faucet. After the First World War there was a terrible succession of race riots and lynchings by civilian mobs. Some of the lynchings had been of Negro soldiers to demonstrate that Negroes must neither seek nor expect the "social equality" which they had experienced in France and other European countries.

During the Second World War we heard many disturbing rumors that a number of Southern cities and towns and a few in the North had invested huge sums in machine guns, grenades, tear gas, armored trucks, and other riot-quelling equipment. This material was to be used, as some of the officials of these cities and towns frankly admitted, in case of trouble caused by two groups—Negro veterans and organized labor.

I was permitted to see the variety and quantity of the preparations which had been made by one Middle West industrial city. There had been a sudden shift of police commissioners. The new commissioner had been a long-time friend of mine and he invited me to visit him the next time I was in his city. When I did so he showed me enough guns and ammunition to cause me to feel that I was overseas again in a battle area. "My predecessor bought all this," he told me, "to take care of any 'bad niggers' who come home with any fancy ideas about occupying a different status from that they knew before they left."

A new technique, according to quite authentic rumors which we checked as thoroughly as possible, was to be used. As soon as any trouble threatened, especially where Negro veterans were involved, a cordon of policemen, deputy sheriffs, state highway patrolmen, or National Guardsmen would be thrown about the Negro section. If this show of force did not quell the trouble, whatever peace officers had been assigned to the job were to move into the Negro area with blazing machine guns to put the fear of the law into any Negroes who refused to be cowed. Not only legalized violence of this character but mass arrests with the imprisoned held incommunicado and whatever other methods were necessary to break the spirit of Negroes or organized labor were to be used. Those who planned such handling of racial or union trouble were certain that no general criticism would be leveled against them since everything had been done by officers of the law in a perfectly "legal" manner.

We had to wait only six months after V-J Day to learn where the first attempt would be made to implement this plan. I was awakened early one morning by a long-distance telephone call from Nashville, Tennessee. In near-by Columbia, my caller informed me, state highway patrolmen were riddling Negro homes and business establishments to quell an "armed insurrection" by Negroes. I was aboard the first plane on which I could obtain a seat out of New York for Tennessee. But action had to be taken even more quickly than a plane could get me to Tennessee, if anything was to be done to prevent murder and destruction. Fortunately Donald Jones, one of our field secretaries, was at the time in Chattanooga conducting a membership drive. I telephoned Donald to tell him about the trouble and to ask him to locate if possible a trustworthy white lawyer who could be engaged to get to Columbia as quickly as possible to protect the interests of the beleaguered Negro citizens.

"I know just the man for the job," Donald almost shouted. "He is Maurice Weaver, a young Navy veteran who had just resumed practicing law here in Chattanooga." A few hours later Weaver was on his way to Columbia. Feeling was running so high in the little country town that no Negro lawyer could have entered it without grave danger. Even Maurice's white skin and Southern birth were insufficient to save him from threats of being killed. As soon as he made it known that he had been employed to represent 106 Negroes who had been arrested and denied permission to see either attorneys or families, local hostility grew to such an extent against him that his life was constantly in danger. But neither violence nor the threats of violence had the slightest effect upon the young Tennessean. It was my impression that Maurice reveled in the danger as did Z. Alexander Looby, West-Indian-born member of our national legal committee, who was engaged with Weaver as our Tennessee counsel.

The violent outburst had developed out of circumstances which were so simple and ordinary that the extent of the damage done was a remarkable barometer of the fear and prejudice which haunted the community. Mrs. Gladys Stephenson, an exceedingly quiet colored woman who cooked for one of Columbia's leading white families, had gone with her nineteen-year-old son James to a local radio repair shop to pick up a portable radio which had been left there for repairs. Although he was only nineteen years of age, James was a three-year veteran of the Navy, having served most of his enlistment in the Pacific. In the shop an argument arose when the proprietor demanded a sum more than twice what he had estimated the work would cost. To avert trouble Mrs. Stephenson paid the larger sum, only to discover that the radio would not work. When she insisted that the repairs for which she had paid be made, the proprietor and another white employee of the store became infuriated and began striking and kicking the colored woman. James rushed to his mother's rescue and knocked one of the men through a plate-glass window, injuring him slightly but not seriously.

At this point, police officers who had been attracted by the altercation arrested, in typical Southern fashion, Mrs. Stephenson and her son instead of the white assailants. News of the altercation spread rapidly through the small town and threats of lynching became so prevalent that the sheriff advised respected and well-to-do Negroes of Columbia who sought to post bail for the Stephensons to let them remain in jail for safety. Later in the day, however, the sheriff telephoned Sol Blair, wealthy patriarch of the Negro community, to urge him to post bail and arrange to get the Stephensons out of town before nightfall as a mob was forming to storm the jail. The sheriff also urged seventy-six-year-old Sol Blair and other Negro leaders to close all business establishments in the Negro neighborhood at nightfall and to advise all colored people to remain in their homes.

Shortly after dark a mob attacked the jail and dispersed only when convinced that the Stephensons had been spirited away. The only two members of the unmasked mob who were arrested were men so intoxicated that they were unable to walk. These two men were allowed to sleep it off overnight in the jail and were released the following morning.

Somewhat later several police officers started to drive down the darkened main street of the Negro section. A voice shouted, "Here comes the mob now!" and a volley of shots aimed at the automobile rang out, wounding two of the policemen. Additional highway patrolmen were ordered to the scene to strengthen the cordon around Mink Slide, the name which Negroes resented but which the white Columbians derisively applied to the ghetto. Just before daybreak the peace officers moved in, raking Negro homes and stores with streams of gunfire. Plate-glass windows and mirrors were demolished. The office of a Negro dentist and all of its expensive equipment was smashed beyond repair, and the desk, typewriters, and files of the local office of an Atlanta insurance company were destroyed. Cash registers in stores were looted, ice cream and other food consumed, and cigarettes and cigars confiscated in various Negro stores. Watches and other jewelry, fountain pens, and other valuables were openly and unashamedly stolen from Negro homes as the helpless owners watched the looting.

We had to apply for writs of habeas corpus before we were even allowed to talk to the imprisoned Negroes. Two of the 106 who were arrested were shot and killed in the jail for "attempting to escape" and for "attempting to kill police officers" in a room of the jail thronged with heavily-armed policemen and deputy sheriffs. Thurgood Marshall arrived a day or two later to arrange with Maurice Weaver and Alexander Looby for the difficult and perhaps perilous trial ahead. Meanwhile I devoted the major portion of my time to an effort to arouse and coordinate public opinion, white and Negro, for the defense. Before leaving New York I had telegraphed Governor Jim McCord, requesting an appointment to discuss the Columbia situation. The Governor's office telephoned me shortly after arrival that he would see me that afternoon. I asked Reverend William J. Faulkner, dean of the chapel of Fisk University, and Z. Alexander Looby, Nashville attorney and member of NAACP national legal committee, to accompany me. We arrived at the Governor's office a few minutes ahead of the appointed hour and were greeted in peculiar fashion by an opinionated and verbose young Southerner who introduced himself as Bayard Tapley, secretary to the Governor. His manner toward me was one of scant courtesy, but it was insulting to the two darker-skinned men with me.

"These fellows with you?" he asked me, as though they had no business in the Governor's office. When I told him that they were present at my request, he informed me that the Governor was not feeling very well but would see me for a few minutes but that "he cannot see these other fellows any time."

His face flushed angrily when I informed him that unless the Governor could see all three of us I did not care to talk with him. Grudgingly he ushered us into the Governor's office, sat down at the head of the table, and put his feet atop it. The Governor entered the office a few minutes later and sat quietly as Tapley dominated the conversation. He proceeded to inform us that he had evidence that the Negroes of Columbia, Tennessee, and "niggras" all over Tennessee and the United States, had been purchasing huge quantities of arms to stage an uprising. When Mr. Looby challenged this statement and cited in disproof of the allegations the fewness of the weapons found in Negro homes, Tapley burst into a rage.

Tapley's mind was no match for that of Alexander Looby, who again and again caught him in contradictions. On one occasion the secretary could answer only by shouting, "Don't you tell me what I said! I'm telling *you* what I said!"

It became necessary eventually for me to tell Tapley sharply that I had not come to the Governor's office to hear him talk but wished instead to secure the Governor's attention. Later newspapers published a story to the effect that I had made the statement—which I had not made—that though we had not seen eye to eye with the Governor, "after hearing the facts" we thought the situation had been handled rather well. Neither the anti-Negro *Nashville Banner* or the slightly more liberal *Tennessean* printed a contradiction of Tapley's statement which we requested, although the *Tennessean* promised to do so. Although I had encountered many Southern officials similar to McCord and Tapley, this experience stands out as one of the most disheartening of its kind.

The details of the court actions which followed are too numerous to permit recital here. But the story is one of as great hardship and bigotry as has ever attended a court trial in the United States. At the same time it was dramatic evidence of how human decency can rise above environment. We moved for a change of venue from Columbia because it was evident that the inflamed state of public opinion made a fair trial impossible there. Our contention was proved accurate when two of the defendants were tried and swiftly convicted, although their convictions were later set aside on appeal. Twenty-five of the defendants were granted a change of venue with what must have been malicious joy to the prosecution. They were ordered tried at Lawrenceburg—in which no Negro was permitted to remain overnight. Until a short time before the trials were ordered there signs had been posted on roads into the sleepy hamlet reading NIGGER, READ AND RUN. DON'T LET THE SUN GO DOWN ON YOU HERE. IF YOU CAN'T READ, RUN ANYWAY.

The twenty-five defendants had to travel one hundred miles daily on the round trip from Columbia to Lawrenceburg and return. Each day of the trial, the lawyers, including Looby, Ransom, and Weaver—who being white might have been able to find lodgings at Lawrenceburg, but who chose to share the hardships of his Negro fellow attorneys—traveled two hundred and six miles between Nashville and Lawrenceburg daily.

Not only were they unable, as were the Negro newspapermen, to remain overnight in Lawrenceburg, but they were unable to secure food or drinking water or even to use the toilets. Room had to be reserved in each car for luncheon baskets and kegs and thermos bottles of drinking water. It is doubtful whether any other trial, in the history of America was ever conducted under more explosive conditions. Open threats were made by the unshaven, overall-clad spectators that the lawyers who dared defend Negroes would wind up in Duck River, a stream near Lawrenceburg which the lawyers had to cross twice daily between Nashville and the scene of the trial. The judge and prosecuting attorney played openly upon the prejudices of the jury and audience. Every possible opportunity to refer to "niggers" and "damyankees" and the Reconstruction Era was utilized. An attempt was made to inject the issue of "communism" into the trial. At the outset not one of the major press services or newspapers paid attention to the trials with the exception of the anti-Negro *Nashville Banner*, whose reporter made no secret of his prejudice against Negroes, and the Communist *Daily Worker*, whose correspondent Harry Raymond wrote brilliant factual accounts of the trials.

I was desperately concerned at the indifference toward the trial and its significance. A pattern of police and public behavior was in process of formation which would be disastrous for the country as a whole if not exposed and stopped. We decided to attempt two remedies. We first invited a group of organizations and distinguished individuals to meet in the Willkie Building in New York to discuss the situation. We included not only minority, church, labor and other groups concerned with the problem of civil liberties, but a number of employer, newspaper, and other more conservative groups which we felt should be concerned with this issue. Most of the latter sent regrets—to our own regret. Again I was depressed with the apparent blindness of those who should have been concerned, if only for reasons of self-interest, with attacks upon the democratic process. I wondered again when they would awaken to the realization that unless they fought for the principles in which they believed those principles would be destroyed by inanition.

But fortunately a very representative group gathered to form the National Committee for Justice in Columbia, Tennessee. The cochairmen chosen at the meeting were Mrs. Roosevelt and Dr. Channing H. Tobias of the Phelps-Stokes Fund. Because the handling of the legal defense in the case was satisfactory to the Committee it was decided to concentrate on two tasks which needed desperately to be done—obtaining more adequate and impartial press coverage, and the raising of funds for the defense. But we soon learned that we were caught between two opposing forces and that the consequences of their actions would have to be reckoned with. One of these, of course, was the determined group in Tennessee which looked for political, racial, and other reasons, to do everything in its power to obtain convictions. The other group was made up of Communists and Communist-sympathizers who had an impassioned interest in the cases but at the same time were more concerned with using the plight of the defendants for Communist purposes than they were with seeing the Negroes free.

The danger from the latter quarter appeared immediately when the Civil Rights Congress announced that it had "signed up" two of the defendants and wished on that basis to appear on a coequal basis in the cases. The chief spokesman for the Congress was George Marshall, son of the late Louis Marshall. The charge had been made that prominent members of the Congress had Communist affiliations. We knew that our already difficult task would be made doubly difficult if any Communist or Communist-front organization participated in the defense. The same question arose when a sincere Washington woman, herself of Southern birth and convinced thereby that every possible ally was needed in the struggle against Southern reaction, urged that the Communist Party be invited as one of the cooperating defense organizations.

Mrs. Roosevelt bluntly opposed such a step. She pointed out that the Tennesseans who were bent upon conviction of the accused Negroes and perpetuation of "white supremacy" would like nothing better than to be able to pose as the defenders of Tennessee against communism. We were in total agreement with her position. It was obvious that the odds against us were already so great that any additional handicap would almost certainly seal the doom of defendants who were wholly ignorant of the fantastic charges which had been made against them.

Just as we believed that this problem had been licked, we found that there were new complications from this direction. I received an alarmed telephone call from Nashville that Robert Minor had gone to Columbia and formed at a Negro church an "Independent Voters League." Bob Minor is a gentle, affable, and courageous individual, completely and honestly devoted to communism. But we were informed that his connection with the Communist Party had not been divulged by him to the colored citizens of Columbia with whom he had talked convincingly about the corruption of the Crump political machine in Tennessee and the necessity of forming an independent political movement. Here was a friendly white ally who used none of the patent condescension which most white Tennesseans manifest toward Negroes. He was trusted and his suggestion of a voters' league was adopted. Handsome and patriarchal Sol Blair, the seventy-six-year-old chief defendant, was elected as president of the Voters' League and all of the other officers were codefendants with Blair.

News of the formation of the organization was seized upon gleefully by the *Nashville Banner* and the prosecution as conclusive "proof" that Tennessee was about to be taken over by the Communist Party. I talked frankly with Mr. Blair and other officers of the League. I pointed out that the idea of an independent voters' league in Tennessee was an excellent one, but that to organize such a movement under Communist auspices was a tragic mistake, particularly while the trials were pending. I advised that the defendants and the Negro citizens of Columbia disband the organization and reform it under auspices completely independent of any political party at a later date. But even as I gave this advice, which was followed, I again was depressed with the failure of non-Communist political parties who said they believed in the democratic process to demonstrate as much concern with, and freedom from, race prejudice as did the Communists.

Equally trying was the task of convincing press services and newspapers of the necessity of intelligent and unbiased coverage of the trial. The Associated Press was using the very biased stories of the prejudiced *Nashville Banner* reporter, when mention was made of the case at all in AP dispatches. The United Press had no reporter present at the outset of the trial. Appeals which I made to both news services appeared to have little effect. We were appalled by the realization that a procedure of legalized mob violence was in the making which could be checked only by the telling of the truth. But even the Negro papers appeared to believe this to be only another trial like countless others which had preceded it.

In desperation, I telephoned the distinguished correspondent and writer, Vincent Sheean, at his home in Vermont to ask him to go to Tennessee to cover the trials. I proposed to him that we would try to raise the funds to supply whatever he wrote to whatever newspapers were interested in publishing his accounts. Although I knew it was superfluous, since Jimmy Sheean (as he prefers to be called) and I had been friends for many years, I assured him that there would be no censorship nor other attempt on our part to influence his opinion. Jimmy was feverishly writing against a deadline on a novel at the time, but he readily agreed to come to New York to discuss the case. He suggested that I get in touch immediately with Mrs. Helen Reid and George Cornish of the *New York Herald Tribune*, for which paper he had frequently written.

The next day it was decided at a conference in the *Herald Tribune* office that he should go to Lawrenceburg as an official representative of the *Herald Tribune* and of such other newspapers as would subscribe to his dispatches to write the truth as he saw it, wholly independent of the influence of any of the agencies concerned with the case.

Jimmy's accounts dealt not only with the trial itself but even more with the background out of which such a racial clash could develop. They were featured prominently on the front pages of the *Herald Tribune*, the *Washington Post*, the *St. Louis Post-Dispatch*, and other widely read and respected newspapers throughout the country. They constituted what in the opinion of many persons was one of the soundest jobs of reporting which has been done during recent years. National attention was focused on the trials and soon the little town of Lawrenceburg found itself the center of attention from all parts of the country through the presence of reporters from a large number of wire services and individual white and Negro newspapers.

What had been confidently counted on as a quiet, routine lynching suddenly was transformed into an embarrassing *cause célèbre*. The disregard of the constitutional rights of the defendants by the judge and prosecutor were pitilessly exposed, to their embarrassment. They were increasingly angered by the unfavorable publicity and became less cautious. But we wondered with apprehension about the reaction of the jury. Would they cast their sympathies with the beleaguered judge and prosecutor? Or would they see the court officials as they were being pictured in the news dispatches, be ashamed of their tactics and the ill fame they were bringing upon Tennessee? There was no possible way for us to learn the answer until the trial was finished. Most of the jurors were farmers and small businessmen whose lives had brought little contact with the outside world. As far as had been humanly possible we had tried to eliminate from the jury through peremptory challenges all known members of organizations such as the Ku Klux Klan and the United Sons of Dixie. But we feared that in such an atmosphere environmental prejudices might conceivably cause the best jury obtainable to ignore the evidence and to vote for conviction.

It was a haggard jury which filed into the courtroom to announce its verdict. Twenty-three of the twenty-five defendants had been adjudged "not guilty." Two had been found guilty and were subsequently sentenced to five years' imprisonment. The basis on which these two were selected for verdicts of guilty remains a puzzle to us to this day. The evidence against them was the weakest of that against any of the twenty-five. They had not even been in Columbia the day of the alleged rioting!

But the verdict of acquittal of twenty-three of the defendants delighted us as proof that even mountain whites in an isolated village like Lawrenceburg would be so shocked by the behavior of the judge and prosecutor that they would react violently enough to vote acquittal for men they believed to be persecuted. Our faith in the inherent decency of persons who had been subjected all their lives to organized race prejudice was further strengthened when new trials were ordered for Robert Gentry and John McKiven, the two who had been convicted at Lawrenceburg. They too were acquitted, this time on recommendation of the Attorney General himself, who had become convinced that there was no evidence to support the charges which had been made against the defendants.

But Columbia experienced little change of heart. When the retrials of Pillow and Kennedy, who had been convicted at Columbia, were held in December 1946, an effort was made to punish the lawyers, and particularly Thurgood Marshall, for daring to appear for the defense. Thurgood Marshall told the story of what took place in the following letter which he wrote to the Department of Justice:

The trial of William Pillow and Lloyd Kennedy in Columbia, Tennessee, was completed a short time after 7 P.M. with a verdict of guilty for Kennedy and acquittal for Pillow. The courtroom was almost empty at the time. . . .

We left the courtroom and went down to the area referred to by some as "Mink Slide," went into the drugstore of Mr. Julius Blair and purchased soft drinks and crackers. We then got into the car of Mr. Z. Alexander Looby and started for Nashville with me driving, at, I would say, approximately 7:30. We went over the bridge from Columbia and on going up a main road to Nashville a very short distance, which I am unable to estimate, I noticed what appeared to be a grey automobile standing on the pavement and a state highway patrol car on his right off the pavement. I believe there was a filling station at the same place. A car was coming in the opposite direction and I slowed down for the car to pass and blew my horn in an effort to have the car parked in front of me move off the highway and when it did not move I pulled around it still headed for Nashville. We had gone a very short distance down the road when we heard a siren blowing. As I was slowing down to pull off the road a car with men in civilian clothes pulled up opposite flashing flashlights and with their doors open telling me to pull off the road, which I did. This car pulled in front of us and approximately four men came back and told us they had a warrant to search the car for whiskey and that we should all get out, which we did. When we got out we noticed a state highway patrol car parked behind our car and another car parked on the right of the car with a spotlight turned on the car, which made three cars in all. A man read the search warrant and the car was searched. However Mr. Weaver and myself watched carefully to make certain that no whiskey was placed in the car by the men searching it. Mr. Looby, another of the attorneys, and Mr. Harry Raymond, a reporter for the *Daily Worker*, was also in the car and stood by.

After the car was searched and no whiskey found some question was raised as to whether there was a warrant to search our persons. There didn't appear to be any warrant and we were not searched. We then asked if we might move on and we were told to go ahead. I got into the driver's seat. There had been some difficulty in the hydromatic system of Mr. Looby's car and while I was trying to get it started, the suggestion was made that Looby should drive and I agreed to this. I got out of the car and changed places with Looby and as we started off flashlights were flashed again and there was much yelling to halt and to stop, which we did. Then the group gathered around the car again, flashing lights in everyone's face, stating that this man was not driving when we drove up. Someone immediately pointed me out and they asked me for my driver's license. They took my license, examined it and returned it to me and we were told again we could go ahead to Nashville.

As we started off again the same procedure was followed, lights flashed, and there was yelling to stop. The rear door opposite where I was seated had opened and someone in the group said: "We have got to arrest you for drunken driving." We all, of course, stated that I was not drunk nor had I been drinking but I was told to get out of the car and did. I was placed in the rear seat of the car and four men got in the car with me, all appeared to be deputy sheriffs or constables. Mr. Looby and the others were told that they were free to go to Nashville. Instead of going back on the main highway to Columbia, the car I was in turned left down the road leading toward the famous Duck River. Mr. Looby instead of driving toward Nashville followed the car, whereupon the car turned left twice back to the main road and on to Columbia.

When we reached Columbia someone got out of the car I was in and I asked what was next and they told me to go over to the building across the street to the Magistrate's office. I told them that if we went over there we were all going over there together since I wasn't going by myself inasmuch as I was under arrest.

When we went into Mr. Pough's office, Mr. Weaver came in as my attorney and Mr. Pough wanted to know what was going on and he was told that I was arrested for drunken driving and he should issue a warrant or some other paper. Mr. Pough went over to his desk to fill out the papers and Mr. Weaver told him that this was a "frame-up" and that he would appreciate it if he, Mr. Pough, would smell my breath. Mr. Pough agreed to do so and on examining my breath, said: "This man isn't drunk, he hasn't even had a drink." Whereupon all of the men left the office except the man who swore out the original warrant to search the car and he agreed with Mr. Pough that I wasn't anywhere near drunk. Mr. Pough refused to sign any papers and told me I was free to go. When we went out into the street we noticed that the streets were deserted in the business section of the town with the exception of cars of local police and deputy sheriffs circling around. We returned to "Mink Slide" and left Columbia in another automobile entirely different from Mr. Looby's car and made the trip to Nashville without incident. Some friends of ours brought Mr. Looby's car to Nashville the following day.

The Department of Justice made an investigation but nothing came of it. We learned from authoritative sources that it had been planned to manhandle Thurgood and some of the group had wanted to lynch him for his courage and ability. Had Looby and Weaver obeyed the order to drive on to Nashville—which they had no intention of doing —and failed to follow the car into which Thurgood had been put down the dark road toward the Duck River, there is little doubt that he would never have been seen again.

Ironic emphasis was given the episode by the widely heralded insistence during that period by Secretary James F. Byrnes that the rights of minorities in the Balkans should be guaranteed in democratic fashion.

XXXIX

Johnny (Black) Comes
Marching Home

Early on the morning of July 26, 1946, I received a long-distance telephone message which told me that four Negroes, two men and their
wives, one of the men recently honorably discharged from the United
States Army, had been lynched the previous day in Walton County,
Georgia.

I immediately telephoned Atlanta to find great surprise and doubt
that such a lynching had taken place since no news of it had been
published there. But because my informant was utterly reliable I asked
that the most competent and trustworthy investigators, white and
colored, who could be secured be sent to Walton County as quickly
as possible.

Georgia was torn asunder at the time by one of the most bitterly
contested gubernatorial elections in its dark and bloody history. The
notorious "Gene" Talmadge was using every possible appeal to bigotry to get himself elected governor again. Walton County was one
of the strongholds of the rural electorate which followed Talmadge
and his kind with blind devotion.

Monroe, the county seat of Walton County, was an attractive little
Georgia community. In proportion to population it had an unusually
large number of churches. It numbered among its citizens several
whites who were as appalled by the lynchings and condemnatory of
the mob as were the Negroes. But few of them dared express their
opinion. Most of their fellow townsmen and even a larger percentage
of the farmers who traded in Monroe were rabid believers in the

Ku Klux Klan, Gene Talmadge, lynching, and white superi

The facts discovered by our investigators revealed a sordid background of twisted, sadistic sexuality. One of the lynched Negroes had become involved in a fight with a white man over the attentions which the latter had been paying to the Negro's wife. The white man went to the hospital and the Negro to jail. In a manner which unmistakably established official connivance with the mob, the Negro had been released from jail and driven down a back road by the white man on whose plantation he worked. In the car were also the Negro's wife and another Negro friend and his wife. The car was driven directly to the spot where the mob was lying in wait. We turned over to the FBI and the Georgia Bureau of Investigation the evidence gathered by our investigators, naming seven ringleaders of the lynching party. We offered a reward of ten thousand dollars for the arrest and conviction of these men, which, added to the rewards offered by the State of Georgia through Governor Ellis Arnall and other groups, brought the total sum to more than one hundred thousand dollars. But even this sum, which was undreamed-of wealth to the impoverished backwoodsmen of Georgia, was insufficient to cause them to risk physical violence from the lynchers and their supporters. A reign of terror and fear swept over Walton County and effectively shut the mouths of both whites and Negroes. One man was beaten almost to death for having testified before the Federal Grand Jury. Even nation-wide condemnation of the lynchings had no more appreciable effect than water on a turtle's back.

A fortnight later a less-publicized but even more brutal lynching of another Negro veteran occurred at Minden, Louisiana. Honorably discharged Ex-Corporal John Jones had been thrown into jail charged with "loitering" in the backyard of a white woman resident of Minden. Jones had been kept in jail along with his seventeen-year-old cousin Albert Harris, despite the fact that the woman had steadfastly and indignantly refused to prefer charges against them. It was later revealed that Jones had incurred the enmity of a local white citizen for refusing to give the latter a war souvenir which he had brought back from overseas.

One night Jones and Harris had been told by the jailer that they were free to leave because the charges against them had been proved groundless, but there was something about the manner in which this news was imparted which aroused Jones' suspicion. He refused to leave the jail and insisted on remaining there until daybreak, whereupon he was seized by several of the jailers and carried forcibly from the building and put into an automobile filled with armed white men. His young cousin was forced into another car also filled with hostile whites. The two men were driven to a lonely spot. Jones was beaten terribly and left for dead. A blowtorch so charred his flesh that the undertaker described him to us later as having been jet black in color though his skin had been light yellow. The handsome and terrified seventeen-year-old Albert Harris had been beaten also unmercifully in a futile attempt to force him to "confess" that he and Jones had been in the white woman's yard. Albert had been struck on the forehead with the butt of a forty-five caliber pistol and also left for dead. But he did not die. Reviving some time after the mob had gone, he heard his cousin moaning in agony and crawled to his side to hear the dying man beg for water. Albert, using a shoe for a dipper, had brought him water from a stream and had held the war veteran's head in his arms as he died.

Despite his weakened condition from the terrible beating, the boy made his way by back roads to his father's house. The family knew that if it was discovered that Albert was still alive, he would surely be killed, to prevent his testifying against the mob (which included a number of prominent men of Minden and vicinity and several deputy sheriffs). Albert and his father climbed into the family automobile and set out under cover of darkness for a town in Arkansas where the boy could be hidden with a relative.

I telephoned the president of the NAACP branch in that town and asked him to put the Harrises on a plane and send them to New York. I wanted first to get them out of the clutches of the mob which, we learned from Daniel Byrd of our New Orleans branch who had gone at my request to Minden, was already on its way to the Arkansas town to complete its job of killing.

But hour after hour and day after day passed with no arrival of the Harrises. I talked with the Department of Justice and the FBI and solicited their aid in locating and protecting them. But even the vast and efficient manhunting machinery of the FBI was unequal to the

task. We learned of other relatives of the Harrises in Texas and
information from them, thinking that the Harrises might have lea...
of the mob seeking them in Arkansas. Our search in various parts of
Texas was equally unsuccessful. We spread our search and eventually
found them in a small town in northern Michigan after one of the
most taxing and exciting manhunts in which we had ever engaged.

But even in Michigan we feared for their safety. The very success
of the efforts we had made over the years to arouse public opinion
against lynching and to stir the machinery of the federal government
to activity against lynchers might have increased their danger, wherever they were. We knew from our representatives in Louisiana that
the lynchers were so terrified by the prospect of being arrested and
convicted in federal courts that they would let nothing be left un-
done to close Albert's mouth forever. We notified the Department of
Justice that we had found the Harrises and I was asked to send them
to Washington to tell their story. I sent Madison Jones, administrative assistant in our national office, to Michigan to bring them to New
York, and Robert Carter of our legal staff and I took them to Washington. Never before had we been able to locate an eyewitness who
could and would give firsthand evidence of what had taken place during a lynching.

Indictments of several members of the mob were handed down by
the federal grand jury after Albert Harris, heavily guarded by U. S.
marshals and by NAACP representatives, had gone from Michigan
to Louisiana to testify. But a jury acquitted the lynchers despite the
fact that the Department of Justice had utilized every possible section of the ineffective federal statutes which were then in effect.

Still another veteran was the target of violence during that terrible
summer of 1946. After three years in the Army, fifteen months of
which was spent in the jungles of the South Pacific, Isaac Woodard
was discharged from the Army at a camp in Georgia. He eagerly
boarded a bus for his home in North Carolina to see his wife and family after the long absence. On the bus he asked to be allowed to go
to a restroom and, when he returned, was cursed and threatened by
the driver because he had been gone longer than suited the driver's
wishes. At a town in South Carolina, the name of which Woodard
did not know, the driver asked the chief of police to arrest the veteran

for being "drunk and disorderly," although Woodard did not drink. When Woodard protested that he had been neither drunk nor disorderly the chief beat him unmercifully with a blackjack and struck him in both eyes with the end of his nightstick, blinding him forever. The soldier was then thrust into a cell and kept there overnight without food or medical treatment.

The next morning his cell door was opened and a policeman ordered him to go with him to court to be tried. He told the officer that he was unable to see. The policeman led him to a sink where he could wash the blood from his face and then conducted him before the judge. The latter promptly found him guilty and fined him fifty dollars and costs. The veteran fumbled in his pockets and proffered the contents totaling forty dollars in payment of his fine. This was peremptorily refused and he was told that the full amount must be paid in cash or he would return to jail. Woodard also had a severance-pay check of six hundred and ninety-four dollars which he was told he could sign to obtain the balance of his fine. Woodard shrewdly refused to do this, suspecting from the treatment which had been given him and from his own knowledge of the South that, being blind he would receive very little of the check. The court officials were apparently afraid to endorse the check themselves lest they get into difficulties with the federal government. By this time, moreover, the condition of Woodard's eyes was apparently so terrifying that either the consciences or the fears of the court were disturbed. A telephone call was put in to the U. S. veterans hospital at Spartanburg to ask that doctors be sent to examine him and take the Negro veteran to the Army hospital. Examination by Army doctors revealed that Woodard had been beaten so brutally that the corneas of both of his eyes had been injured beyond repair.

Orson Welles read of the case and with magnificent fury devoted most of the time of several weekly broadcasts to denunciation of the barbarism and a demand for punitive action, bringing about unsuccessful efforts on the part of Southern groups to have him removed from the air. Veteran, church, labor, and other groups joined us in our work of tracking down the culprit and insisting upon action.

The investigation launched by the FBI and the NAACP was hampered by the fact that Woodard didn't know the name of the town

in which he had been beaten, imprisoned, and tried. But ev
we located after long search civilian and military fellow pas
on the bus who were able to identify the place of the assault and the
man who had administered the barbarous beating as the chief of police. The chief of police was eventually indicted, so great was the
public indignation against him, but upon being brought to trial he was
acquitted to the cheers of a crowded courtroom. The U. S. Army denied our appeal in Woodard's behalf for a pension on the ground that
his disability had not been incurred in service despite the fact that an
Army ruling makes a discharged veteran subject to army discipline
until midnight of the day of his discharge. We sought damages from
the bus company but a jury ruled against Woodard. We arranged a
tour for Woodard, accompanied by Franklin Williams, to publicize
the case and to raise money for Woodard's relief. With the money
obtained in this fashion, and through voluntary contributions totaling ten thousand dollars, we purchased an annuity to aid him.

There are two poignant memories connected with Isaac Woodard
which I shall never forget. The first of these was the occasion when
Woodard was led by his cousin into my office for the first time. Fal-
tering with the unsureness of the newly blinded, Woodard extended
his hand into open space in greeting, pathetically attempting to find
my hand through the sound of my voice. Not yet skilled enough, his
hand wavered a full two feet away from where my hand was, in the
manner of one feeling his way in the darkness of a strange place.

"I saw you, Mr. White, when you visited my outfit in the Pacific,"
he told me. "I could see *then*."

The other memory is of the day when we invited representatives
of several organizations and other individuals to meet in the Willkie
Building to hear Woodard tell the story of what had happened to him.
Although he could not see the audience, he was terrified by the ordeal
of making a speech. I had to tell him over and over again that he need
do no more than relate the facts and to assure him that his auditors
were friends. It was one of the most moving speeches I have ever
heard. With not the slightest trace of either bitterness or self-pity, and
in a voice almost totally devoid of emotion, he told of the long and
trying months in the Pacific and how eagerly he had looked forward
to the end of the war when he could rejoin his family and resume

normal civilian life. His voice swelled with modest pride as he told of receiving and reading his honorable discharge from the Army. We shared with him his impatience and anticipation as he waited for the bus which would take him to the North Carolina town where his wife awaited him. He made us in simple fashion look forward to the trip he and his wife were planning to New York to visit his mother and father. And we suffered with him the agony he endured during the unmerciful beating, the long night of pain without medical attention or food in a filthy prison cell, and his uttermost despair when he was told that he would be blind the rest of his life. Such was the pathos and understatement of Woodard's story that many in the audience, including hardboiled New York newspapermen, hardened to tales of misery and brutality, had tears in their eyes as he finished.

We were certain that the next morning's papers would give prominent and lengthy treatment to the story. I wanted this very much, because it had become evident that only the pressure of public opinion could force any redress for Woodard and stop the terrifying epidemic of violence against Negro veterans which threatened to spread. I knew from conversations with many veterans and from the reports of other conversations which members of our staff had had with Negro soldiers that a dangerous rebellion was rapidly growing among them. Many of them were beginning to feel that their service in the Army and Navy had intensified prejudice instead of diminishing it, and that there was no defense for them except that which they gave themselves.

But during the very time when Woodard was telling the story of what had happened to him in South Carolina, a Negro named Caraway killed the wife of a Long Island banker and shot and criminally attacked her daughter. This terrible crime, for which Caraway was later executed, was emblazoned in enormous headlines on the front page of every New York newspaper and the Woodard meeting was totally unmentioned by most papers and only briefly reported by the others.

XL

The President Is Helpless

The Caraway case demonstrated, however, that efforts over the years to develop a more enlightened and discriminating public opinion had not been in vain. It is possible and even probable that such a crime a decade before would have so disheartened or frightened some of the church, labor, professional, and educational organizations as to cause them to lose interest or to withdraw from the National Emergency Committee Against Mob Violence which was formed in August 1946. Just the opposite occurred. What Caraway did was recognized as an isolated crime which might have been committed by an individual of any race or color. When examination by psychiatrists and physicians ordered by the court revealed that Caraway was of subnormal mentality and a drug addict and that he had no memory of criminally assaulting the daughter, public indignation against him was not lessened but the terrible crime he had committed was understood in a manner which was gratifying.

We worked out a comprehensive program to build as swiftly as possible an active body of public opinion to counteract the activities of the hate organizations which were stirring up violence. It was decided to ask every church leader in the United States to preach special sermons and to urge the members of their congregations to refuse to join hate groups and instead to oppose them actively. We asked chambers of commerce, manufacturers' associations, employers' associations, and trade unions to activate their members against mob violence. We asked local units of national organizations to talk personally with their senators to urge amendment of the Senate rule to permit ending of filibusters by a majority instead of a two-thirds vote and to talk with their congressmen regarding amendment of the rules of the House of Representatives to prevent throttling of legislation by the oligarchic House Rules Committee. We asked them also to confer with their governors, attorneys general, mayors, sheriffs and chiefs of police to offer their aid in the devising of programs to stop violence and prejudice at their inception. We urged them as consumers to use their organized strength in persuading newspaper and magazine editors and radio and moving picture executives to use those media against violence.

The immediate action which was voted to be taken first was the sending of a small but representative delegation to Washington to confer with President Truman and Attorney General Tom Clark. Either individually or as a member of a delegation, I had been to the White House on numerous occasions to discuss this question with presidents from Coolidge to Roosevelt. I frankly doubted that our efforts on this occasion would be any more rewarding than had been those we had made with any of Truman's predecessors. There was considerable delay in gaining an appointment because the President was absent from Washington and there was almost as much difficulty because of vacation schedules in assembling the kind of representative delegation we desired. Our efforts to interest conservative and representative business organizations were utterly fruitless.

On September 19 six of us went to the White House. Labor was represented by James Carey, Secretary of the CIO, and Boris Shishkin of the AFL. The church was represented by Dr. Herman Reissig of the Federal Council of the Churches of Christ in America and education by Dr. Channing H. Tobias, Director of the Phelps-Stokes Fund. Leslie Perry, administrative assistant in our Washington Office, and I completed the delegation.

I was asked to be spokesman. The President sat quietly, elbows resting on the arms of his chair and his fingers interlocked against his stomach as he listened with a grim face to the story of the lynchings in Georgia and Louisiana, the flood of viciously anti-Semitic, anti-Catholic, anti-labor, and anti-foreign-born literature with which more than sixty hate organizations were inundating the country, and of the blinding of Isaac Woodard. When I had finished, the President exclaimed in his flat, Midwestern accent, "My God! I had no idea it was as terrible as that! We've got to do something!"

Carey, Shishkin, and Tobias related other stories of the rising wave of violence and voiced their convictions that unless some deterrent was found, even more serious trouble was inevitable. Numerous ideas were proffered, analyzed, and discarded as being either impracticable or inadequate. The President's face became even more perplexed and pessimistic as we fumbled for an answer to the question which had brought us there.

"Everybody seems to believe that the President by himself can do anything he wishes on such matters as this," he complained. "But the President is helpless unless he is backed by public opinion."

David K. Niles, Assistant to the President, entered into the discussion at this point for the first time to suggest the appointment of a committee to investigate the entire subject of violation of civil liberties and to recommend a program of corrective action. My first reaction which was shared by other members of the delegation was skepticism. President Roosevelt had made a somewhat similar suggestion several times to me but I had invariably gained the impression that he had made such proposals as a means of postponing decisions on issues which would bring him into conflict with belligerent anti-Negro Southern congressmen and senators. I pointed out to President Truman that if an attempt was made to establish such a commission by act of Congress, the House Rules Committee, which was at the time heavily weighted with Southern and conservative Republican members, would bottle it up and defer action indefinitely. Even after that delay had been overcome a prolonged and vitriolic filibuster would be inevitable in the Senate. The President nodded his head in agreement as he said, "I'll create it by executive order and pay for it out of the President's contingent fund."

I believe it was Channing Tobias who raised another objection—that such investigations were usually so time-consuming that the creation of such a committee would defer action too long a time for safety's sake and provide an excuse to weak-kneed members of Congress for non-action. The President, after we had discussed this serious hurdle, thought that it could be overcome by enjoining the committee to **do** work as speedily as possible and to have the report completed by e date of the opening of the 80th Congress in January 1947 if that could be done.

Mr. Truman then asked our advice on the composition of the committee. It was manifestly desirable to make it as broadly representative of every important segment of American thinking and activity as possible. Once again I voiced my conviction that however able a study was made and however sound its recommendations, the report would have little impact on public opinion if the committee were made up wholly or predominantly of especially interested persons like myself. I particularly urged onee again that intelligent representatives of business and finance should be included in the personnel of the committee. The President asked us each to suggest to him individuals to be considered for this important job. I told the President as I bade him good-by of a story I had heard for whose authenticity I could not personally vouch but which, if true, indicated one of the industry representatives who ought to be on the committee.

The story was one of a conversation between Charles E. Wilson, President of General Electric Corporation, and a friend who was asked by Mr. Wilson what he considered to be the most important question facing America. The friend had replied that it was either our foreign relations or labor-management relations. Mr. Wilson had vigorously disagreed, stating to his companion's astonishment that he was convinced that the race question was the most important of all American problems and that some day he hoped to be able to do something about it.

Whether the story be true or not, the record of Mr. Wilson as chairman of the President's Committee on Civil Rights has set a precedent which conceivably may be far-reaching in view of Mr. Wilson's prominence. The caliber of the other fourteen members of the committee was equally distinguished in various fields. They included Charles Luckman, the spectacularly successful young president of the Lever Brothers soap company; the Most Rev. Francis J. Haas of the Catholic Church; the Rt. Rev. Henry Knox Sherrill of the Protestant Episcopal Church; Mrs. Sadie T. Alexander, energetic Negro lawyer of Philadelphia; James B. Carey of the CIO, Boris Shishkin of the AFL, Rabbi Roland B. Gittelsohn, whose eloquent prayer at the dedication of the Iwo Jima Cemetery is one of the most superb professions of faith of our time; Presidents Frank P. Graham of the University of North Carolina and John S. Dickey of Dartmouth College; Dr. Channing H. Tobias; Franklin D. Roosevelt, Jr.; Mrs. M. E. Tilly of Atlanta, Georgia, one of the outstanding figures of the Methodist Episcopal Church South; Morris L. Ernst, famed fighter for civil liberties; and Francis P. Matthews of Omaha, Nebraska, former head of the Knights of Columbus.

The report which these representatives of business, labor, education, the law, and the public generally presented to the President and the American public in the autumn of 1947 under the title *To Secure These Rights* is without doubt the most courageous and specific document of its kind in American history. There are of course some omissions and deficiencies. But these are so minute in importance and number as to be insignificant when compared to the explicit recommendations of things to be done by the Congress, administrative bureaus of the federal and state governments, by state legislatures and by private organizations and individuals. An almost perfect yardstick was thus established by which can be measured the gap between what Americans say they believe and what they do.

No attempt will be made here to summarize the findings or the recommendations of the committee. I would prefer instead to recommend the reading of the report in its entirety. It may be obtained from the United States Government Printing Office, and from Simon & Schuster, who issued the report in a trade edition. It deals with denials of decent housing, jobs, justice, and hope to many millions of Americans because of the God they worship, the place of their birth, or the color of their skins. Underneath the report is the ominous rumble of a warning that if these rights are not secured to all Americans, there soon will be no rights for any.

I did not know the role I was playing in the growing conflict between the left-of-center and the more extreme left factions of the United Automobile Workers-CIO until the performance was over. Victor Reuther, the scholarly and almost shy director of the educational division of the world's biggest trade union, invited me to speak at a meeting in Cleveland in 1946 of the educational directors of

UAW-CIO unions from all parts of the United States. Victor estimated there would be between five and six hundred of these key individuals whose job it was to utilize films, lectures, literature, and personal contact to interpret the union's policies to its vast and turbulent membership. Instead more than twelve hundred showed up at the Hollenden Hotel, now somewhat shabbily genteel but once one of the great hotels of America.

The morning we registered was a cold rainy one. The rococo lobby and corridors, once the rendezvous of dignified gourmets, were filled with the voices of men accustomed to making themselves heard over the roar of factory machinery. There was much slapping of backs by ham-sized hands hardened by manual labor but becoming less calloused now that their owners were devoting themselves to the work of education instead of the work of making automobiles.

But there was an undercurrent of tension and caucusing. Walter Reuther's crowd was growing in strength and determination to oust by whatever means were necessary all Communists and fellow-travelers from the UAW-CIO. Equally determined not to be ousted, but instead to throw out redheaded Walter Reuther were the Communists and those who, wittingly or otherwise, voted with the left-wingers. Throughout the day the business of buttonholing in the long dark corridors and the rooms of the Hollenden proceeded feverishly. No quadrennial convention to select a presidential candidate by any of the political parties was ever more steeped in political maneuvers than the Cleveland meeting, although no officers were to be elected there. But the lines were already tightly drawn for the annual meeting of the UAW-CIO to be held in Atlantic City a few months later when either Reuther or the Thomas-Addes-Leonard faction would win control of the powerful union.

Walter Reuther and I were the speakers at the mass meeting to be held that evening in the Grand Ballroom. Long before the meeting was scheduled to begin every available seat and bit of standing room was occupied. Several of the UAW-CIO officials apologized to me because I was scheduled to speak first. I did not at the time understand the reason for such explanations, because it seemed to me perfectly proper and right that the president of the union should be the final speaker. I talked briefly, saying that the fate of minorities, whether they be racial, religious, or economic, are inextricably intertwined. I cited two or three historical instances of bigots attacking the most vulnerable minority and then, when that group had been crushed, extending their denial of elemental rights to the next most defenseless group and from that one to the next one until liberty for all had been circumscribed or destroyed. I talked frankly and specifically about the job which the UAW-CIO had started but was a long way from completing—eliminating prejudice of their Southern white and some of their Northern white members against Negroes and suspicion of trade unionism and of the attitude of their white fellow workers among Negroes.

There was little which was new and certainly nothing brilliant in my speech. But fortunately my audience seemed convinced that it was an honest speech and they were amazingly generous in their applause as I sat down. Some of my listeners had winced when I reminded them sharply that internal political quarreling or factional fights to satisfy personal ambitions or grudges could mean destruction of the union. Walter Reuther was given an ovation when he was introduced although I noticed some in the audience who sat glumly silent as they refrained from applauding. It was Don Montgomery, the quiet and erudite economist of the UAW-CIO, who looks more like a college professor or writer than a labor leader for the very good reason that he was a teacher, who told me after the meeting was over what had happened. Some of Reuther's enemies had planned to stage a demonstration against him when he rose to speak. But after the audience had reacted so spontaneously and cordially to my remarks, Don and Victor Reuther told me, the anti-Reutherites decided to call off the demonstration.

Later Victor Reuther wrote me a letter which I treasure, in which he told me that my speech had helped to turn the tide against the attempts of Communists to capture the meeting.

XLI

Children Grow Up

Every parent goes through a mental and emotional metamorphosis when suddenly his children burst through the chrysalis of childhood and emerge as adults, and, to a certain extent, strangers. For Gladys and me the process was complicated, as is everything in the life of a Negro, by the circumstance of race.

During my career with the NAACP, I had filled each year an increasing number of lecture engagements at American colleges and universities. Sometimes these contacts with students had caused my incurable optimism regarding the inherent decencies of human beings to develop to such an extent that not infrequently I would be brought up sharply by encounters with the bigotry of older persons. But the reverse was fortunately also true, when I would leave the dismaying atmosphere of a filibuster in Washington or the scene of a riot or lynching to speak on a week-end to eager and courageous students. My dreams of a more just and decent world were kept alive frequently only by talking with young people who were sloughing off the prejudices of their parents and environment.

For a variety of reasons Smith College in Northampton, Massachusetts, was the institution with which I had most frequent contact. The beloved William Allan Neilson, president of Smith, devoted a great portion of his extracurricular activity to service as a member of the board of directors of the NAACP. Before the decline of his health and eventual retirement from Smith, Dr. Neilson came down to New York from Northampton the second Monday of every month to attend and actively participate in NAACP board meetings. He and I frequently dined together and occasionally went to a movie between board meetings and the night train to Northampton. On those occasions and those of my visits to Smith, I learned to love him as a friend and to admire him as one of the greatest educators I have ever been privileged to know. I used to accuse him of using me as a sounding-board and avenue of release from campus academic problems since I could make no claim to scholarly erudition.

Thanks to Dr. Neilson and others on the Smith faculty, the college maintained leadership among American educational institutions in ignoring artificial lines of demarcation based on race, social position, wealth, or place of birth. Few colleges I have known have been more free from cant and hypocrisy or more ready to examine new ideas than Smith.

It was, therefore, quite natural and inevitable that Gladys and I wanted Jane to receive her college education there.

Jane's four years at Smith did more than provide her with a college degree. They gave us ringside seats from which we, as parents, could witness the growth of intelligence and thinking on social questions of students of Jane's generation. Jane herself was the central figure, unwittingly, in one of the most significant and dramatic of these episodes.

On matriculating as a freshman, she was assigned to live in Morris House. She had hardly arrived before a sizable commotion was created by a white student from Florida, assigned to the same house, who objected strenuously to Jane's presence and delivered an ultimatum that unless Jane was removed she herself would leave Smith College.

It was probably the worst jolt the girl ever received when she was firmly informed that if she could not comply with the principles and practices of the college her place would be filled immediately by another girl. The young woman decided to remain in college.

Three years later, during the annual campaign to elect officers of the class which would be seniors the following year, the most indefatigable campaigner on the campus was the young Floridian. She was not working in her own behalf—but to elect Jane as president of the house of representatives. Jane was elected by an overwhelming majority.

After Jane's graduation from Smith College she revealed that she wanted above everything to devote her life to the theater. But for her the disadvantage of skin color was greater even than that faced by dark-skinned Negroes. If her skin had been darker, she could have secured (assuming that her ability were great enough) so-called Negro roles in the increasing number of Broadway plays in which there were Negro characters. But her delicate ivory color and regular features caused her to appear un-Negro behind the footlights even with the use of dark makeup. And the stage was not yet ready to permit a Negro actor or actress to portray any except Negro roles.

When she tried out for the part of a young woman in a play about India, the author and producer were enthusiastic about her performance, declaring that her appearance, diction, and acting ability ideally suited her for the role. But from a higher level came the indignant objection that it was "unthinkable" to cast a Negro girl in an Indian part (in spite of the fact that Jane's color was lighter than that of most Indian girls). Another girl was given the part.

Jane's debut in the theater was made in the dramatization of Lillian Smith's novel of the south, *Strange Fruit.*

On the blizzardy night of the New York opening we had a party for Jane which lasted until nearly daybreak. Helen Hayes and Charlie MacArthur, Canada Lee, Jean Muir, Fredric March, Edna Thomas, Marc Connelly, Poppy Cannon, Kenneth Spencer, Edwin Embree of the Rosenwald Fund, Richmond Barthe the sculptor, Fania Marinoff, Carl Van Vechten, John Bright, J. J. Singh, Marcella Powers, and many others filled our small Harlem apartment to launch Jane and the other members of the cast on the all too brief New York run of the play.

Jane and Mel Ferrer, who played the leading male role, received excellent notices from the critics in the white press. Some of the Negro newspapers, using the occasion as a political grindstone, were less kind. I had opposed the making of a sordid moving picture called *St. Louis Woman,* and defended Lena Horne's refusal to play in it. It had been planned to produce the story first as a play and then as a picture. Although written by two able Negro writers, Countee Cullen and Arna Bontemps, who were my friends, it had pictured Negroes as pimps, prostitutes, and gamblers with no redeeming characteristics. Even one role supposed to portray a decent person—that of a pious churchgoing woman—represented her as having had several children, each by a different father without benefit of clergy. I had been shocked on reading the script to find every cliché and stereotype of the minstrel Negro included in it. My disapproval had angered a number of people, particularly some of the Negro actors and actresses in Hollywood who feared the loss of employment through the abolition of movie stereotypes of Negroes as perennial and incurable buffoons or feeble-minded menials.

While I would have written *Strange Fruit* quite differently had I been fortunate and able enough to write so successful a best-seller, its story and motivation were vastly different from that of *St. Louis Woman*. Lillian Smith had written her tragic story of racial hate in Georgia as honestly as any author had ever put word to paper. Considerable as were its faults it had an integrity and realism which were totally absent from *St. Louis Woman*. My enemies and critics, happy to find what they believed to be inconsistency between my attack on *St. Louis Woman* and my support of *Strange Fruit*, charged that Jane had been given the role only to silence criticism from me. It was a foul business but I was very proud of the manner in which Jane withstood the attack, although Gladys and I could see that she was deeply hurt.

My son Walter's emergence from childhood was similarly marked by problems created by racial prejudice. As a child of ten he had announced, with a singular adultness of mind, his belief that war was "immoral" and futile. He gave no evidence of any change in this attitude until he was sixteen, when, to the consternation of Gladys and me, he announced one morning at breakfast that he wanted to join the paratroopers, because, though he had not changed his ideas about war, he thought that Hitler and Hirohito and Mussolini stood for everything against which I had been fighting all my life, and he wanted to do what he could on the right side.

The age of adolescence in children is a difficult time for parents. They have not yet quite sloughed off their habit of thinking of their offspring as infants, and a proposal such as Walter's stimulates pictures in their minds which are shockingly incongruous.

Suddenly it seemed as though it had been only yesterday that he had come home from the maternity hospital in his mother's arms. I loathed to a degree beyond expression in words the ruthlessness and unscrupulousness in mental attitude with which I knew paratroopers were necessarily indoctrinated. I hated the thought of a sensitive, healthy, and idealistic boy being taught to gouge eyes, hit below the belt or anywhere else opportunity offered, as the men dropped behind enemy lines were taught to do. Because he loved photography, I suggested both seriously and banteringly, that if he was seeking sudden death he should join the signal corps and ask for advanced combat duty. At least, I reminded him, he would be learning a useful skill instead of that of gutter fighting. But when I saw that he was not to be discouraged, I told him that I would sign whatever papers would make it possible for him to enlist at his age.

But Gladys and I needn't have worried about it, had we thought the thing through. When he applied for acceptance, he was informed that "the United States Army is not enlisting Negroes as paratroopers."

It was two years later, after he had entered Swarthmore College, that he received his "greetings from the President." The day of Japan's surrender was not one of jubilation for him because on that very day he was ordered to take his physical examination for the Army. "Were the war still going on I'd not object, Dad," he told me, "but now that peace has come I don't want to interrupt my college career just as it begins."

There was nothing I could do. Were I to ask any favor for my own son in the form of a deferment, which I could freely ask for any other man's son if the facts justified asking, inevitable criticism would descend on the Association and hurt its good name. Already some critical remarks had come to me because Walter was unusually tall and large for his age. The statement had been made, interestingly enough by Negroes, that Walter was being kept out of the Army through my "influence" while the sons of less publicized parents had had to serve.

Induction came several months after V-J Day in the middle of Walter's second semester at Swarthmore. He was ordered to Camp Dix in New Jersey, where he remained for a long time during the period of uncertainty after the war when neither the War Department or Congress could make up their minds on what kind of a national defense

America would need. Then one night he telephoned us that he was scheduled to leave early the next morning for Camp Robinson in Arkansas.

I became almost physically ill. That very morning I had received a carefully documented account of the killing in cold blood of two Negro soldiers at that camp because, having been born north of Mason and Dixon's line, they had unwittingly violated one of the South's unwritten laws on the way in which Negroes should defer to whites. It was too late to do anything even if there had been anything which could be done without harming the Association. I dared not tell Gladys of my dismay although I knew she sensed it. Cold terror filled me as I thought of what might happen when Walter, accustomed only to a somewhat more civilized section of the country where he could come and go almost as he pleased, unwittingly failed to say a properly deferential "sir" to a white Southerner. Even more paralyzing fear gripped me all through the night as I visualized what might result when my son gave his name as "Walter White." I tried desperately but unsuccessfully to forget the rewards which had been offered in Arkansas and other Southern states to anyone who would "get Walter White" following my investigations of race riots and lynchings which several times had disclosed the names of the killers. I wished heartily for Walter's sake at that moment that there had not been so much publicity of that work which made my name so loathed by the Ku Klux Klan and its like-minded organizations. I got little sleep that night.

We never found out what happened that next morning at Camp Dix. Walter was lined up with the other miserable and unhappy draftees on the railroad station platform awaiting his turn to step aboard the Arkansas-bound train. Suddenly a sergeant's voice barked a command to eight or ten men, including Walter, to step out of line and return to camp. A few days later he was sent to Camp Lee in Virginia. I was delighted because Lee had a reputation of being the best-run training camp with the least racial friction of any in the South. Its commanding officer, General George Horkan, and two majors, Jack Tierney from Goshen, N. Y., and Andy Gray from Boston, were my friends.

Gladys and I felt confident that between General Horkan and

Majors Gray and Tierney Walter would not exactly be mistreated at Camp Lee. Our peace of mind, however, did not last long, through no fault of theirs. Although his induction and other Army records listed Walter as "colored" he found on his arrival at Camp Lee that he had been assigned to a "white" barracks. He telephoned us in great perturbation. "What will be the effect," he demanded, "on the NAACP of my being assigned to a 'white' outfit? Won't colored people think I'm passing and won't it hurt your work?"

I was deeply touched that he did not think of himself but only of what harm might come to my work. I tried to reassure him by reminding him that the NAACP had vigorously fought racial segregation in the Army and Navy and perhaps, now that the war was over, the armed services were beginning to practice some of the democracy they allegedly had fought for. But my half-jesting, half-serious quip gave him no consolation. "Your son is the last person they should choose for the experiment," he told me. I promised to telephone General Horkan and get the matter straightened out if I could, and he seemed to feel somewhat relieved.

It had been a mistake, I learned. Walter is tall, ivory-skinned of color, not bad-looking according to our friends, and speaks with an accent not usually associated with Negroes. So the Army officer who made the assignment apparently had not bothered to look at the designation of race and had assumed that Walter was white instead of Negro. George Horkan arranged a transfer to a Negro unit.

Thus Walter was introduced to a way of life which was a painful and trying transition from the quiet culture of Swarthmore. On the day before his transfer there had been two knifings and other brawls in the colored unit. Most of the men had come from the levee towns and rural areas of the deep South where life had been tough and advantages few. Walter had been rudely awakened to the realization that a lot of his fellow Americans were not like those at Fieldston (his preparatory school) and Swarthmore by his contacts with men in the barracks at Dix and Lee. But now, perhaps because most of the Negroes he had known in our home had been men and women of great gentility like James Weldon Johnson and William Hastie and Marian Anderson, the ones he was living with in the goldfish-bowl life of Army barracks were a distinct novelty to him, to put it mildly.

"I can't even understand them," he told me plaintively over the telephone.

But he made his adjustment gallantly and we were glad when later he brought to our house some of the men he had learned to know and respect.

XLII

No Road Back to Atlanta

The years since World War Two have passed swiftly, bringing their mixture of the old discouragements and the new hopes.

The end of the war brought many signs that the patience of the Negro was wearing thin. There were many ways in which this was visible—some of them gratifying, others of a nature which complicated the problems we were attempting to solve. Despite the economic hardships suffered by Negroes through closing down of many war industries in which they had found employment, and rising commodity prices, the NAACP continued to grow in membership and influence. Not only Negroes, but also a growing number of white Americans, both Southern and Northern, became increasingly active in the Association's work. Frequently I was embarrassed by the necessity of rejecting the applications of many young white men and women who were eager to work to eliminate race prejudice.

A much less commendable and often quite embarrassing evidence of the Negro's resentment became more frequent—hypersensitive belligerence and surliness of Negroes toward whites. On numerous occasions I found myself the victim of such ill-will until I escaped from the situation or was forced to let it be known that I was not white. This situation could have been even more embarrassing and dangerous had it not been for the persistent campaign of Negro newspapers like the *Pittsburgh Courier* and *Chicago Defender* and of church, civic, and other groups.

Another proof of disillusionment which caused us difficulty was the attempt of Communists to infiltrate a few branches and youth councils of the NAACP after the shooting war was over. During the days of the Scottsboro case, the strategy of the Communists had been to discredit the NAACP and to destroy the faith of its members in the organization. The Negro issue had been dropped with conspicuous abruptness during the days of the Hitler-Stalin pact and it had been played down by the Communists during the war. Some of the abler and more honest Negro Communists had made no attempt to conceal their conviction that the success of the defense of Russia should take precedence over the fight for Negro rights in the United States. During that period of Russian collaboration and of Communist Party alliance in the United States with anyone who directly or indirectly contributed to Russian military victory, the NAACP encountered little criticism or conflict with American Communists. But as soon as the war had ended in victory and the unity created by military necessity had begun to deteriorate, we began to see Communists try to gain control or at least to influence the policies of some of our local units.

Their method was comparatively simple. Members of the Communist Party joined some of the local branches of the Association and worked indefatigably on projects against discrimination. Nothing was said about membership in the Communist Party nor was there any attempt to spread obviously Communist doctrine. In one of our California branches two Communists became members of the legal redress and legislative committee. They did an excellent job.

Soon they proposed that it be made into two committees since the amount of work was too great for one. Without consultation with the national office this was done. On the newly created "political and legislative committee" were appointed the two Communists, two sincere but politically inexperienced members of the branch, and a fifth person who, though not a Communist, liked publicity and was delighted with the energetic fashion in which the two Communists worked.

On September 15, 1946, at a meeting which was attended by approximately 300 of the 1600 members of the branch, the "political and legislative committee" presented a report recommending that the branch endorse a slate of candidates in the bitterly contested California elections of that year. The proposed slate was headed by the name of the Communist candidate for governor and included both Democrats and Republicans.

My first knowledge of the action of the branch came in a telegram from a member of the branch asking if branches of the NAACP had authority to endorse political parties or candidates for political office. I promptly informed the inquirer that such endorsement was unequivocally prohibited both by the national board of directors and by action of the Annual Convention. At the same time I telegraphed the president and secretary of our San Francisco branch "immediately to withdraw its endorsement of political candidates which is in direct violation of Association policy. . . . Branch is further instructed to notify National Office of such repudiation and to issue statement to newspapers that it has repudiated endorsement of political candidates." When this telegram was not answered immediately the president of the branch was informed that unless such retraction was issued by the branch within twenty-four hours, the national office would repudiate the endorsement and at the same time suspend the charter of the branch. This brought action. A special call meeting of the board of the branch rescinded its previous action and the news was given to the press.

Equally swift action was taken when efforts were made in ten or twelve of the other sixteen hundred branches, youth councils, and college chapters of the Association. We were determined to permit no political organization, whether Communist, Republican, Democratic, or of any other political persuasion, to "capture" local units or to utilize the Association's machinery for selfish and partisan political purposes.

Counterattack, the Weekly Newsletter of Facts on Communism, edited by former agents of the Federal Bureau of Investigation, spotlighted the situation in its November 28, 1947, issue. Its leading item told of Communist plans to capture the National Association for the Advancement of Colored People, "the great mass organization of Negroes" which "is respected and supported by Negroes everywhere." *Counterattack* reported that its investigators had learned that the Communist National Board had "decided last summer that the time had come to move on from infiltration of the NAACP to actual capture of it," had liquidated the National Negro Congress as part of the plan, and added that "the party has ordered them (its members) to behave discreetly a while . . . to refrain from pushing the party line conspicuously . . . and thus to quiet the suspicions of Walter White, Secretary and main leader of the NAACP, and prevent him from acting against them before they get too strong for him to stop them."

Newspaper reporters who thought they smelled an exciting story were somewhat baffled when I refused to become alarmed. I informed them that I saw no reason to worry about former leaders of the National Negro Congress "capturing" the Association when they had so conspicuously failed to attract any mass membership for their own organization. I also told reporters that the issue would be decided, not by the NAACP or any other organization, but by the capacity of the capitalist system to prove its right to continue to exist. If racial bigotry continued to dominate the domestic and international policy of the United States and of the white capitalist world, I could see no possible hope of survival of that system. But if democracy and a system of free enterprise were able to abolish inequalities, guarantee security and a decent way of life to every man on the basis of his ability, we would have nothing to worry about from communism. I said this, incidentally, to Frederick Woltman, *New York World-Telegram* reporter who won the Pulitzer Prize for his exposé of communism in the United States, and as a result I was bitterly denounced in the *Daily Worker* by Benjamin J. Davis, New York City councilman whom I have known since he was a boy in Atlanta.

On April 9, 1947, I called on President Truman at the White House to invite him to speak at the Lincoln Memorial in Washington on June 29, 1947, at the closing session of the Thirty-first Annual Conference of the NAACP. Although I knew it was unnecessary for me to do so, I reminded the President of how acts of discrimination against minorities were being used abroad to discredit the United States and convince the people of the world that Americans were incurably addicted to bigotry. A forthright and unequivocal statement by the President was necessary, I urged, to let the people of the world know that while Americans frequently failed to live up to their declarations of democracy, we were constantly at work to narrow the margin between our protestations of freedom and our practice of them.

"Send me a memorandum," he said, "of the points you think I ought to emphasize in my speech."

We both laughed as I told him that if he included even one half of the things I thought he ought to say, the Southern Democrats would probably want to run him out of the country.

We invited also as speakers Mrs. Eleanor Roosevelt and Senator Wayne Morse of Oregon, and it was decided by the committee on arrangements that I should introduce the President and utilize the occasion to state simply and unequivocally the position of the Negro. All four major networks—CBS, NBC, ABC, and Mutual— and most of the independent radio stations generously agreed to broadcast the President's and my speeches. The State Department arranged to send the program by short wave to all parts of the world. A number of local networks and independent stations in addition agreed to rebroadcast the speeches one or more times in addition to carrying the program directly from Washington as it was in progress.

Anticipating the explosive report of the Committee on Civil Rights which was destined to bring down upon his head vilification and denunciation from the South as great as that heaped upon Abraham Lincoln, President Truman called for federal, state, and individual action against lynching, disfranchisement, the poll tax, educational and employment inequality, and the whole caste system based upon race or color. The applause when he finished was hearty but not overwhelming. I thought again of Lincoln—of the cool response which had been accorded the Gettysburg Address. I did not believe that Truman's speech possessed the literary quality of Lincoln's speech but in some respects it had been a more courageous one in its specific condemnation of evils based upon race prejudice which had too long disgraced America, and its call for immediate action against them.

As he sat down, the President turned modestly to ask how I liked his speech. When I told him how excellent I believed it to be, he assured me, "I said what I did because I mean every word of it— and I am going to prove that I do mean it."

If he had any premonition of the savage assaults which were destined to be made upon him by Southern governors, senators, and congressmen when he asked the Congress to act upon the issues he had discussed in his speech, or if he had any fear of the consequences, he showed no signs of it.

Radio authorities estimated that several hundred million listeners in all parts of the globe heard the speeches. It was by far the largest single audience in history to hear the story of the fight for freedom for the Negro in the United States. One of the members of our board of directors, Bishop W. J. Walls of Chicago, wrote me from Vienna that the program had been very widely publicized and discussed there. And one of the most touching of all responses was a letter from the remote Pacific Island of Tinian which I had visited during the war. The writer, Lewis Harris, Jr., said that he and a number of other American soldiers had listened to the broadcast in a miserably hot tent and had been so stirred by it that they had immediately afterward raised among themselves a contribution of $59.25 to help carry on the work of the NAACP.

And then there was the Freedom Train.

By invitation I attended a conference at the White House shortly before our Washington meeting. The meeting had been called by the American Heritage Foundation, which had been organized to promote the Freedom Train on which original documents pertaining to the American struggle for freedom, such as the Declaration of Independence, the Bill of Rights, and the Emancipation Proclamation, were to be exhibited throughout the United States.

I agreed with some cynics that it was a ballyhoo stunt—but I was equally convinced that it was good ballyhoo which would reawaken in the minds of Americans the passionate devotion (which at times appeared almost to have been totally lost) to the belief that all men are equal and should be given equal opportunity.

Names on the roll of conference delegates read like a super *Who's Who* of the business, professional, and civic leaders of the United States. Winthrop W. Aldrich, Louis Novins, Attorney General Tom Clark, and Thomas D'A. Brophy were the speakers. The theme of the meeting was voiced by Mr. Brophy in the slogan. "We must work at democracy to make democracy work." Later we were guests of Mr. Aldrich at luncheon at the Statler Hotel at which a variety of eloquent speeches were made by Eric Johnston, William Green, and Mrs. Robert Patterson, wife of the Secretary of War. After the formal address individual after individual rose to speak in support of the Freedom Train. Many of the statements were brief and to the point. Several others of the speakers, however, talked glibly and at length of a freedom which their own organizations had notoriously denied to other Americans.

I found myself increasingly annoyed by some of the statements in praise of freedom when I knew that the acts of the speakers belied their words. I kept remembering a headline in the morning's newspapers which to me at least marked a tragic gap between the phrases which were being spoken and what was really going on in the United States. I had not intended to speak but suddenly I found myself standing, attempting to gain recognition from Mr. Aldrich. I was determined, even at the risk of being guilty of spoiling an otherwise pleasant occasion, to speak the plain truth. At last Mr. Aldrich nodded in my direction. Fearing that some of those present might not know my race, I announced my name and said that I was secretary of the National Association for the Advancement of Colored People, emphatically stressing the word "colored." I suggested as an objective "a program to teach Americans the real meaning of the Bill of Rights and the Constitution" and said that the first place at which the Freedom Train should stop was Greenville, S. C., in which on the night before "twelve good men and true . . . had freed twenty-eight self-confessed lynchers."

Startled faces turned to stare at the individual who had dared to tie in a grim reality of this embarrassing nature with the talk about freedom. I did not relish the experience but I could never have felt right afterward had I not spoken. There was a stunned silence for perhaps fifteen seconds and then applause which filled the room. Irving Berlin put his arms about my shoulders as he congratulated me, while some of the newspapermen were generous enough to tell me they were delighted that someone "had the guts to get up and tell the truth."

Shortly afterward Charles E. Wilson, president of General Electric Corporation and chairman of the President's Committee on Civil Rights, introduced a resolution in a meeting of the board of directors of the American Heritage Foundation that the Freedom Train be withdrawn from any city which attempted to segregate those who wished to visit the train. It was passed unanimously.

I was startled when shortly thereafter the Communist Party ordered its members to discredit whenever possible the Freedom Train as a "plot to fool the people." With some justification and considerable accuracy they charged that some of the most prominent sponsors of the project had been guilty of anti-labor and anti-minority statements and practices.

But more direct were the assaults from the right on the Freedom Train. Memphis, Tennessee, that bastion of feudalism ruled by the notorious Boss Crump, bluntly refused to abandon racial segregation for the duration of the scheduled appearance of the Freedom Train in that city. Promptly the American Heritage Foundation canceled the showing there. For one of the very first times in history the rest of the country had called the bluff of the reactionary South. Mortified by the unfavorable publicity caused by the cancellation, many of the citizens of Memphis dared the wrath of Crump by protesting vigorously and loudly.

When the Freedom Train visited Nashville shortly afterward, space was purchased by citizens of Nashville in the Memphis newspapers inviting Memphians to come to Nashville where they could see the original Bill of Rights which Crump had not let them see in Memphis. Other Southern cities, including several small ones in Mississippi, besieged the American Heritage Foundation to send the train to those cities on the days which had been allotted to Memphis and to Jackson, Mississippi, which also refused to abandon segregation and also suffered cancellation as a consequence.

Birmingham, Alabama, warned by the fate which had befallen Memphis and Jackson, came up with the bright idea of justifying segregated lines because of state laws requiring separate waiting rooms for whites and Negroes on the Birmingham railroad station. The two lines were scheduled to merge a few yards from the train with alternating groups of twenty persons from each racial line admitted to the train.

Inquiry speedily revealed that since the train was to be exhibited in the railroad yards and not in the railroad station, the excuse of separate waiting rooms required by law was obviously fallacious.

The issue was finally settled when the American Heritage Foundation discovered that deliberately false statements had been made about the arrangements by some of the Birmingham city officials. The showing in Birmingham of the Freedom Train was promptly canceled. Other Alabama cities like Montgomery and Anniston received the train without segregation. Their local newspapers pointed out that Negro and white citizens stood in the same lines to pay taxes, make bank deposits, and purchase stamps in local post offices, and that it would be ridiculous under these circumstances to require segregation on the Freedom Train.

Another victory, although a modest one, was scored for democracy when other Southern cities which had in one form or another insisted on segregation, withdrew their demands after the Birmingham exhibition of the Freedom Train was canceled. It was increasingly apparent that the stigma of bigotry attached to the South by politicians, opportunists, and bigots was beginning to lose its talonlike effectiveness.

Perhaps if enough Northerners *and* Southerners who are ashamed of being constantly pictured as morons and bigots achieve such understanding, decent Southerners can be elevated into a position where they instead of the Talmadges and Rankins shall be the real spokesmen of the South—both white and Negro.

The increasing importance to world peace of the problem of racial minorities, and the inextricability of all race hatreds, one from another, were emphasized by events centering around the controversy in the United Nations over the partition of Palestine, when once more the United States needed the help of black Haiti. For the first time on a major issue in the United Nations, the United States and Soviet Russia were lined up on one side against Great Britain and the Arab states on the other. Haiti had announced that she would vote against partition as had also the black Republic of Liberia. I was bombarded by pro-partition organizations and individuals in the United States and one highly placed American official importuned me to do what I could to persuade Haiti to change her vote.

In my own opinion both the wisdom and the practicability of partition were doubtful. But no other solution had been devised or discussed. I did not like the self-segregation of Zionism, nor did I approve of the attitude of many Jews who had made it a sacred cult. But I reluctantly supported partition only because Palestine seemed the only haven anywhere in the world for nearly one million Jews of Europe.

My efforts to persuade the Haitian government to reconsider its decision to vote against partition were not made any easier by the attitude of some of the advocates of partition. One exceedingly able and experienced woman who telephoned my office and home incessantly during the UN debate imperiously demanded of me one day, "Don't the Haitians know that the best friends they have on earth are Jews?" Annoyed at her manner, I brusquely informed her that both the Haitians and I would like to have evidence of her statement. Her reply was so vague and evasive that I suggested that she would be more successful in her efforts to win support for partition if she refrained from overstatements of that character.

For a time I hoped that the passionate partisans of partition were making such statements only to me because I knew them well enough for them to feel free to talk frankly. But I soon learned that this was not so and that as a result the UN representatives from Haiti, Liberia, and the Philippines and other small countries were becoming increasingly annoyed at the imperious way in which attempts were made to dictate to them the way they should vote. It was quite clear that some of the most active workers for Palestine, although by no means all of them, labored under the delusion that the Haitians and Liberians should accept without question the mandates of the white pro-partition advocates. In one or two instances the racial arrogance toward the small countries because they were black and poor was little different from that shown by the most intransigent Southern politicians toward Negroes.

I had been serving for some months on the Citizens Committee on Displaced Persons under the chairmanship of Earl G. Harrison, the distinguished Dean of the law school of the University of Pennsylvania. I had written a number of syndicated columns to do what I could toward creation of public opinion in favor of the Stratton Bill, the purpose of which was to bring about the admission of displaced Europeans to the United States. The reaction to some of these columns had been startling, to put it mildly, revealing widespread and intense anti-Semitism. A number of letters, usually anonymous and couched in obscene language, denied the accuracy of my statements that eighty per cent of the one hundred thousand displaced persons which the Stratton Bill proposed should be admitted to the United States per year for four years were non-Jews. These figures had been vouched for by all responsible governmental and private agencies.

It was nauseating to see how effectively the vicious propaganda of both the Adolf Hitler of Nazi Germany and the native American Hitlers had poisoned with hate the minds of so many Americans. I remember ruefully the experience during the war when I had been invited to luncheon by a well-known New York banker. We ate in one of New York's most famous university clubs. My host had telephoned me after hearing me speak at a meeting at Carnegie Hall. I had pointed out that throughout the history of bigotry, bigots had selected as their victims the most vulnerable minority in any given area against which prejudice and fear could be most easily created. Acts of violence or denial of justice to that minority usually created protests at the inception of such a campaign. But, in time, the recurrence of such episodes became less and less noticed until there was common acceptance of such patterns of prejudice.

I had gone on to point out that after the most vulnerable minority had been victimized, the bigots had extended their activities to the next most defenseless group and from that one to the next until liberty was either destroyed or gravely restricted for all. I had cited the development of the Know-Nothing and the KKK movements in the United States, nazism in Germany, and anti-Semitism in Czarist Russia and Poland as examples.

My luncheon host had been most extravagant in his over-praise of what seemed to me a simple statement of fact. He told me of his abolitionist ancestry and of his own contributions to support of Tuskegee Institute. He tactfully mentioned that he was financially able to make a sizable contribution to the NAACP and asked me to send him literature descriptive of the Association's work which he wanted to use in persuading his friends and relatives to make contributions also.

"But," he told me, "you are making a serious mistake and doing grave injury to your cause by linking it with that of the Jews." I was so startled at the swift transition that I paused involuntarily in replacing my coffee cup on the saucer, holding it suspended in midair.

"Most Americans really *like* Negroes, but they hate Jews," he finished, almost spitting out the last three words. I left him soon after that, and he probably wondered why I was so cool to his praise of the NAACP, and his vague offers of help. I had long since learned that no faith can safely be reposed in any man who believes he has no prejudice against one minority while he indiscriminately hates another one. The problems of persecuted minorities differ in historical background and in certain details. But in a basic fashion they are identical in that persecution always arises from the same desire for selfish individual or group security and gain, from the same ignorance, from the same unreasoned and baseless fears.

To return to the UN debate on partitioning of Palestine. I talked with representatives of Haiti, Liberia, the Philippines, and several other countries whose votes on the issue were destined to be important. I freely admitted that partition seemed to be only a very temporary expedient but I suggested that for humanity's sake it would be wise to vote for the only immediate remedy which had been proposed in the hope that thereby time could be gained to work out a more lasting solution, if there was any lasting solution.

A seemingly unrelated and minor episode (save that all episodes in the story of race hatreds are related) added to the difficulties. I read in the *New York Post* one October afternoon a huge advertisement of the revival on Broadway of *The Birth of a Nation,* the distorted David W. Griffith film of the Reconstruction Era which glorified the Ku Klux Klan and grossly libeled the Negro as a brutish rapist.

I knew the owner of the theater. His son and my son had been classmates at the Ethical Culture School in New York City. He had invited me on several occasions to be a week-end guest at his home in a New York suburb. I telephoned him at his home on reading the advertisement and he was most cordial until I told him the purpose of my call. He denied that he had ever heard that the infamous film glorified the Klan or defamed Negroes. He told me that he had exhibited the picture more than four hundred times during the past twenty-five years in various theaters he owned, and had never been told that it had created riots and other disorders or that, because of this, it had been banned in a number of cities. He bluntly refused to consider withdrawing it and added gratuitously, "I have been a friend of *your* people, but of course I don't expect any gratitude." I restrained with difficulty the anger which welled up within me at the condescension of his statement and repressed the temptation to tell him of the friendship I was exhibiting toward *his* people through the work I was doing for the partition of Palestine. The conversation ended when he informed me that he had a number of theater guests who were waiting for him.

When the picture opened the following morning, we threw a picket line in front of the theater. The picketing proceeded peacefully through Saturday and Sunday with almost complete abstention of the public from entering the theater. On Saturday afternoon a representative of the theater, waving his hand at the pickets, proposed to me, "If you will get rid of all this, we will see if we can put in another picture on Monday." His offer was swiftly and unequivocally refused.

Sunday afternoon the quiet and effective picket line was inundated by a large number of lusty-lunged members of an organization which had recently changed its name from the Young Communist League to American Youth for Democracy. We knew that participation by real or alleged Communists in the picketing would label the affair "just another Communist demonstration" and would imply our involvement with extraneous political ideologies. We, therefore, promptly withdrew our pickets and explained to the newspaper reporters why we did so. Fortunately, the AYD pickets disappeared shortly thereafter and we resumed our picketing until the film was withdrawn the following Friday.

But I had to answer repeatedly the question from some of the

Haitians and Liberians as to why we fought for partition when an
anti-Negro film like *The Birth of a Nation* was exhibited on Broadway by a member of the race we were trying to help. I had to
explain over and over again that what one individual did should
not be held against the other members of any racial, religious, or
national group and to point out that the most dangerous of all
practices from which Negroes had suffered most was the attachment
of odium to an entire group because of the shortsightedness of one
member of that group.

When the vote on Palestine was taken, Haiti, Liberia, and the
Philippines voted for partition instead of against it as they had
previously declared their intention of doing. Those three votes decided the issue.

The NAACP's growing conviction that the battle for the Negro's
freedom must be fought on a world-wide, rather than a merely
American, front, involved me in the affairs of the West Indies in
1947. When a conference on the West Indies was announced for
September 1947, by Sir Arthur Creech-Jones, British Colonial Secretary, a meeting of West Indian and American leaders was held
in my office. We talked at length about the desperate plight of the
overwhelming majority of the British West Indian people, impoverished because most of the profits of their agriculture were
reaped by absentee landlords in England. We were also gravely concerned because, although the problems of the peoples of the various
islands were largely identical, the difficulty of intercommunication
between the islands had prevented united consideration of the basic
problems.

Increasing squalor, misery, and poverty, combined with the deterioration of the British Empire as a result of World Wars One and
Two, have fanned the flame of demand for freedom in the West
Indies as it has all over the world. In Jamaica, where one half of the
three million inhabitants of the British West Indies live, a shrewd,
rabble-rousing soldier of political fortune named Alexander Bustamante had risen swiftly to power by capitalizing on the misery of
the oppressed classes of that island. In conflict with wiser leaders
whose objective was federation of the British West Indian islands

and the attainment of dominion status, Bustamante demanded complete independence, although he presented no program for solution of the almost insuperable economic problems facing the islands as a result of centuries of exploitation.

There were present at the meeting in my office A. A. Austin, a successful real estate operator in New York City, Dr. Lucian Brown of New York, and several others. Before the meeting ended the American Committee for West Indian Freedom was formed with Mr. Austin and myself as cochairmen.

The preliminary conference of leaders from the various islands at Kingston, Jamaica, under the auspices of the Caribbean Labour Congress was extraordinarily successful. Although the fiery Bustamante bitterly opposed the proposal to create a federation of seven British West Indian islands, he later voted for federation. There was frank presentation to the Colonial Secretary of the problems of the islands and insistence upon greater self-government through federation and eventual dominion status. Although complete unity appears to be more a hope than an achievement and although the perplexing problem of economic security must yet be solved, a very marked advance toward the solution to the economis and political problems of the British islands in the Caribbean has been made.

World-wide attention was focused on the problem of color by the presentation to the United Nations of an appeal on behalf of the Negro American which had been prepared under the direction of Dr. DuBois. He had written the first section and several chapters had been prepared by Dr. Rayford Logan of Howard University, Professor Milton Konvitz of Cornell University, Earl Dickerson and W. Robert Ming of Chicago, and Leslie Perry of Washington, D. C. In one hundred and fifty-five carefully documented pages the grim story of legal proscription, economic injustice, and mob violence against American Negroes had been set forth in temperate and unanswerable language.

The appeal created an international sensation. We were flooded with requests for copies of the document, particularly from nations which were critical of the United States, including Russia, Great Britain, and the Union of South Africa. It was manifest that they were pleased to have documentary proof that the United States did not practice what it preached about freedom and democracy. But it was equally apparent that Russia, Great Britain, and the Union of South Africa were morally afraid that acceptance of the appeal on behalf of American Negroes and action on the document would establish a precedent giving the United Nations authority in those countries.

Dr. DuBois spent several futile weeks in correspondence and telephone calls to Trygve Lie's office in an attempt to arrange for a delegation to present the petition formally to top officials of the UN. He was urged to mail the petition to Mr. Lie's office obviously to avoid any publicity for the presentation. Dr. DuBois firmly refused to permit the petition to be sidetracked in this fashion, and we finally presented it in M. Langier's office at the Human Rights Commission. We knew that for the time being at least the UN would use every possible stratagem to avoid any formal action on it. We knew also that its chief value would be its dragging out into the open the grim facts of denial of even elementary justice to human beings because of color. But we were convinced that in time the petition would stimulate other appeals from other minorities in other parts of the world and form a pattern of information which no society of nations could evade.

When the Human Rights Commission met at Geneva later under the chairmanship of Mrs. Eleanor Roosevelt, the Soviet government demanded that the NAACP petition and one other from the International Congress of Women, should be received and acted upon to the exclusion of any other petitions. Mrs. Roosevelt took the sound position that all bona fide petitions should be received and investigated or none at all.

From the time when I first came to New York at Jim Johnson's invitation to join the NAACP until now, I have lived in Harlem. But when, in 1947, I had a heart attack, and specialists told me that unless I reduced my work and slowed up I might develop a serious heart ailment and die in two or three years, it seemed wise to supplement my home with an apartment near the office where I could rest for an hour during the middle of the day. It was also becoming increasingly necessary for me to find a place close to the office where, uninterrupted by telephone calls and visitors, I could write my two columns weekly, articles, this book, and my speeches.

My daughter Jane located one of New York's virtually non-existent vacant apartments through a former classmate whose father was president of a huge apartment house corporation located very close to my office. But just as the deal was about to be closed, Jane's classmate reported that although the apartment was vacant, I could not rent it "because the presence of a Negro would jeopardize the floating of a large bond issue which was being planned to refinance the apartment building." The individuals who made the decision were among the most active advocates of the partition of Palestine.

Nor is that the only time when, in the post war years, and north of Mason and Dixon's line, I have had the cry "Run, nigger, run!" hurled at me. Late in 1947 my article called "Why I Remain a Negro" was published in the *Saturday Review of Literature* and later in *Reader's Digest* and the *Negro Digest*. In it I attempted to tell simply and anecdotally the story of why I had decided not to "pass."

A flood of letters and telegrams poured in in response to the article from men and women like Albert Einstein, Carl Van Vechten, Eric Johnston, Darryl Zanuck, Clare Boothe Luce, and from many whose names were quite unknown to me, and though most of them praised the article, among the latter there were a number that were bitterly hostile. Some of the most sympathetic and understanding comments were written by Southern white women; some of the most bitter came from Northern or border cities. One indignant woman in Iowa demanded, "If you niggers don't like it here, why don't you go back where you came from?"

I was strongly tempted to reply that I did not think Herman Talmadge and Dr. Green of the Ku Klux Klan would want me back in Georgia.

XLIII

All Shadows Are Dark

For over thirty years I have been active in the fight to destroy racial prejudice. When one is fighting against evil his attention is inevitably concentrated on evidences that the evil still is rampant, rather than on those which show that, in some places, it is abating. It would be impossible, through reiteration of wearily repetitious episodes to overstress the cruelties and injustices which Negroes have suffered for centuries, and are still suffering. Yet this book would badly fail to make one of its most important points if it did not call attention to some more hopeful aspects of the matter.

Here, listed briefly, are some isolated evidences, taken at random from many. These things are facts today. They would have seemed to most Negroes only a dream of the millennium even twenty-five years ago.

In 1948, the University of Delaware, influenced by the Supreme Court decision in the Ada Sipuel case, announced that Negro applicants for graduate and professional courses not offered to them elsewhere in the state would be admitted without segregation.

In 1948 the Board of Education of Freehold, New Jersey, abolished the rule which made Negroes go to public schools assigned to them (in fact, segregated schools) and announced that all students could attend the schools nearest them, thus abolishing segregation.

In Trenton, New Jersey, not only has segregation been completely abolished in the public schools, but some Negro teachers are teaching white, as well as colored, children.

The University of Arkansas, following the Sipuel decision, has announced that it will accept qualified Negro students for its law school, though it will teach them in separate classrooms.

In 1948 New Jersey abolished segregation in its National Guard, announcing that it would carry out its plan, even if the United States government (still insisting on its archaic and cruel policy of segregation in the armed forces) withdrew support.

Encouraged by the New Jersey action, the late Governor James L. McConaughty of Connecticut renewed his efforts to have segregation abandoned in the Connecticut National Guard.

On May 3, 1948, the United States Supreme Court handed down a unanimous decision outlawing restrictive covenants in real estate deeds—i.e., clauses which forbid the sale of property to a buyer because of his race. This marked the culmination of a thirty-one-year fight waged by the NAACP at a cost of more than $100,000 to break the pattern of the ghetto for American racial and religious minorities. The unequivocal language and the unanimity of the Court made constitutional authorities present in the crowded courtroom call the decision the most important assertion of civil rights handed down by the Court since the notorious Dred Scott decision of 1857 which declared that "Negroes have no rights which a white man is bound to respect."

In several New York City offices of which I have firsthand knowledge (and in other cities) Negroes and whites work side by side most amicably in responsible positions, and it is a common sight to see mixed groups of laborers repairing New York's perpetually torn-up streets. But a friend has reported to me something which goes a step beyond this, and which would probably be incredible to several Southern senators. On a street in lower Manhattan, in this Year of Grace 1948, he watched a gang of a dozen white street laborers working under the direction of a skilled Negro foreman. Time does march on!

Negroes are today teaching in more than seventy-five nonsegregated American colleges and universities and the demand for additional teachers is steadily increasing, some of the institutions seeking such teachers being ones which until recently admitted no Negroes as students.

There are today more than one million Negroes who are registered voters in the South and cast their ballots without difficulty. The number steadily increases and rival wings of the Democratic Party in many Southern states and towns are bidding for the Negro vote. Of less publicized but equally important influence upon the Southern scene is the circumstance that our fight to enfranchise Negroes has played a considerable part in enfranchisement of whites and a greater interest in who is elected to office.

More than 1,500,000 Negroes are today members of trade unions and many of them serve as officers of nonsegregated locals, elected by the white as well as Negro members. The loyalty and industriousness of many of these Negro unionists has been a marked influence in causing most of the unions to become militant fighters against racial discrimination.

All officers' training schools of the armed services, all of them located in the Deep South, are completely integrated: infantry at Fort Benning, Georgia; aviation at Randolph Field in Texas; field artillery at Oklahoma's Fort Sill; armored infantry at Fort Knox, Kentucky; and airborne at North Carolina's Fort Bragg. There have been no friction and no untoward circumstances in the total obliteration of segregation in these schools, the arguments of the segregationists that "it can't work" to the contrary notwithstanding.

Book publishers and editors of magazines and newspapers with but a very few exceptions today welcome forthright writing about the Negro from both Negro and white writers, asking only that the authors write well and have something to say.

This is only a smattering of the sound evidence that the leaven is working. These things I have seen, and many more like them, and I have found deep satisfaction in them. If I have said little of them in this book it is only that there are so many more events of the sort I have reported, and I am convinced that until the balance swings the other way, democracy, and even human civilization, are in grave danger of destruction by racism.

And at the root of my anger and my frequent deep discouragement, is the knowledge that all race prejudice (save that which is deliberately uttered in base attempts to gain political or economic advantage by men and women to whom the phrase "honesty of purpose" has no meaning) is founded on one of the most absurd fallacies in all thought—the belief that there is a basic difference between a Negro and a white man.

There is no such basic difference.

More and more scientists, realizing the dire importance of the race problem to human welfare, are going out of their way to state unequivocally the falseness of the belief that such a difference exists. Only the other day I read such a brief statement in a book by a famed biologist, though the book was essentially about the crying need for soil conservation. "The saying 'We are all brothers under the skin,' " he wrote, "has a basis in scientific fact. . . . The antipathies of nations and races, the cults of 'superior' and 'inferior' races, cannot be founded on biology." [1]

Even the belief that racial markings are apparent in a Negro, no matter how light he is, has over and over been proved false.

Some years ago I met in London Sir Arthur Keith, president of the British Association for the Advancement of Science. Before he spoke a word of greeting, he extended a long, bony hand in welcome and, abstractedly, continued to hold my hand as he examined my features intently.

"The only way I can tell that you have Negro blood is by the shape of your eyes," were his first words.

Startled, I asked him, "What is there in them which reveals my ancestry?"

He did not reply immediately but continued his scrutiny of my face. It probably lasted no more than a minute, but the time seemed much longer. Sir Arthur then shook his head as though trying to rid it of cobwebs.

"No—I'm wrong. If you had not told me in one of your letters that you have Negro ancestry, I would have seen nothing. But because you did tell me, I *thought* I saw some indication. That's unscientific. Sit down, won't you—and let's talk."

Suppose the skin of every Negro in America were suddenly to turn white. What would happen to all the notions about Negroes, the bases on which are built race prejudice and race hatred? What would become of their presumed shiftlessness, their cowardice, their

[1] Fairfield Osborn, *Our Plundered Earth*. Boston: Little, Brown and Company, 1948.

dishonesty, their stupidity, their body odor? Would they not merge with the shiftlessness, the cowardice, the dishonesty, the stupidity, and the body odor of the whites? Would they not then be subject to individual judgment in matters of abilities, energies, honesty, cleanliness, as are whites? How else could they be judged?

As my father lay dying in a jimcrow hospital in Atlanta he put into words for my brother and me the faith which had sustained him throughout his life. "Human kindness, decency, love, whatever you wish to call it," he said, "is the only real thing in the world. It is a dynamic, not a passive, emotion. It's up to you two, and others like you, to use your education and talents in an effort to make love as positive an emotion in the world as are prejudice and hate. That's the only way the world can save itself. Don't forget that. No matter what happens, you must love, not hate."

I have remembered that. I have remembered that when, sitting in the gallery of the House or the Senate, I have heard members of our Congress rise and spill diatribe and vilification on the Negroes. I have remembered it when the Negroes were condemned as utter failures in soldiering.

I remembered it when I talked with my nephew for the last time, as he lay in a bitterly cold, rain-drenched tent on the edge of the Capodichina airfield near Naples. He was a Georgia boy, the youngest of four children. His father, like mine, was a mail carrier. He, like me, could have passed for a white man. By sacrifice and labor his parents provided him with a college education. He won a master's degree in economics, and the next day enlisted in the Army Air Forces, as a Negro. He went to the segregated field at Tuskegee, Alabama.

He hated war, he loathed killing. But he believed that Hitler and Mussolini represented the kind of hate he had seen exhibited in Georgia by the Ku Klux Klan and the degenerate political demagogues. He believed that the war would bring all of that hate to an end. He was a fighter pilot. He fought well. Over the Anzio beachhead he was shot down, bailing out and escaping with his right leg broken in two places. He was offered an opportunity to return home but he refused it. "I'll stick it out until the war is finished or I am," he told a friend. Later, returning from a bomber escort mission to Germany, his plane lost altitude over Hungary, was fired upon by antiaircraft batteries, and was seen striking a tree and bursting into flames. That was the end of one of the men Senator Eastland of Mississippi described as "utter and dismal failures in combat in Europe."

It would be easy to grow bitter over such things, but in remembering my nephew and our last conversation, in which he asked me whether the war would really bring an end to prejudice and race hatred, I remember also the Negro corporal of an engineers unit, who said to me, "This is the only work they would give me, but I don't mind. We learn a trade; we do constructive work. The combat soldiers are taught how to kill. It will bother them. It will stick with them. It will have no effect on us. We will not have to unlearn it."

There have been times when I have felt with a sweep of fear that the patience of the colored man is close to its end. I remember the clamoring stillness and the blood heat of a day in Georgia. I remember how I felt when I stood beside my father and feared that the whites would not let me live, that I must kill them first and then be killed.

Yet I know, I know, I know that there is no reason for this killing, this hatred, this demarcation. There is no difference between the killer and the killed. Black is white and white is black. When one shoots the other he kills his reflection. Only hate, the negative force, can separate them; only love, the positive force, can bind them together.

I am one of the two in the color of my skin; I am the other in my spirit and my heart. It is only a love of both which binds the two together in me, and it is only love for each other which will join them in the common aims of civilization that lie before us. I love one for the sins she has committed and the fight she has made to conquer them—and conquer them, in great degree, she has. I love the other for her patience and her sorrows, for the soft sound of her singing, and for the great dawn which is coming upon her, in which her vigor and her faith will serve the world.

I am white and I am black, and know that there is no difference. Each casts a shadow, and all shadows are dark.

Index

A selected list of MIDLAND BOOKS

(continued on next page)

MIDLAND BOOKS